THE WORLD OF WALLS

THE
WORLD
OF WALLS

The Middle Ages in Western Europe

POLLY SCHOYER BROOKS

and

NANCY ZINSSER WALWORTH

J. B. LIPPINCOTT COMPANY

PHILADELPHIA   NEW YORK

The authors wish to thank the following for permission to quote passages from their publications:

Peter Davies Ltd. for a selection from *Charlemagne* by Douglas Woodruff.

Harvard University Press for lines from the Minnesinger's song from *Eleanor of Aquitaine and the Four Kings* by Ann Kelly.

Houghton Mifflin Company for Richard I's prison song from *Mont-Saint Michel and Chartres* by Henry Adams.

Penguin Books Ltd. for lines from the *Song of Roland* translated by Dorothy Sayers.

Thanks also go to Professor Eleanor T. Lincoln of Smith College for reading the chapter on Chaucer, to Mrs. Carlos Garcia-Mata of New Canaan for suggesting the book's title, to Professor Sumner McKnight Crosby of Yale University for advice and photographs, to Miss Marjorie G. Wynne of Yale's Beinecke Rare Book and Manuscript Library, to the Yale University Library, and to the New York Public Library for their help.

Acknowledgment is made to the following sources for the pictures appearing on the pages noted:

Alinari-Art Reference Bureau. Pages 171, 177.

Anderson, Rome. Page 161.

Archives Photographiques. Pages 69, 160.

Bettman Archives. Pages 13, 14, 41, 185.

Bibliotheque Nationale, Paris. Pages 18, 21.

Bibliotheque Royale, Bruxelles. Pages 59, 200, 219, 243, 249.

Bodleian Library, Oxford. Page 217.

British Museum. Pages 125, 129, 207.

The Fitzwilliam Museum, Cambridge. Page 173. Reproduced by permission of the Syndics.

French Government Tourist Office. Pages 75, 119.

The Frick Collection, New York. Page 181.

Italian Government Travel Office, New York. Page 163.

Kunsthistorisches Museum. Page 22.

Marburg-Art Reference Bureau. Page 47.

The Metropolitan Museum of Art. Page 36 (gift of Mr. and Mrs. Frederic S. Pratt, 1936). Pages 111, 122, 138 (gift of J. Pierpont Morgan, 1917). Page 136. Page 168 (Fletcher Fund, 1947). Page 189. Page 199 (The Cloisters Collection).

Museie Gallerie Pontificie. Page 54.

Museum of Fine Arts, Boston. Page 121 (gift of Mr. and Mrs. Alastair Bradley Martin).

Paul Popper Ltd., London. Pages 135, 239.

Pierpont Morgan Library. Pages 35, 82, 150, 198, 222, 225.

Pierre Devinoy. Page 113.

Radio Times Hulton Picture Library. Page 196.

Smith College Museum of Art. Page 226.

Stiftsbibliothek St. Gallen. Pages 45, 53.

Spencer Collection, New York Public Library. Pages 107, 223.

The Walters Art Gallery. Page 29.

World Publishing. Page 96 from *Weapons* by Edwin Tunis.

To our husbands, Ernest Brooks, Jr. and Edward H. Walworth, Jr.,
and to our friend and first editor, Eunice Blake Bohanon,
for hours of invaluable work

CONTENTS

Part I THE BARBARIAN INVASIONS   13

Part II THE EARLY MIDDLE AGES   19

Gregory the Great   22
The Rise of the Franks   41
Charlemagne   47
The End of the Dark Ages   73
William the Conqueror   78

Part III THE PEAK OF THE MIDDLE AGES   101

Eleanor of Aquitaine   107
Richard the Lion Heart   135
Francis of Assisi   161
Beginnings of English Liberties   185
Simon de Montfort   189

Part IV THE LAST OF THE MIDDLE AGES   217

Geoffrey Chaucer   221

BIBLIOGRAPHY   247
INDEX   253

THE
WORLD OF
WALLS

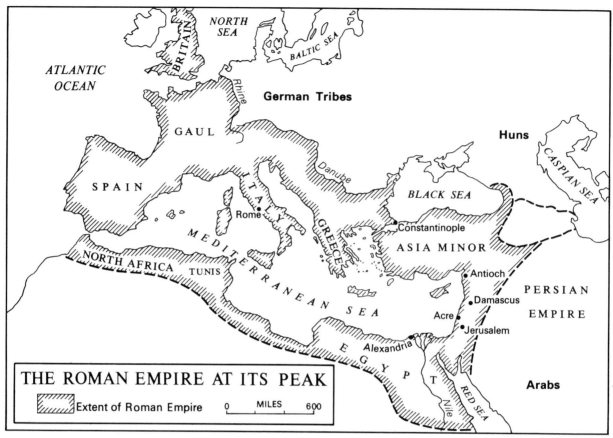

THE ROMAN EMPIRE AT ITS PEAK

///// Extent of Roman Empire   0   MILES   600

NORTH SEA

BALTIC SEA

ATLANTIC OCEAN

BRITAIN

German Tribes

Huns

G A U L

Rhine

CASPIAN SEA

S P A I N

Danube

BLACK SEA

I T A L Y

• Rome

GREECE

• Constantinople

ASIA MINOR

M E D I T E R R A N E A N   S E A

PERSIAN EMPIRE

NORTH AFRICA   TUNIS

• Antioch

• Damascus

Acre •

• Jerusalem

E G Y P T

Alexandria •

Nile

RED SEA

Arabs

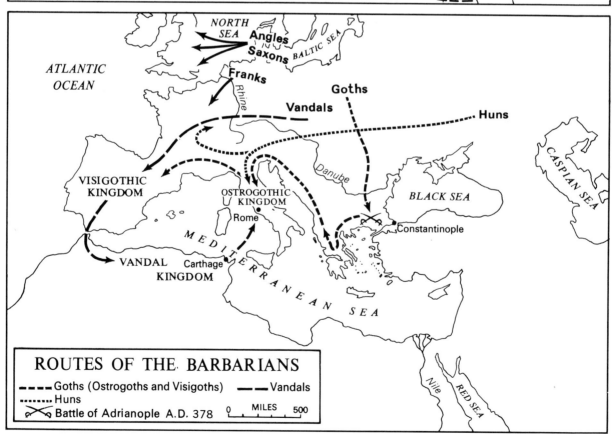

ROUTES OF THE BARBARIANS

- - - Goths (Ostrogoths and Visigoths)   —— Vandals
······ Huns
✕✕ Battle of Adrianople A.D. 378   0   MILES   500

NORTH SEA

Angles

Saxons *BALTIC SEA*

ATLANTIC OCEAN

Franks

Rhine

Goths

Vandals

Huns

CASPIAN SEA

VISIGOTHIC KINGDOM

Danube

OSTROGOTHIC KINGDOM

BLACK SEA

Rome

• Constantinople

VANDAL KINGDOM

Carthage •

M E D I T E R R A N E A N   S E A

Nile

RED SEA

PART I

THE BARBARIAN INVASIONS

The Roman forum at the height of imperial power.

In the untamed forest and swamplands to the north of the Roman Empire countless Germanic tribes were on the move. Seeking lands for their cattle and fertile ground for crops, they naturally eyed with envy the rich and more cultivated lands of the Romans. These tribes had originally migrated from Scandinavia and by the early third century A.D. they were scattered from the Black Sea to the Rhine and Danube Rivers, the northern frontiers of the Roman Empire. They were a blond, blue-eyed, stalwart race. Though uncivilized and uneducated, they had great loyalty to their tribal chiefs, preferring to die with them than to escape or surrender. Their passion was war, their virtue courage. Unlike the Romans they wore their hair long and smeared it with grease. They loved bright colors and ornaments

13

Invading barbarians.

and used animal skins for tunics and capes. They armed themselves with round wooden shields, short axes, and heavy spears.

For hundreds of years the Roman Empire had ruled the Western World, centering around the Mediterranean Sea, but in the third century A.D. the Empire showed signs of decline. Its very size, stretching from Britain to Asia Minor, from the Rhine and Danube Rivers to the Sahara Desert, made it cumbersome. When the limits of its far-flung conquests were reached, its greatest sources of wealth, the booty and spoils of war, ceased. In trying to maintain its power, the government became oppressive and tyrannical. Burdened with harsh taxes and ruled by despots, the Roman people lost the will to work and lost their civic pride.

Finally the Roman government could no longer pay its soldiers adequately, feed its people and maintain law and order. Corruption, anarchy, and civil wars spread and were followed by plague and famine. Gradually the army took over the government, making and unmaking emperors at will. The formerly well-defended frontiers became deserted as population shrank and army men sought profit in the government. As the famous Pax Romana—peace within the Roman borders—vanished, efforts were made to fortify some of the great cities. The capital, Rome itself, was for the first time surrounded by a wall twelve feet thick, with towers every hundred feet. But the Empire had lost its greatness; it was inwardly dead and rotten. It became an easy prey for restless barbarian tribes beyond its frontiers.

Most of these barbarians led a nomadic life and were ever on the move for food and fresh pastures. Only a few tribes were willing to clear and plough the land. It seemed simpler to conquer other people's already cultivated lands.

In the fourth century these restless tribes were themselves menaced by even fiercer tribes, the Mongolian Huns from the East, who, with their slant eyes and black hair and squat bodies which seemed glued to their swift ponies, terrified all who beheld them. They, too, were in search of land and they forced the Germanic tribes south, right to the borders of the Empire.

In the same century, in A.D. 325, the Roman Emperor Constantine, in an attempt to save the Empire, abandoned Rome and founded a new capital on the site of the ancient village of Byzantium, a more strategic area for guarding the frontiers. He named the city Constantinople or City of Constantine and enclosed it with heavy walls. At the same time Constantine embraced Christianity; soon it became the state religion instead of the old pagan one.

Constantine's strong rule held the eastern and western parts of the Empire together but after his death only the eastern or Byzantine part, with its splendid new capital, remained strong and rich. The western half, from the Rhine to North Africa, continued to decline, becoming poor and weak. Most of Constantine's successors were unable to rule both parts of the Empire. The Roman half once more set up its own emperors but they were too ineffectual to defend it against the barbarian infiltration from the north. They even hired barbarians to fill the dwindling ranks of their own legions.

In 376 a whole tribe, the Visigoths, fleeing the terrible Huns, were allowed to settle within the Empire, south of the Danube River. But they were treated as undesirable immigrants, not as equals. In 378

15

they rose in revolt and, aided by a related tribe, the Ostrogoths, they attacked the Roman legions on the plains near Adrianople. Their cavalry completely routed the Roman infantry.

After this decisive victory tribes penetrated the barriers more and more. The Roman legions became filled with uncouth barbarians instead of the once proud Roman citizens. Finally the barbarians became the Empire's real defenders, willing to fight for it against other tribes who kept pressing on the frontiers. During the fifth century these tribes came in wave after wave, heading south and west. When Constantinople, impregnable behind her massive walls, withstood them, they then turned to the western half of the Empire. Soon they became masters of the weaker people of the West.

In 476 a barbarian chieftain, Odovacar, deposed the last of the western Roman emperors, Romulus Augustulus, and set himself up as king of Italy. This was the end of the long dying Roman Empire of the West. But the fall of the Roman Empire was scarcely noticed. The people were so used to sudden revolutions, to emperors being made and unmade (within the last twenty-one years there had been nine emperors, no sooner set up than banished or murdered) that they paid no attention to the disappearance of Romulus Augustulus. Nor were they surprised by the sudden rise to power of an illiterate northern barbarian chieftain. Many other barbarians had already risen to prominent positions and power.

Barbarian kingdoms were set up throughout the western half of the Empire. Visigoths settled in southern France and Spain. Another tribe, the Vandals, after a swift migration from the forests north of the Rhine, crossed to North Africa and gained control of the rich Roman province which had formerly supplied most of the Empire's grain. Angles and Saxons from the Baltic Sea area crossed the North Sea to Britain, already deserted by her Roman legions, and easily overran it. Burgundians spread themselves along the Rhone River valley. The Franks, armed with their deadly tapered throwing axe, the francisca, crossed the lower Rhine and settled between it and the Loire River. The most effective of all the barbarians, they gave their name to France.

Most of these barbarians had not come to destroy the Empire but

Ruins of the emperors' palaces.

to enjoy its wealth. Around them stood reminders of past Roman greatness—beautiful theaters and arenas, huge buildings with pillars and friezes of finest marble, well-paved roads, graceful aqueducts stretching across wide valleys. But many of these structures were beginning to crumble, and the barbarians did not know how to repair them. Life throughout the Roman territories began to change radically. Some of the barbarians took on the worst traits of the decaying Roman civilization and became slothful and idle when not at war. Others, especially the warlike Franks, instilled new vigor into society. The Romans, although outnumbering the barbarians, were apathetic and weak. Former Roman ideals of justice declined as each barbarian tribe brought in its own laws and customs. Roman education deteriorated. Fewer and fewer people knew how to read and write.

But there was one thing which the Romans and barbarians shared in common, one force which promised hope and meaning in an age of violence and despair. This was the Christian religion. By the end of the fifth century most barbarians had been converted. In spite of years of war and disorder they and the Romans gradually became united in the Christian faith. One faith and one creed became as important to them as one emperor had been to the old Roman Empire. The Romans and barbarians, bound together by Christianity, were developing a new civilization, which would last for a thousand years

17

until the Renaissance of the fifteenth century. During this period known as the Middle Ages, men lived in constant fear of sudden attacks from predatory neighbors. The weak sought protection of the strong who built thick-walled fortresses. Below these fortifications grew up walled towns. The more devout retreated to cloistered lives in high-walled monasteries. The Western World became a world of walls.

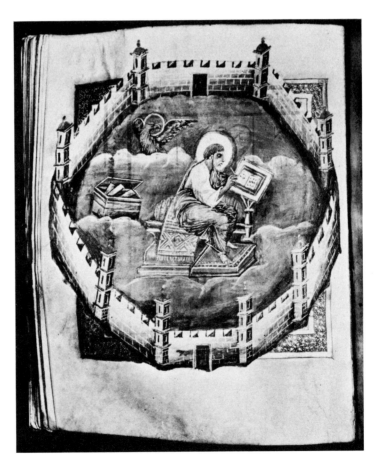

Monk writing within high walls.

PART II

THE EARLY MIDDLE AGES

Monasteries kept some learning alive.

In 476 when the barbarian Odovacar removed the last Roman Emperor of the West from his throne, people could no longer pretend the Romans still had any power. The western Roman Empire from Britain to Spain was in the hands of barbarian kings. The following century, the sixth, was one of the darkest known to western man. Europe went steadily downhill into the Dark Ages—as the first part of the Middle Ages between the fifth and tenth centuries is often called.

On the fringes of Europe, in Britain, were the Anglo-Saxons, who still worshipped stones and trees. In Spain were the Visigoths, and across the straits from them in North Africa were the Vandals. In the north of Gaul were the golden-haired Franks. In 496 their pagan king Clovis and three thousand of his warriors were baptized Roman Catholics; then, with the Church's support, they ruthlessly conquered the rest of the tribes in Gaul. Their kingdom—Frankland (France)—extended from the Rhine River to the Pyrenees. Upon the death of Clovis, his sons and grandsons squabbled over their inheritance and France became the scene of their bloody civil wars fought with dagger and axe. The history of sixth-century France reeks of violence and cruelty, murder and poisonings.

Italy at the start of the sixth century was better off. A remarkable barbarian ruler, Theodoric the Ostrogoth, was determined that his people should get along with the native population. Though his vigorous, illiterate Goths controlled the army, he used educated Romans as magistrates and scribes, and permitted the Roman Senate to handle most of the details of government. Aristocratic Roman families still managed to live in town houses and country villas, with slaves to wait on them. But as these Romans, surrounded by noisy barbarians, saw their children adopt barbarian customs, they despaired. Watching their own culture and power decay year by year, they despised their Gothic conquerors.

After King Theodoric's death in 526, when various Gothic claimants fought over his throne, Italy, like France, became a land of constant civil wars. Education and government sank to a lower level than ever before.

Only in isolated places did learning survive. In 529 St. Benedict founded a monastery on a wild cliff, Monte Cassino, south of Rome. There he wrote the famous Benedictine Rule which taught his monks humility, stability, and obedience. "Let no one in the monastery follow the will of his own heart," St. Benedict wrote. The only important thing was to serve God.

Benedict's rule spread swiftly to other places and countries. Benedictine monks grew their grain, pressed their olives for oil and their grapes for wine, and by hard labor were able to survive no matter how terrible the world was around them. More important, they were teachers and scholars who copied manuscripts which otherwise might have been lost. Thousands of them led selfless, dedicated lives amidst the confusion and desolation of the Dark Ages.

Meanwhile, far away at the eastern end of the Mediterranean, the Byzantine Empire flourished, rich and powerful, in tremendous contrast to the unhappy lands of the West. In 535 a Byzantine emperor, Justinian, was inspired by the idea of restoring the old Roman Empire to its original boundaries. He wished particularly to rescue Italy, the motherland of the vanished Roman Empire, from the barbarian Ostrogoths. His generals sailed over the seas and in 536 recaptured most of Italy, pushing the Goths back into the northern districts.

The Roman population at first rejoiced, thinking they were now going to be once more a wealthy and important part of a glorious empire. They soon discovered that Justinian's generals were not interested in the traditions of empire, but wanted booty. Rome became riddled with graft and poverty. Instead of bringing back the Empire's ancient greatness, Justinian's conquest pushed Rome further into darkness.

A Frankish king murders his wife.

GREGORY THE GREAT

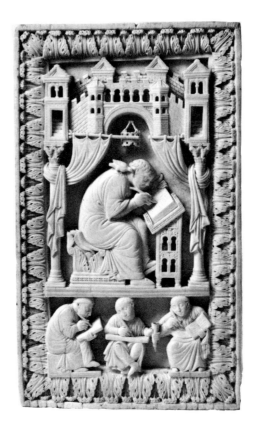

St. Gregory.

The year 540 seemed dark and hopeless to all the people of Rome. Their city had shrunk in population, wealth, and power. Everything was in ruins; there were few shops, no manufacture, and little trade. The Roman Senate, once a group of powerful, aristocratic men, was now a collection of nobodies. Worst of all, the armies of the Byzantine Emperor Justinian, who had pushed the Goths out of Rome four years before, were behaving far worse than the Goths ever did. Corrupt and avaricious, they spent their time looking for bribes and booty in Rome and its suburbs. Rome, buffeted for centuries, sacked by barbarians and now looted by her friends, seemed doomed.

But in the year of 540 a boy was born who was to start Rome on a path of importance once more. Gregory, a bright little boy with yellow-brown eyes and ruddy face, lived in a large palace with a courtyard and many rooms on the Caelian Hill in the middle of Rome. His father, Gordianus the aristocrat, was a wealthy man—unlike most of the Romans—with a large income from Sicilian farms untouched by barbarian raids. In those days there was little for aristocrats to do in Rome, and there was not much social life, but Gordianus tried to keep himself busy as a minor official of the Christian church. Gregory's mother Sylvia, a devout Christian, was a beautiful Roman matron who spent much of her time at prayer. Both parents worried that there would be no future in Rome for their son.

Gregory's parents and the few friends—the last remnant of educated Romans—who came to their house, told the little boy stories of the ancient glories of the city. They described its former splendor: the streets of marble lined with rows of statues; the luxurious public baths and vast arenas jammed with people; the countless buildings with gold-tiled roofs and bronze doors; the thronging, bustling, noisy crowds of soldiers, slaves, workers, officials, and nobles.

All of this was hard for Gregory to imagine, for most of Rome was now a silent city. On Palatine Hill, opposite his parents' mansion, were empty haunted palaces of former emperors. On the Capitoline hill nearby were acres of rubble, the remains of hundreds of mansions sacked by barbarians in the fifth century and never rebuilt. Gregory and his friends walked on cracked pavements full of tree roots and lined with fallen statues, and climbed into huge empty baths—now waterless because the old aqueducts had cracked and leaked. The vast Colosseum where gladiators once had fought to the death and Christians had been eaten by wild beasts, now held only rats and beggars; and the Circus Maximus, built to hold 200,000 spectators for chariot races, could have held the entire population of Rome in one fifth of its seats.

This desolation made a deep impression on young Gregory. He was serious and often sad. From 545 to 552 he saw the city change hands four times as the Ostrogoths fought to recapture Rome; he saw blond Gothic warriors in the streets one year and swarthy Byzantine troops from Constantinople the next. Many times during sieges

23

A mosaic angel on a sixth-century church wall.

the Roman inhabitants were reduced to eating thorns and mice. Famine and despair were everywhere.

The Romans felt that the world was crumbling so fast that soon—as the great Christian preachers St. Jerome and St. Augustine had prophesized—it would come to an end. Daily they clustered to pray and lament in the city's many churches. Some of the churches were huge basilicas; some were small, wooden parish churches. Gregory loved the smell of the oil lamps and the incense, the mosaic saints looking down from the walls, the ceremonies, processions, and chants. The priests and monks as they went about their quiet duties seemed

24

to be the only secure, happy people. The Bishop of Rome—called Pope, or father—was the most respected man in the city. His great basilica with its ninety-two spiraling columns of colored marble and its prized possession, the body of St. Peter lying in a vault below the altar, kept a thin stream of pilgrims coming from far-off places even in those harsh days. Medieval Christian Rome, with crowded churches, monasteries, and pilgrim shrines, was beginning to emerge from the ruins of classical Rome.

In 552 the Goths were forced out of the city forever and in a few more years they were almost exterminated. Governors and generals sent from Constantinople now ruled Italy. Roman citizens started once more to rebuild their lives.

As soon as a school re-opened, Gregory enrolled. He was twelve years old, bright and energetic and eager for more education. Dressed in old-style Roman tunic or a robe for more formal occasions (for Romans still disdained the barbarian fashion of short coats and leggings) the boy walked every day through the Forum to the old academy buildings. He had the Roman aristocratic, thin arched eyebrows, aquiline nose, and high coloring; but he also had a gentle and reflective expression.

Roman education had almost disappeared during the Gothic Wars. Teachers had fled to the bigger, richer cities of the East; pupils had vanished; libraries had been pillaged. Now a few teachers reappeared, scraped together a few manuscripts, and offered courses once more in writing, debating, literature, mathematics, and law. Gregory studied everything he could. His mind was quick and his memory excellent, and he soon mastered everything there was to be offered. People spoke of him as the best scholar in the city.

Gradually Gregory came to the conclusion that most of what he studied was too frivolous for these serious times. The great Roman

An angel weighing souls at the day of judgment.

writings of former days did not appeal to him at all. The church had taught him that the terrible Day of Judgment, when God would send some people to Heaven and others to Hell forever, was coming soon. Gregory thought that his chances of Heaven would improve if he concentrated on the Bible and the writings of the early Christians instead of wasting time on stories of Greek and Roman gods and goddesses and other pagan writings.

After a number of years, when he had completed most of his courses, his father died and his mother decided to become a nun. Gregory inherited his father's wealth and the mansion with its many rooms, but riches and leisure did not suit a young man of his many talents. Although no records of this part of his life survive, he probably worked several years for various departments of the city.

In the middle of the sixties the plague struck Italy. Called the Black Death because of the black lumps that appeared on sufferers' bodies, it was to come again and again during the Middle Ages to the undernourished populace. Thousands of men, women, and children died. A historian of the period described the desolation of the land:

> "Dwellings were left deserted by their inhabitants, and only the dogs kept house. The flocks remained alone in the pastures with no shepherd at hand. Sons fled, leaving the corpses of their parents unburied; parents, forgetful of their duty, abandoned their children in raging fever. The world was brought back to its ancient silence: no voice in the field, no whistling of shepherds."

In 568, before Italy had time to recover from the Black Death, the wild Lombards, last of the migrating Germanic tribes, invaded the north Italian plains whose villas and forts had been emptied by the plague. These men were terrifying to behold; they had long shaggy beards and their hair, shaved far up the back of their heads, fell in long locks over their ears and cheeks. Led by their young King Alboin, so brutal that he killed his wife's father and drank wine out of his skull before her eyes, they moved with little opposition into the fertile valley of the Po River. They cared nothing for Roman civilization and destroyed many northern towns. Everyone feared that they would attack Rome; but fortunately for the time being the few garrisons sent by the Byzantine Emperor staved them off.

Lombard warrior with typical haircut.

Sometime during this desperate period Gregory, then only about thirty years old, became Prefect of Rome, the city's highest political office. With the Lombards remaining in the north of Italy and their immediate threat to Rome removed, Gregory was able to concentrate on running the city's government.

As Prefect, Gregory was responsible for the welfare of Rome and the land around it to the hundredth milestone. Many of the city's departments such as Baths and Theaters had gone out of existence, but there still were important things for the Prefect to supervise: police, river traffic, markets, taxes, provisions, and pilgrims. Many people worked under him. He had the place of honor at all meetings and ceremonies. The Romans still tried to keep up appearances, and their Prefect was given purple robes and four fine horses to pull his carriage, even though the carriage might bounce over wrecked streets and detour around fallen columns.

Gregory was very popular with the people for he was practical and yet tenderhearted. His eyes sparkled with kindness and vitality. But underneath he was unhappy. He felt that the robes and carriage and banquets were signs of vanity. The calm religious life of the mon-

27

asteries attracted him and he longed to get away from the frustrations of politics and the strain of running a bankrupt, threatened city. He withdrew more and more to ponder and pray.

Then to the consternation of all the young Prefect gave up his title and became a Benedictine monk. Renouncing the life of politics and government, he gave all his riches and properties to the Church and turned over his beautiful mansion to the monks of St. Andrew for their monastery.

To this former home Gregory returned as the humblest of monks. The people of Rome, accustomed to the dark-haired young Prefect in elegant robes and jewels, hardly recognized him with shaven head and rough gown. His face, once ruddy, was thin and pale through fasting and long hours of prayer.

The life into which Gregory entered was common to all the monasteries of Europe throughout the Middle Ages. Every hour was planned for him according to the Rule of St. Benedict. Gregory had no more decisions to make for himself. He obeyed the Abbot of the monastery in everything; he had no possessions—even his black robe, sandals, and blankets belonged to the monastery—and he lived in complete humility and simplicity.

He and his brother monks rose every day in their bare dormitory two hours before the first light of dawn and assembled by torchlight to kneel and pray on the cold stone floors of the chapel. Gregory did not feel the discomfort of the hard floor; as the Latin chants echoed against the low walls, he felt only the nearness of God. He did not feel hunger as he went about his work, although there would be no food for almost twelve hours.

Every monk had a place in the labor of the monastery. Educated monks like Gregory copied manuscripts which otherwise would have been worn out and lost forever. They also taught children given to the monastery by parents unable to feed and educate them properly at home. Some monks were bakers, others carpenters or gardeners. Even a city monastery like Gregory's had a garden and a small orchard to tend. The heaviest work was done by young monks. Everyone took his turn at housekeeping tasks—sweeping, scouring pots, cleaning lamps—and was also given time for meditation and study.

A father gives his son to monks to educate.

In summer when there was outside work to be done, two meals were served, at midday and late afternoon. In winter the monks ate only once—at three o'clock. All meals were eaten in silence, broken only by the voice of the monk reading the day's holy lesson. Gregory received a daily cup of wine and a pound of bread with perhaps vegetables or fruit. Sometimes as a special treat there would be eggs, fish, or cheese, but never "meat of a four-footed beast." Once in a while Gregory's mother sent him fruit on a silver dish—the last, much loved possession of their family. At regular intervals bells called the monks to prayers, sometimes in the chapel, sometimes wherever they happened to be standing, in field or kitchen. The last chapel service was said before bedtime which came very early—about five in the dark winters, a few hours later in the summers. And then complete silence was observed until the prayers of the following early morning.

Gregory endured this strict life cheerfully and even fasted and kept vigils longer than the Rule required. He often went without food until he sank from weakness and illness, but prayers carried him past the breaking point. Although he ruined his health this way, he always remembered the three years of seclusion in St. Andrew's monastery as the happiest in his life.

One day during these years as he walked through the Forum, still the chief business place of Rome, he noticed some fair-haired, white-skinned slave boys for sale in the stalls of Frankish merchants. They were a startling contrast to the olive-skinned, dark-haired children of Rome. Gregory was told that they were from the island of Britain.

Like most Romans in the sixth century, Gregory knew little about this faraway island and its inhabitants. There had been little contact between Rome and Britain since the Roman legions had withdrawn from it more than a hundred years before. Gregory asked whether these boys were Christians. When the merchants told him that they were pagans, he sighed heavily. He asked the name of their tribe and was told they were Angles. Gregory could not resist a pun. "They are well-named," he said, "for they have the faces of angels."

Gregory could not stop worrying about the souls of these boys, which he of course believed were sentenced to Hell forever. He resolved to convert the heathen in Angle-land (England) and he begged Pope Benedict for a leave of absence to go on this dangerous mission. The Pope, no match for Gregory's persuasion and charm, gave permission, but neither man realized how much the people of Rome would object to his departure. They had known Gregory and been proud of him as a little boy, a brilliant student, a Prefect—and then had admired him even more when he sacrificed everything to become a monk. When it was learned that Gregory had left the city, angry mobs formed around Pope Benedict as he made his way to St. Peter's. "What have you done? You have offended St. Peter! You have destroyed Rome! You have sent Gregory into exile!" they cried.

Gregory had gone only a few miles on his mission and was resting by the side of the road when messengers from the Pope caught up with him, commanding him to return at once. Then the Pope removed Gregory from his cloistered life and made him a deacon of one of the church districts of Rome. Gregory dared not disobey. Humility and obedience were part of the monastic code, and though he regretted going into public life once more he felt that God had called him.

In the year 578, Lombard bands made a sudden drive southward. The new Pope Pelagius II felt almost overwhelmed, for Rome's garrison consisted of only a handful of Byzantine troops and a feeble citizens' militia. The thought that the city of St. Peter might fall to these terrible people was unbearable, and he looked around for possible help. The only solution seemed to be to send Gregory as his ambassador to Constantinople to ask for troops and money.

In 579 Gregory set out with some senators and churchmen for Constantinople. After a long journey by sea and land his party arrived at the city's formidable walls. Chariots, litters, wagons, gold-harnessed mules carrying important people, crowds of many races and tongues jostled him on the magnificent road that led through the tall gates. Gregory rode by the Emperor's palace, a series of buildings almost a mile long connected by covered passages, with its own private harbor at one end. He saw the busy Forum, the great Hippodrome for chariot races, the Senate House, the shops, the bustling university and law courts, the public baths, the innumerable ships tied up at the wharves. Most impressive of all was the great new Christian church, Sancta Sophia (Holy Wisdom) towering one hundred and eighty feet tall above the marble pavements. Its many-colored marble columns, dazzling mosaics, and solid gold altar were "like a meadow full of flowers in bloom." Its huge dome "seemed to hang from heaven on a golden chain." Gregory had never seen such a dome in the West; in fact, he had never seen anything like the crowds and the splendor about him. This beautiful and rich city, which the Emperor Constantine in 325 had called "New Rome," was an impressive contrast to Old Rome. All the builders, artisans, scholars, riches, and glory seemed to be here in the East.

Gregory presented his credentials to the Byzantine Emperor Tiberius, who, in silks and jewels, sat on a golden throne surrounded by guards in golden armor. The glittering courtiers, the ladies with rouged cheeks and dyed yellow hair, the splendidly costumed bishops from Egypt and Syria looked curiously at this pale man with shaven head and simple robe.

Tiberius listened politely to Gregory's request for troops and money, but made only a few vague promises; his armies were needed on the Persian frontier. Every so often during the following months —which were to stretch into years—he sent a few troops to Italy, but never enough to satisfy the worried Pope.

Gregory lived as simply as possible amidst all the glitter and lux-

31

ury. There was too much oriental splendor for his modest tastes. Even the language—Greek—was strange to the Latin-speaking Gregory. With the few monks who had accompanied him, he retired as often as he could to a small Latin monastery and church.

In 585 the Pope finally summoned Gregory home, for the Lombards temporarily had ceased to threaten Rome. Though Gregory had accomplished little, he had learned much that would later be important to him. He had seen how diplomacy was carried on, he had observed how a huge empire was governed, he had met influential people from all parts of the world. But at the moment these things were of no concern. Exhausted, feeling his mission a failure, he asked the Pope to let him go back to his beloved monastery. The Pope could not say no to the man who had labored faithfully for him six years in a frustrating job.

The monks of St. Andrew's welcomed him joyfully and elected him their abbot—a very important position in the Middle Ages. An abbot managed monastery lands and buildings, ran the monastery schools, choirs, and hospitals; gave alms to the poor and entertained important visitors. He was absolute master of the monks, who called him "Dominus"—Lord.

Abbot Gregory ruled his monks strictly. He punished them when they disobeyed the rule about possessing money, when they wasted food or broke dishes, or were lazy, or dreamed at their devotions. But he loved them as a father. His own example of kindliness, hard work, and sacrifice inspired them all. The monastery won the reputation of being a "school of saints." Gregory was happy there, but after five years events drew him back into the turmoil of sixth-century life.

In 589 great floods desolated Italy. In Rome the river Tiber overflowed its banks, bringing snakes and "a dragon, large as a stout beam" (according to an eyewitness) which passed through the city and descended to the sea. Thousands of bushels of wheat, stored in church granaries to feed the poor, were ruined.

As the floods subsided, the Black Death returned to the stricken city. Pope Pelagius caught it and died. The clergy and the people of Rome with one accord chose Abbot Gregory to be the next Pope.

Few men would have been willing to accept such an anxious burden, but Gregory's Roman and Christian sense of duty was strong. Rome needed him and the Church needed him. In September, 590, when formal consent had arrived from the Byzantine Emperor, Gregory was ordained Pope in St. Peter's basilica. He knew all too well the problems he would have to face, with the prestige of his church at a low ebb and its very existence threatened by the Lombards. He wrote:

> "I, unworthy and weak, have taken charge of an old and grievously shattered ship—for on all sides the waves enter, and the planks are battered by a daily and violent storm."

The interruption of Gregory's monastic career was a fortunate event for Europe in the dark sixth century. Though he would have preferred a cloistered life, his energies were needed in a world where too many competent men had given up the fight against barbarism and retired to monasteries. Someone was needed to bring a new sense of purpose to the age.

When Gregory ascended the papal throne he was fifty years old. He was of average height, bald and bearded, and his face had a gentle expression that drew people to him. His hands were beautiful and expressive, with long, tapering fingers. Though in bad health, with constant pain from his severe fasting as a monk, he never relaxed and was always busy. There was plenty to keep him busy—so much that a lesser man might not have attempted half of what he did in the fourteen years that he was Pope.

Even though he was now elevated to the office of the highest bishop in the Church, he preferred to live in simplicity. He substituted monks and priests for the usual overdressed papal servants and pageboys. In the privacy of the Palace of the Popes he continued to wear coarse monks' robes and to eat plain food. In public he wore vestments of white linen without embroidery and a simple belt of only a thumb's width.

Gregory's first duties were to help the paupers, refugees, and plague-stricken families of Rome. Fortunately, although most of Rome had grown poorer during two hundred years of barbarian invasions, the Roman church had grown in wealth as rich Romans, fleeing from Italy or joining monasteries, gave it their lands, houses, and jewelry. The Pope had all this wealth at his command. He ordered alms to be distributed on the first day of every month from the porches of each church and monastery in Rome—corn, wine, cheese, bacon, oil, fish, whatever was in season. He ordered dishes of cooked food to be carried to invalids and old people. To those of noble families who were too proud to beg he would send food from his own table and say in a most tactful way that it was a present from St. Peter.

Unlike many Popes before and after him, Gregory spent little on building churches or ornamenting them with gold and silver, but gave all that he could to the poor. "Let a bishop have a liberal hand," he wrote. "Let him believe the wants of others to be his own." The list of his charities is enormous. If he heard that a bishop of another town was threadbare, he sent him blankets and a warm tunic accompanied by a sympathetic note. If he heard that a vineyard of a little monastery had failed, he sent enough money to support the monks until the next harvest. He ordered a thousand pecks of wheat to be given to some starving Greeks, and blankets and horses to hospitals in Jerusalem and Sicily. He sent ransom money both to the Lombards for captives and to the African markets to rescue Christian slaves.

In order to be sure his funds would not dry up, Gregory kept a watchful eye on the Church's properties. No detail was too small for him as he carefully studied the reports from these estates. In a collection (fourteen volumes) of hundreds of letters which the busy Pope wrote to all sorts of people, there are many to his overseers and agents, telling them how many cows, ewes, bulls, and mares to sell; how many trees to cut down for timber, and how much rent to collect. While Gregory protected the Church's properties in this way, he also protected the peasants on them who were robbed in countless ways by dishonest bailiffs. He wrote many stern letters ordering his agents to correct these injustices.

When his agents saw that the Pope meant business, and when the people knew that he would protect them, the lands prospered. Gregory is justly famous as one of the best landlords the Church ever had.

Immense crowds of all ages followed the popular Pope whenever he rode on horseback in solemn procession to preach in one of the

city's many churches. Sometimes he was too ill to preach and someone read the sermon in his place; but when he did speak the people
were spellbound, and called him "golden-mouthed." The uneducated people in the congregation could understand him for he spoke
simply. His favorite theme was the coming end of the world and the
necessity for people to mend their ways. Everybody loved his deathbed tales, particularly of dying sinners seized by the devil, shrieking,
"The dragon has me! His foaming mouth is licking my face, he is
choking me, my arms are held fast and he has swallowed down my
head!" Gregory pictured the entrance to Hell as a volcano with its
mouth growing wider as its load of sinners increased.

The mouth of Hell.

Gregory was as popular a writer as he was a speaker. His book
about holy men who stopped avalanches and fires, cured blindness
and fits, and even made the dead alive again, became one of the most

A statue showing the miracle of a martyred
saint holding his head.

influential books of the Middle Ages. People believed these stories
and were comforted by them in their harsh lives. It is hard for us
to realize that a man of Gregory's keen mind and education believed
all that he wrote. But he lived in an age of belief, not of scientific
proof, when anything unusual—a fire or flood suddenly subsiding,
a raiding Lombard falling dead, a sick person unexpectedly recovering—was interpreted as a sign of God's personal intervention. Gregory had come to the conclusion long before he finished his education
that faith was far more important than learning, and this conclusion
greatly influenced the thinking of the Middle Ages. For centuries
stories of saints and miracles interested people far more than did the
ancient classics. The more carefree days of pagan antiquity had given
way to the spirit of the Middle Ages with its emphasis on sin, Heaven,
and Hell.

Gregory also encouraged people in the belief that to touch saints'
bones, or hair from their heads, or even the dust from their coffins,
would bring them nearer Heaven. There were many such relics in
Rome, but the body of St. Peter was the most famous of all. Gregory

rebuilt the crypt around St. Peter's bones and widened the aisle for throngs of pilgrims. To this day one can discover sixth-century initials scratched on the crypt.

Not satisfied with the singing of hymns in the city's churches, Gregory would go to the choir school and listen to the choirboys practice. Because of his poor health he would lie on a couch and keep time with one hand; with the other—like all teachers of the age—he held a rod to beat any boy who droned or sang through his nose. His choirboys did not sing hymns as we know them, but simple unaccompanied chants. Lines, notes, and rhythm marks had not been developed, so each tune was memorized and handed down from generation to generation. Some historians believe that Gregory composed hymns himself and taught them to the choir. Whether he did or not, many of the chants sung in Roman Catholic services today are called Gregorian chants in memory of the great Pope.

In trying to extend his influence in other lands, Gregory found that he had no real authority over the hundreds of bishops around the Mediterranean from Spain to Constantinople, Alexandria, and Carthage. Many of these bishops had grown powerful and did not welcome interference. Gregory felt it was vital to bring them all under one control; otherwise the Church might be divided just as the Roman Empire had been divided—and had fallen.

Gregory's letters to bishops everywhere reminded them that the watchful eye of the Pope was on them. One bishop was scolded for plowing on Sundays, another for being too lazy to destroy stone idols, another for taking a gold pin from the family of a man he had buried. But to take the sting out of his words, Gregory mixed compliments with his advice. He was especially shocked at the behavior of the Frankish bishops whose morals were so low that they often took bribes and even stole Church property. He persisted in writing these wicked men even though his letters did not have much effect, for he knew how important it was for Frankland, far richer and larger than Italy, to keep its allegiance to the Pope. Gifts and tactful letters to the warring rulers of the rival Frankish kingdoms also paved the way for future alliances of great importance between the French and the Popes.

Because of Gregory's firm letters to rulers and churchmen, all Christian lands began to respect the Roman Pope. Though he had no military might, his moral power achieved more than armies. This extension of the influence and power of the Pope was Gregory's greatest achievement. The unity of the Church began to have real meaning.

One nation in the West, once in the Roman Empire, remained outside of Gregory's influence—England, overrun by barbarian Angles, Saxons, and Jutes for almost two hundred years. Gregory had not forgotten the blond English slave-boys in the Roman market and the cancelling of his mission to convert the English. He could not rest until he sent another mission to these far-off pagans.

In 596 Gregory appointed a monk, Augustine, to head up the small group of forty monks who were to have a vast impact upon English history. Gregory's correspondence with the Frankish monarchs and churchmen now proved useful, for he was able to arrange a safe passage for his missionaries through their turbulent land. By the spring of 597 all had arrived on the northern shores of France and crossed in small, flat-bottomed boats to England.

The Anglo-Saxon King Ethelbert decided to hear what these strange, black-robed visitors had to say. He was the most powerful of all the petty rulers on the island, and he had a Christian wife, daughter of one of the Frankish kings. It was not too long before he was persuaded to become a Christian. By Christmas Day more than ten thousand of his subjects had been baptized. Gregory's dream of converting the English had come true. Churches and monasteries soon took the place of pagan temples in England and Latin chants echoed through the countryside. The English Benedictines developed schools whose influence was to spread to the outposts of Europe.

In Rome the great Pope rejoiced as messengers told him of the mission's success. He had brought the Christian religion with its order, traditions, and teaching to an important land.

During these busy years, Gregory had a constant worry. It was of little use to plan a great unified church with Rome as its center if Italy was to be torn apart by Lombard enmity. Two fierce Lombard dukes had established large duchies near Rome and might cut off

Rome's food and trade at any time. At one point, Lombard raiders had come so close to Rome that Gregory, looking over the walls, saw them lead off Roman peasants "with ropes around their necks like dogs." The blood of his senatorial ancestors rebelled.

Though he had no political or military authority, he decided that he alone could save Rome. The determined Pope selected a commander to defend Rome, another to defend a nearby town, and sent soldiers to the frontiers. He even advised on strategy against the Lombard dukes. His predecessors would not have dared take these steps without the Byzantine emperor's permission, but Gregory had given up waiting for the emperor.

But these were stopgap measures and bound to fail sooner or later. Another way had to be found to persuade the Lombards to lay down their swords. Bitterly calling himself the "paymaster of the Lombards," Gregory used his precious funds to bribe the Lombards to stop their raids. But soon they were back for more gold.

From Queen Theodelinda's treasury.

Then he knew he must negotiate. Swallowing his pride, he sent representatives to the Lombard King Agilulf. The Pope also sent presents to Agilulf's beautiful and pious Queen Theodelinda and her children—crosses, crowns, rings, glass bottles of holy oil from the tombs of martyrs. The queen, who had great influence on her warrior husband, recognized Gregory's good intentions and did a great deal to ease the bitterness between the Romans and the Lombards.

Over a period of six years definite boundaries were established; the Lombards kept certain lands and towns, the Roman others. The far-off Byzantine emperor, at first outraged by Gregory's illegal meddling, finally agreed to his plan and in 598 ordered a treaty of peace to be drawn up. By acting as a statesman and not merely as a churchman, Gregory had saved Rome.

At the turn of the century, Pope Gregory's health, never very strong, began to worsen. He suffered cruelly from rheumatism, gout, and indigestion, and gradually took to his bed, hardly able to get up to celebrate Mass for his beloved Romans. For four years he thought himself daily at the point of death, and as his pain increased, began to long for it.

In A.D. 604 he died and was buried in St. Peter's basilica. The Church soon made him a saint, later centuries added "Great" to his name—and both were well deserved. Standing alone, courageous and devoted, in the ruined capital of a suffering country, he dominated the last half of the dark sixth century. At a time when the new barbarian kingdoms in Europe knew little of law, order, and education, the vacuum of European leadership was filled by this remarkable man. From now on, Popes would have political as well as spiritual power. As the shadows of the Dark Ages lengthened, he created the strong Church that would bind Europe together through centuries of invasions and petty wars. As hundreds of new principalities and kingdoms groped their way throughout the Middle Ages to a new society, the medieval Church would serve as a center of faith, education, and tradition because of the groundwork laid by Gregory I, first medieval Pope.

THE RISE OF THE FRANKS

Charles the Hammer at the battle of Tours.

Pope Gregory's dream of unity of the Christian world was shattered soon after his death by a new invasion, the biggest and most far-reaching of all the invasions which had threatened the Roman and Byzantine world.

Under the leadership of the great prophet Mohammed a new religion arose in the desert country of Arabia. After Mohammed's death in 632, his followers, the Moslems, needing land and fired with the enthusiasm of their burning new religion, swept through country after country with extraordinary swiftness. From Arabia to Syria, Egypt, North Africa, and Spain they came as conquerors, carrying their new faith and their language. They penetrated the very heart of Christian centers, Jerusalem, Damascus, Alexandria, and Tunis which soon became centers of the Moslem faith and culture. By the early eighth century they had conquered Spain in the West and had advanced to Constantinople in the East, but the city's strong walls held and its powerful navy defeated them in 717.

While the Byzantine Empire vied with the Moslems for control of the Mediterranean, Western Europe became more and more isolated. Its trade shrank to almost nothing. Luxuries, spices, and silks from the East, oil from Africa, and papyrus from Egypt, nearly disappeared. Money became scarce and payments were made by cattle, grain, wine, and above all by land. Cities of the former Roman Empire, once connected through trade under one central government, gradually changed to walled fortress towns, hardly communicating with one another at all. The West became more dependent on agriculture than on trade. Large self-sufficient estates with their own mills, forges, and wine presses replaced the old Roman urban civilization. A more simple frontier-type of life took over.

After the Moslems had captured Spain in 711 they began to raid the country of the Franks, north of the Pyrenees. Searching for booty and conquest, they approached the sacred city of Tours, in the heart of Frankland, where they knew that the great shrine of St. Martin contained vast treasure.

Luckily for the Franks a new champion had appeared, the mighty warrior, Charles Martel, who wielded the heavy battle hammer with such skill that he has forever been called Charles the Hammer. Charles, the bastard son of an important East Frankish nobleman, had broken loose from a dungeon where his step-mother had confined him, and had become the real ruler of the East and West Franks, whose kings had become so feeble that they were known as the "do-nothing" kings.

By the fall of 733 the Moslems, ravaging and looting the country-side, neared the city of Tours but Charles had been alerted and was there to meet them. The Moslems found the old Roman road to Tours blocked by the formidable Franks, who, armed in mail and protected by their huge round shields, stood like an iron wall. In the battle which ensued the Franks hurled their barbed spears and tapered throwing axes with such ferocity that many Moslems, including their leader, were slain. As darkness brought a halt to the fighting, each side retired to its camp. Early the next morning the Franks, creeping toward the Moslem tents, were surprised to find them deserted; the leaderless Moslems, panic-stricken, had fled during the night. All Christians hailed Charles as a hero who had saved the West from the infidels. The Christians now looked to the Franks as defenders of their faith.

Charles the Hammer realized that he must make his army even stronger to maintain his power over the vast Frankish lands which stretched all the way from the Rhine River to the Pyrenees. He began to build up a cavalry—the mounted knights whose fighting ability had been increased by a valuable device which had recently appeared in the West. This was the stirrup which, by supporting the rider's legs, gave him a firm seat and enabled him to fight freely, without fear of being unhorsed. The stirrup made the horse and rider a single fighting unit; with the combined weight of himself and the horse behind it, a knight could now thrust a lance with great force.

But to equip and arm a knight was costly business and to maintain a cavalry was expensive. Charles soon solved this. He knew that the Church was rich in land—the main source of wealth in the West then—and decided to help himself to Church property and give it to his warrior knights as pay. The produce of the large estates enabled them to equip themselves with arms, armor, and well-trained horses. Charles' knights became his sworn followers or vassals, swearing to serve him faithfully all the days of their lives. He in turn promised to support them. This contract or two-way deal to support a cavalry in exchange for military service was the basis of what is called feudalism. Feudalism eventually affected all classes of medieval society, each person owing service to someone higher up. The man with the most vassals was the strongest. By offering knights estates or fiefs for their military service Charles attracted more vassals than the Frankish kings who had demanded military service but had offered nothing in return.

Charles' son, Pepin the Short, was more of a statesman, though

Frankish cavalry.

less of a warrior than his father. He was respected and admired by the Pope and the great Anglo-Saxon missionary, Boniface, for his efforts to convert the heathen north of the Rhine River. Like his father he was the real ruler of the Franks though not their king. He decided it was time to put an end to the "do-nothing" kings and have himself crowned. In 751 he sent messengers with an important question to the Pope in Rome: "Who should be king, he who has the power but no title or he who has the title but no power?" The Pope gave Pepin the answer he wanted and King Childeric, last of the first Frankish royal line, who had nothing to call his own but the vain title of King, was trundled off in an oxcart to end his days in a monastery.

Pepin called an assembly at the town of Soissons, where he was raised upon a shield and proclaimed King of the Franks. He was also anointed with holy oil by his friend, Boniface, so that he was not only king, but king by the grace of God, with divine rights.

44

Pope Stephen, in desperate need of help against the Lombards who, a hundred and fifty years after Pope Gregory, were again encroaching on papal lands and threatening Rome, determined to seek the aid of the newly anointed Frankish king. Leaving Rome in October, 753, the aged, frail Pope crossed the Alps and arrived in Frankland by January where Pepin's envoys met and escorted him to the royal villa. With the envoys was a tall gangling youth with reddish-blond hair and piercing blue eyes. This was Charles, Pepin's oldest son, destined to be one of the greatest rulers of the West.

The Pope told Pepin of his troubles with the Lombards. Young Charles noticed with interest that the Pope went down on his knees and humbly begged King Pepin's help. And, as if to thank Pepin for his promised aid, the Pope not only anointed him for a second time but also anointed Charles and his brother and gave them the honorary titles of Patricians of the Romans, hoping thus to make the new royal line of Franks protectors of Rome.

With this new honor and the papal blessing went obligations which Pepin was prompt to keep. He led his army over the Alps, defeated the Lombards, and gave the disputed lands to the Pope forever. This made the Pope a large landowner of states stretching across the center of Italy but it did not endear the Franks to the Lombards.

Charles the Hammer and Pepin the Short had united the earlier Frankish conquests. Supported by the Church and blessed by the Pope, the Franks now took the lead of the Western World. The center of their large realm was in the north, near the Rhine River, a land of deep forests, mists, and swamps. It bore little imprint of the past Roman civilization, for the Romans had preferred the south, the land of olive groves, vines, and orange trees near the warm Mediterranean Sea. But a new civilization was beginning with this line of Frankish kings, and northern Europe now became the focus of the West. Here Pepin's son Charles, the future Charles the Great, was to cast a beam of light in the Dark Ages and to create a new Christian empire.

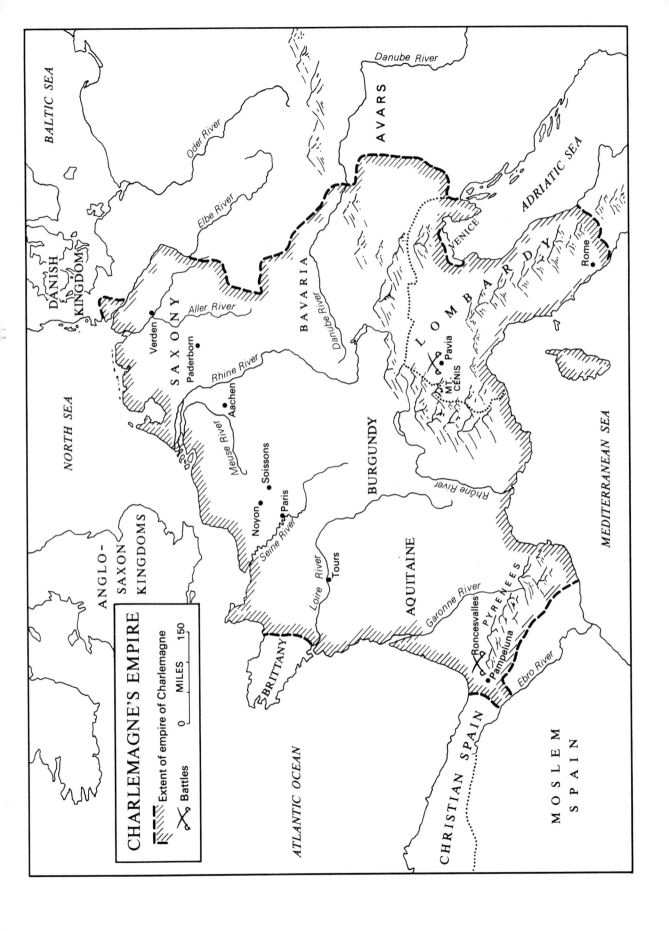

BALTIC SEA

Danube River

AVARS

ADRIATIC SEA

Oder River

DANISH KINGDOM

Elbe River

L O M B A R D Y

VENICE

SAXONY

Aller River

BAVARIA

Rome

Verden

Danube River

NORTH SEA

Paderborn

Rhine River

MT. CENIS

Pavia

Aachen

Meuse River

Soissons

ANGLO-SAXON KINGDOMS

Noyon

Paris

Seine River

BURGUNDY

Rhône River

MEDITERRANEAN SEA

CHARLEMAGNE'S EMPIRE

Extent of empire of Charlemagne

✕ Battles

0   MILES   150

Loire River

Tours

AQUITAINE

Garonne River

PYRENEES

Roncesvalles

BRITTANY

Pampeluna

Ebro River

ATLANTIC OCEAN

CHRISTIAN SPAIN

M O S L E M   S P A I N

CHARLEMAGNE

*Charlemagne. This fourteenth-century bust encloses his skull,
a sacred relic. Artists always showed him with a beard
although he never had one.*

Carolus Magnus or Charles the Great, Karl der Grosse to the Germans, best known to us by his French name of Charlemagne, ruler of Franks, Saxons, Lombards, and Bavarians, founder of the

Holy Roman Empire, combined the warrior skill of his grandfather, Charles the Hammer, with the statesmanship and piety of his father, Pepin. He became more famous than either of them and his life was immortalized in song and legend throughout the Middle Ages.

Charles was born in the northern part of Frankland in 742. He learned early to hunt the wild boar and stag in the dark forests of oak and elm trees. Holding his shield in his left hand, he could hurl a javelin or throw an axe with his right, while his horse galloped full speed. He was an excellent swimmer and famous for his strength. He grew to be six feet four inches tall and legend said that he could fell a horse and rider with one blow of the fist. His large penetrating blue eyes were usually friendly and merry, but when angry they flashed so that no one dared look him in the face. His forehead was prominent, his nose long and his voice strangely high-pitched. According to the Frankish custom his reddish-blond hair was long and he wore a moustache.

Charles preferred the ordinary dress of the Franks to the ostentatious fashion of some of his nobles. When he noticed them parading around in short silk capes, embroidered and fringed, he scornfully said, "What is the good of those little napkins? I cannot cover myself with them in bed and when on horseback I cannot shield myself with them from the wind and rain." Charles usually wore a plain, long blue cape, short on the sides to allow freedom to wield his sword or axe. Under his cloak he wore a coarse linen tunic. In cold weather this was of otter or marten skin. His most precious possession, his sword, never left his side.

Though Charles had little formal education he learned things of value to a future king. He always went with his father's court when it traveled from place to place. Unlike the old Roman Empire which had one seat of government, the Frankish court had no special home and was always on the move. There was little trade in Frankland at this time and when food and supplies were exhausted on one estate, king and court moved on to another, taking all their belongings with them. Charles saw much of the vast country he would someday rule.

He also attended the national assemblies, which were held twice a year. The fall assembly was a select affair where the king and his most

A Frankish king holding assembly.

intimate vassals, his "paladins," discussed problems of the realm and
made decisions to present to the big assembly in the spring. To the
spring assembly, held outdoors in an open field, came all the great
men of the realm, royal vassals, bishops, priests, and freemen, any
who held land. Charles sat on the grass, watching and listening. The
long robed churchmen sat apart from the laymen, but all discussed
the decrees which the king presented for their approval. They also
brought to the king's attention certain problems—a vassal who had
deserted his lord, poachers in the royal forests, and any dangers which
threatened the frontiers. But the main topic was war, and the able-
bodied came equipped for it. The spring assembly nearly always
meant war.

Charles accompanied his father on several military expeditions and,
at the age of nineteen, helped subdue the rebellious Aquitanians in
the south of Frankland. He was being trained in the statesmanship of
the day, to be a warrior and a defender of the Christian faith.

When King Pepin died in 768, the kingdom was divided between
Charles and his younger brother, Carloman, according to the Frank-

ish custom. At the town of Noyons, Charles was raised upon his shield amid the clanging of spears and the shouts of "May the king live forever. At the same time his younger brother, in a similar ceremony, was proclaimed king in the nearby town of Soissons. Pepin had arranged the division of the realm so that Charles, the older and stronger, inherited the borderlands and seacoast which, like an arc, partly encircled his brother's lands. He would have to guard the dangerous borders.

There was little love between the two brothers and in the first year of their joint kingship they quarreled. When Charles summoned Carloman to help quell another revolt in Aquitaine, his brother refused. Charles, with only a small force, went alone. Actually he was rather pleased to prove his prowess singlehanded. He counted on speed and surprising the enemy; his success was more than he expected, and the revolt was quickly put down. Charles became popular overnight but Carloman's reputation suffered.

Charles returned north to his wife, Himiltrude, and their little hunchback son, Pepin. Charles had married Himiltrude several years before he became king and she had produced only this one, deformed son. When Charles' domineering mother suggested that he marry a princess, the daughter of the Lombard king, he was enthusiastic. Though the Franks had been Catholics since the fifth century, they were rather casual about the marriage sacrament, and cast off one wife for another in spite of the rules of the Church. And Charles' mother felt this marriage would avert war between her sons. Because of the marriage alliance between Charles and the Lombards, Carloman's land would be completely surrounded and he would be powerless to start trouble.

When the Pope got news of this alliance between his friends and protectors, the Franks, and his enemies, the Lombards, he was beside himself with fear and rage. "How," he asked, "could the glorious race of Franks ally with the perfidious and stinking Lombards?" He called down a curse upon the marriage, reminding Charles that it would not be lawful since Himiltrude was still his true wife. He warned the Franks that all who consented to it would be doomed to everlasting Hell. These were strong words but the Pope had every reason to be angry. The Franks had promised to protect Rome against the "unspeakable" Lombards and now they were allied with them. The Pope's message came too late. By the time it reached him, Charles was already married to the Lombard princess.

Charles soon realized his mistake. He had been made King of the Franks and Patrician of the Romans by the Church and he knew he had obligations to the Pope. Within a year Charles sent his bride back to Lombardy. This was, of course, a grave insult to the Lombards and it caused his first rift with his mother. Henceforth, he would decide things for himself. He promptly married a third wife of his own choosing, a lovely young Frankish noblewoman, named Hildegarde. The Pope was so relieved to have the Franks break their alliance with his enemies that he made no objection to this marriage. But the Lombards did not forgive Charles.

In 771 Carloman died. Charles hastened to claim his brother's land and, at an assembly, was proclaimed King of all Frankland. He was now sole ruler of the largest realm in Western Europe.

There would be no war between brothers, but war with the Lombards seemed unavoidable. Yet Charles decided to let the Lombard problem wait while he coped with trouble in the north, beyond the Rhine River. This was the land of the Saxons, fierce barbarians who worshipped heathen gods and, it was rumored, even practiced human sacrifice. Charles' father and grandfather had tried to subdue these heathens and the great missionary, Boniface, had tried to convert them, but the Saxons burned the missionary churches, destroyed Frankish forts along the borders, and refused to pay their annual tribute of three hundred horses. Charles felt they needed to be subdued and, above all, they must be converted to Christianity—by the sword if necessary.

If he could strike at the heart of their heathen religion Charles felt he could accomplish their conversion and bring them to submission. Watching for ambushes from the thick forests, he moved his army swiftly and cautiously along the banks of the Lippe River. A sacred grove of mighty trees lay hidden in a valley. In the center was Irminsul, a huge tree trunk, thought to uphold the universe. Around it the Saxons made their blood sacrifices and beneath it lay a vast treasure,

51

tribute to the pagan tree god. The Saxons had no time to prepare defenses nor to remove the treasure before the Franks, armed with sharp axes, burst into the grove and hacked down the sacred tree. The Franks eagerly seized the treasure of gold, silver coins, goblets, and plate and then destroyed the crude wooden buildings of the pagan priests. As though to reward the Franks for their victory over the heathens, what seemed a miracle occurred. Exhausted by the midsummer heat and parched with thirst, the Franks were amazed to see a "tremendous volume of water suddenly gush forth from the dry bed of a stream." They felt that God was pleased with them.

Now Charles had to attend to the urgent pleas for help from Pope Hadrian. The Lombard king was again encroaching on the Pope's lands. Charles called an assembly at Geneva near the borders of Lombardy and told his Franks of his obligation to defend the Church and Pope's lands. He called for war on the Lombards and the assembly consented.

The great Frankish host was an impressive sight when it gathered that May of the year 773. The mounted horsemen came first, riding into the field of war in separate groups, each under the banner of his count, followed by the foot soldiers. All had to provide their own equipment, shield, lance, bow with two strings, and twelve arrows. The mounted knights also had to provide their own horses, mail coats of interlocking steel rings and iron helms. This was Charles' cavalry, the most important part of his army. Only the wealthy vassals could afford a knight's equipment. Foot soldiers wore tough hide jackets with scattered metal rings, and sometimes caps reinforced with iron bands. Last came the baggage train of wagons drawn by oxen. Food for three months and clothing for six were loaded into the tightly covered wagons along with crude siege weapons, stones, axes, and spades.

To cross the Alps, Charles divided his army into two sections, one to go by the St. Bernard pass, and the other, which he would command, to go over Mont Cenis. After days of struggling up the perilous path, Charles' army reached the summit and started down the Lombard side into a narrow gorge, only to find it blocked by fortifications. But Charles was not to be stopped and by using unexplored passes he and his Franks appeared unexpectedly behind the Lombards who, terrified, retreated to the base of the mountain. The other Frankish army appeared from St. Bernard's pass and joined Charles. Panic ensued among the Lombards, who fled through the valley of the Po River to their walled city of Pavia, pursued by the formidable Franks.

It was said that the Lombard King Desiderius and one of his dukes shut themselves up in a tower and watched the approach of the Franks. King Desiderius, trembling with fear, kept asking if Charles were yet in sight. " 'Not yet,' said the duke, 'not yet. When you see the plain bristle with a harvest of spears, when rivers of black steel come pouring in on your city walls, then know that Charles is at hand.' Hardly had he finished these words than there came from the west a black cloud, which turned the bright day into horrid gloom. Then could be seen the iron Charles, helmeted with iron, his hands in iron gauntlets, and iron his breastplate. He held aloft an iron spear in his left hand and his right hand rested on his iron sword, his shield

An early medieval siege.

was all of iron. The fields and open spaces were filled with iron. The rays of the sun were thrown back by the gleam of iron. 'There is your Charles whom you would see,' said the duke and he swooned like one dead."

Such was the tale of Charles' might but actually he could not breach the walls of Pavia right away. He set up camp in the plain below the city and settled down to wait for starvation to force the Lombards' surrender.

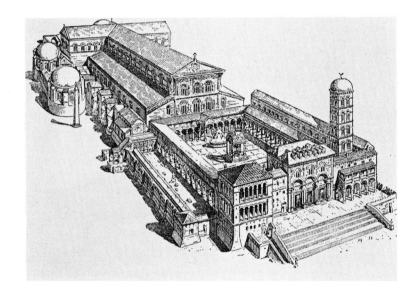

St. Peter's basilica in Charlemagne's time.

Charles, always a restless man in action, soon tired of waiting and set out for Rome. The Pope sent dignitaries to meet and escort the Frankish host. Charles was greeted with enthusiasm. Children lined the streets, waving olive branches and singing hymns; bishops and priests, bearing sacred banners and processional crosses, advanced to meet him. At the sight of the crosses Charles dismounted and continued on foot to the steps of St. Peter's basilica. Then, filled with awe and piety, he fell on his knees and kissed each step as he slowly mounted. At the top he stood and clasped Pope Hadrian's hand and together they passed through the vast atrium into the church itself and on down to the holy of holies, St. Peter's tomb.

The next day was Easter, and High Mass was followed by a great feast at the Pope's Lateran palace. Charles was impressed by Rome's beautiful buildings and thought of the crude wooden houses and squat little stone churches in his Rhine country. The Romans chanted hymns in perfect unison with correct words and musical rhythm. How different this was from the poorly intoned hymns of the Franks. He dreamed of building a great capital near the Rhine River where art and learning would flourish.

In June Charles was back in Pavia where he received a formal surrender of the Lombard kingdom. He was now King of the Lombards as well as King of the Franks and Patrician of the Romans. The Lombard nobles took an oath of fealty to their new king, promising him obedience and service in time of war. King Desiderius was sent off to a monastery—a convenient way of getting rid of a rival. With the surrender of Lombardy came enormous treasure and all its wealthy estates, useful to pay for Charles' incessant wars and to reward his warriors.

On his return to Frankland, Charles was discouraged to find that, in his absence, the Saxons had been raiding his borders again. This was a constant problem. Again and again he went into the untamed land of the Saxons, which stretched northeast from the Rhine to the Elbe River. Again and again he defeated certain tribes, bringing home hostages as pledges of good faith and submission to Christianity. But no sooner did Charles turn his back than raids on Frankish forts and churches started once more and the converted Saxons went back to their pagan religion. Now a new chieftain, Widukind, was uniting the tribes and rallying their fighting spirit against the Franks, telling them that their oath to the Christian Charles was treason to their own gods.

Charles, bitter at the endless Saxon disobedience and defiance, was determined on "Christianity or death" and started a ruthless policy of devastation. His pressure aroused fear, and the speed with which he moved his armed knights began to tell. In 777, when he suppressed a revolt led by bold Widukind, he found little resistance; the enemy humbly submitted to his demands and underwent baptism. Heartened by this success, Charles called an assembly at Paderborn, a new fortress town in Saxon land and summoned the recently converted Saxons to attend. Confident that the worst of the war was over, he was in a gay mood and ordered a chapel to be built to celebrate the conversion of the heathens.

During celebrations at Paderborn, a strange embassy appeared. Three dark-skinned men from Moslem Spain rode into the fortress town on their swift Arab horses. Dismounting, they bowed before King Charles, asking his help. Spain was in the midst of a civil war, one faction of Moslems trying to overthrow the one in power. Ibn-al-Rabi, spokesman for the rebel cause, told of the oppression of the Moslem caliph. He described how the few Christians in northern Spain suffered under the tyrant's rule. He promised rich rewards of land and cities if the Franks would aid in overthrowing the caliph, and added that he would have a large rebel host waiting to join Charles in the city of Saragossa. Eager to champion persecuted Christians and to push the Moslems further south in Spain, Charles agreed to this request.

Charles gathered the largest army he could muster. In the spring of 778 he left the Rhineland, starting south on the old Roman road to Tours where fifty years before his grandfather, Charles the Hammer, had defeated the same enemy. In the sunny land of Aquitaine the army, already weary from its long march, paused to rest before proceeding to the Pyrenees, the mountain barrier between Frankland and Spain. Exalted by his mission to conquer the infidel but also filled with a sense of foreboding on entering this unknown country, Charles led his men successfully over the mountains and approached the Christian city of Pamplona. To his dismay no Christians came out to greet the Frankish host. The Christians were even hostile; apparently they were not at all unhappy under the "tyrant" rule and had no desire to rebel against their Moslem caliph. Charles and his warriors had to fight their way through Christian lands to reach the Moslem city of Saragossa where they expected Ibn-al-Rabi's rebel army to join them and throw open the gates. But the rebel army never appeared and the gates of the city stayed shut. Charles' crude siege weapons could not break down the city's strong walls. The Franks felt trapped and suspected treachery. Frustrated and angry, Charles gave the order to retreat. Gathering his host, he led them back to the Pyrenees, to the narrow pass of Roncesvalles.

"Fair was the day and bright shone the sun," as the Franks wound their way through the narrow mountain pass. They were happy to be going home. Charles led the bulk of his army successfully through the pass and descended safely into Frankland. The rear guard, with the baggage train of supplies, contained many of Charles' best warriors, his closest and most trusted companions in arms, among whom was Count Roland. The men, marching at their ease, were followed by the slow-moving ox-drawn wagons, when suddenly there swept down from the overhanging cliffs a horde of wild mountain men. Taken by surprise, the rear guard was completely at the mercy of the attackers, who hurled down boulders and let fly their swift arrows. Then, with swords drawn, the mountain men leaped down on the Franks in the narrow defile below and killed them to a man. As darkness fell, the assailants escaped with all the booty of the baggage train.

From this defeat, the first rebuff that Charles and his Franks had encountered, grew the famous legend of Roland which was later put into verse. It became the favorite poem of the Middle Ages, carried throughout Europe by wandering minstrels to every town and inn along the pilgrim highways. In the song Roland became a mighty hero, who had conquered many lands for his aged white-haired uncle Charles (really only thirty-six at the time and no relation to Roland) and preferred to die fighting than to sound his horn for help. Sad and angry, Charles returned to look for his rear guard.

> High are the hills, the valleys dark and deep,
> Grisly the rocks and wondrous grim the steeps.
>
> . . . .
>
> Vespers draws on and shining is the day;
> Against the sun glitters their armed array,
> Hauberk and helm flash back a mighty blaze,
> So many shields their painted flowers display
> Such store of spears with gilded pennons gay!
> The Emperor rides right wrathful on his way.
> And all the French in anger and dismay;
> There is not one but weeps for very rage;
> For Roland's sake they're grievously afraid.

The song reported how Charles found the pass littered with the dead bodies of his rear guard and evidence of Roland's brave struggle.

> Red with the blood of all our chivalry!
> He feels such pity he cannot choose but weep;
> And sees his nephew stretched on the grassy green.
> It is no wonder if Carlon's woe is keen.

Heavy of heart at such a loss, the real Charles journeyed north through Frankland. His hopes of rescuing Christians and extending his rule into Spain had come to nothing and he had lost the flower of his army. As he drew near Paris he heard news of famine. But famines were common enough in those days and Charles was more distressed by the news that Widukind was still active and had rallied the Saxons to another serious revolt.

Still smarting from his defeat in Spain, Charles now bent every effort to crush the Saxons. He set up a Saxon law so severe and harsh that it could only cause resentment. It stipulated death for any crime, no matter how small, and if any Saxon tried to avoid baptism the law said, "Let him be punished by death."

When Charles heard that more of his best warriors had been wiped out in a battle in the far north, near the frontier town of Verden, he hurried there and rounded up the Saxon nobles, ordering them to produce Widukind or lose their heads. The Saxon nobles, fearing for their lives, betrayed their fellow men. Widukind, who kept vanishing like an evil spirit, could not be found but forty-five hundred of his loyal men were delivered up to Charles. On the banks of the River Aller, which flowed by Verden, Charles had them all beheaded. Deep within him had stirred the old barbarian feeling of blood revenge. But even this ruthless act, the worst blot on Charles' life, did not break the proud, fierce spirit of the Saxons.

Soon after this terrible day, Charles' wife and mother died. Some thought that God was punishing Charles, though most Christians applauded the massacre of the heathen Saxons, but he was more determined than ever to subdue and convert the pagans. Only after years of cruel devastation, of setting fire to villages, and laying waste the land, could the better-armed Franks wear down and break the Saxons' spirit. The Saxons were finally forced to sue for peace and even Widukind, realizing the hopelessness of the situation, agreed to surrender. When the fallen hero submitted to baptism, thousands followed and embraced the Christian faith. The Saxons were a beaten people but they were Christians and Charles was hailed for his good works. The Pope ordered a three-day celebration to be held throughout the realm.

A medieval conception of the baptism of the Saxons.

Charles now began to organize Saxony as a Frankish province; soon it became an integral part of Frankland. Under the influence of his gentle scholar friend, Alcuin, Charles softened his policy towards the Saxons. "What is the use of baptism without faith? A man may be forced to baptism but cannot be forced to believe," Alcuin wisely said. Charles relaxed his iron rule and gave the Saxons a measure of justice. With land cleared and made fertile by missionary monks, with walled towns rising from the forts, Saxony grew into a great center of medieval Christendom, the future northern Germany. The Frankish kingdom now stretched from the Elbe to the Pyrenees.

Soon after Hildegarde's death, Charles married a fourth wife—he was never long without a wife. Very much of a family man and a devoted father, Charles enjoyed having his many sons, daughters, and grandchildren near by. He was training his favorite son and namesake, Charles, to rule the main part of his realm. He had another son crowned King of Italy and the youngest, Louis, when but an infant, crowned King of Aquitaine.

Besides his devotion to his family, Charles' extraordinary energy and determination to improve as well as expand his kingdom touched all phases of life. He had wisely asked Alcuin to take charge of his palace school. Charles could not have picked a better person. Alcuin, "skilled in learning beyond all others," came from the great cathedral school of York, in England, where, by the eighth century, learning had reached a much higher level than on the continent. Alcuin, who could read and write the pure Latin of the ancient Romans, found Frankish education in a deplorable state. There were only a few poor monastery schools using badly copied texts with incorrect Latin. Few people outside the Church could read and write.

The informal palace school was attended by Charles and his family and anyone else interested in learning. Charles felt strongly that those who, "by the gift of God are able to learn, according to the capacity of each individual, should be educated." When he and Alcuin organized church schools throughout the land, Charles urged that children of the poor not be charged a fee. His aim was free education for all who wanted it.

Charles had a curious and penetrating mind and was one of Alcuin's most eager pupils. He was honest about his own ignorance and set to work with great diligence. He took up arithmetic at the age of fifty and was still trying to master manuscript writing when an old man. He learned to read Latin and understood some Greek.

The main purpose of learning in those days was to reach a better understanding of the Bible and other sacred writings. Arithmetic was used largely to calculate dates of church festivals. The great writings of ancient Romans were studied for correct spelling, good use of language, and eloquence, not as an end in themselves but as a training towards understanding Holy Scripture. All education was reli-

This script with its capitals and small letters is the basis for our modern script.

gious; Greek science had long since been forgotten. To a question such as "What is the moon?" even the learned Alcuin answered, "The moon is the eye of night, the giver of dew, the foreteller of storms."

Charles was concerned about the correct use of words. "What good," he asked, "are good thoughts if you cannot express them clearly?" He and Alcuin worked hard to correct books poorly copied by ignorant monks, and to increase the number of these books. In the monasteries they set up scriptoria, rooms where monks copied old manuscripts. Papyrus, formerly used by the Romans, was no longer available so the monks wrote on sheepskin (parchment) which was difficult to prepare and had to be used sparingly. In order to get more words on a page, the monks developed a fine penmanship known as the "Caroline minuscule," from which our modern script has developed. Alcuin saw to it that the monks wrote clearly and beautifully. They often used gold lettering on purple-dyed parchment and decorated the margins. These manuscripts were creations of great beauty and, more important, they are our greatest source of knowledge of the old Latin writers. Hidden away in monasteries, they survived the upheavals of the next centuries and many were found in perfect condition by Renaissance scholars of the fifteenth century. For this the world owes much to Charles and Alcuin.

61

Charles' conquests seemed never ending; as soon as he conquered one country he was drawn into conflict with another. In 787 Charles had annexed the Christian Duchy of Bavaria, the land between the Alps and Danube River, thus uniting all the continental Germanic peoples. Bordering Bavaria on the east was the land of the heathen Avars who, like the Huns, were swarthy, black-haired people with slanting eyes. Excellent archers and horsemen, they terrorized their neighbors by swift, plundering raids. They had amassed enormous treasure, the accumulation of two centuries, which they kept hidden and safely protected in the center of their strange settlement, known as the Ring, which cast a sense of awe and wonder on Christians of the West. It consisted of nine huge concentric rings of land, each separated from the other by fortified earthworks and high palisades. Each ring contained villages and farms; gates through the fortifications led from ring to ring. It was said that the outer one was thirty miles in diameter. The peal of trumpets, to warn of an approaching enemy, could be heard from ring to ring.

Charles felt that the heathen Avars must, like the Saxons, be brought into his Christian realm. He laid elaborate plans to conquer them, summoning several of his armies to converge on the borders of Avarland. For three days his armies halted by the Raab River, fasting, singing hymns, and praying for victory. Luckily for the Franks, dissension and civil war broke out among the Avars. Revolts within the villages enabled the Franks to break through the fortifications and fight their way to the center of the Ring. Here they stormed the palace where the great hoard of treasure lay. "In no war within the memory of man had the Franks won such great riches." It took fifteen wagons, each drawn by four oxen, to carry the gold coins, precious jewels, jeweled swords, chalices, and silken garments to King Charles, who awaited its arrival in his new palace at Aachen. Charles was generous with this enormous treasure, sending much of it to the Pope and churches throughout the land and rewarding his vassals lavishly. Avar messengers soon appeared, humbly surrendering. Charles had learned his lesson with the Saxons and decreed that baptism for the Avars would follow instruction in the meaning of Christianity. The "most mild Charles," as he was often called, was emerging. After the destruction of their Ring, the Avars gradually disappeared, leaving no trace of their strange civilization. Frankland now extended from the Elbe River in the north to the Pyrenees in the south, from the Atlantic Ocean in the west to the Danube River, almost to the Byzantine Empire.

During the Avar war, Charles' fourth wife died. His fifth and last wife, Liutgard, was gentle, wise, and beautiful. With her Charles began to spend more and more time in Frankland. His favorite spot was Aachen, in the lush green valley between the Meuse and Rhine Rivers. Nearby, warm sulphur springs spread into pools where Charles and his friends could bathe. He built an enormous marble swimming pool in which a hundred people could swim in the health-giving waters. He decided to make Aachen his capital and, to fulfill his dreams of making it a beautiful, splendid city, he called in masons and carpenters from far and near. The Pope sent mosaics and marble from Rome and Ravenna to adorn his palace and chapel. The palace, on top of a hill, was joined to the chapel at the foot by a covered gallery. Besides a large reception hall and rooms for Charles' family, it contained a treasury, a library, baths, and weapons room. But the chapel, modeled on a church in Ravenna, was Charles' pride and joy. He had it built in the shape of an octagon, roofed with a lead dome. He decorated the inside lavishly with silver and gold, mosaics, and different colored marbles and installed doors of solid brass. In it he placed a gift of most sacred relics, a robe of the Virgin Mary and the swaddling clothes of the Infant Jesus for all to worship. They are still there, encased in a lovely gold shrine, which is opened every seven years for pilgrims to venerate.

Beyond the palace and chapel enclosure, a town sprang up to serve the needs of the royal family, to house servants and foreign dignitaries who came to see the king. Food was brought from nearby estates in ox-drawn carts. Peddlers and merchants displayed their wares—wool, fur, and slaves from the North and, on rare occasions, silks from the East. Beggars and cripples swarmed to Aachen, hoping for alms from the rich. It was a busy bustling town, but it hardly compared with the former great cities of the Roman Empire. Aachen, for all Charles' dreams, was a simple place, with borrowed art and decoration. But to the unsophisticated Franks it was a city of glory.

As he grew older Charles became more and more interested in

Biblical studies and interpretations of the Christian faith. He even called his own church council and even dared to disagree with the Pope on matters of church dogma. The Pope was upset and began to wonder if Charles considered himself head of the Church as well as of the State. Charles had indeed raised a question which caused conflict all through the Middle Ages: Who was the real head of the Christians of the West, Pope or king?

In 795 Charles sent a message to the newly elected Pope, Leo III, advising him to be, "a shining example of perfect holiness," and "to follow the statutes of the Holy Scripture." The king seemed to be preaching to the supreme head of the Church but the new Pope Leo made no objection and answered Charles in a most humble letter, swearing allegiance to the king and asking for his protection. He needed Charles' mighty sword to save him from enemies who wished to depose him and set up their own Pope. They even accused Leo of all sorts of dreadful crimes. While messages were going back and forth between Rome and Frankland, the Pope's enemies got out of hand. During a religious procession they fell upon the Pope; his unarmed companions fled in terror as he was dragged from his horse. The conspirators disrobed and beat him, tried to slit his eyes and tongue, then left him lying in the street. Later they crept back and bore him off, a prisoner, to a monastery. His eyes and tongue soon healed as if by a miracle. Late one night a trusty servant helped him escape by a rope down the monastery wall to the sanctuary of St. Peter's church. When Charles heard the shocking news, he sent escorts to rescue and convey Leo to Frankland.

Forty-five years had passed since a Pope had first gone to the Franks for help. King Charles was waiting for his guest in the frontier town of Paderborn, far north of the Alps. He tried to greet the Pope with as impressive a display as possible. Surrounded by his knights, who held brightly colored banners, and bishops, who stood under the banner of the cross, Charles was dressed in shining armor and a golden helmet. As Pope Leo approached, the Franks waved their spears and clashed their shields together. Trumpets sounded and banners waved.

Pope Leo stayed three months at Paderborn. Convinced of Leo's innocence, Charles agreed to put him back on the papal throne. It was clear to Charles that he would have to manage the weak and discredited Pope. Had not Alcuin said to him recently, "Upon you alone rests the salvation of the churches of Christ"? More and more Charles felt his power as the leader of all Christian peoples of the West and considered that the Pope's role was purely spiritual, to pray for souls and for the king's victories in defense of Christianity.

In the fall of 799 Leo returned to Rome, escorted by a powerful Frankish bodyguard. Charles planned to go to Rome the following year to settle the Pope's difficulty. He was confident that he alone could restore the Pope's prestige and position.

Late in November of the year 800 Charles, accompanied by a large army, came in sight of Rome again. A great pageant greeted the king as he neared St. Peter's basilica. Charles swung from his horse and strode up the steps. This time he did not go down on his knees to kiss each one.

St. Peter blessing Charlemagne and Pope Leo who are shown as equals.

Charles insisted on a public trial of Pope Leo to convince the Romans of his innocence of the charges against him but the assembled council soon agreed that it could not judge the Pope, that he was above judgment. The Pope should clear himself by compurgation— by publicly swearing his innocence. Two days before Christmas Pope Leo mounted the pulpit and faced the enormous crowd gathered in St. Peter's. Laying his hands on the Bible, he swore his innocence before God and St. Peter. Franks, Romans, and clergy burst into "Te Deum," praising God and the saints for preserving their Pope.

On Christmas Day the multitude again pressed into St. Peter's to hear High Mass. Charles and his family could be clearly seen as they knelt before the high altar. Charles was not wearing his usual blue cape and short tunic, but a long white Roman robe, bound with a gold belt; on his feet were jeweled sandals. On the altar above him, glittering from the light of three thousand candles, lay the imperial gold crown. The rest of the great basilica was in semi-darkness for only a pale winter light filtered through the small glazed windows. Purple hangings covered spaces between the marble columns, incense filled the air. As Charles rose to his feet at the end of the Mass, Pope Leo lifted the crown and placed it on the king's head. The people burst into a chant, "Charles Augustus, crowned of God, the great and pacific Emperor, long life and victory!" Three times they repeated the chant. Pope Leo fell at Charles' feet and kissed the hem of his robe. The imperial throne of the Western Empire had been empty for over three hundred years. Now a Frank, whose barbarian ancestors had been scorned by the Romans, had been crowned their emperor.

This was a great tribute to the Frankish warrior king and to some it meant the revival of the old Roman Empire. But the old Roman Empire had been unified by one government and one law for all. Charles' empire was a collection of different peoples, living according to their own laws and customs. Its one sense of unity was the Christian faith.

Charles spent only that winter in Rome; he never returned to it for Aachen, not Rome, was to be his capital. Charles' new title gave him prestige and power, but his Franks rarely used it—to them he was still just their king. He had little of the pomp and ceremony which surrounded the Byzantine emperor in Constantinople. Charles was respected and loved for himself, not his title, and was more often called, "the most fearless, the most wise, or the most pious," than Emperor. Yet Charles was uneasy that the Byzantines had not recognized his new position. This was the one thing that bothered him on the momentous Christmas Day. Patience, pressure, and bargaining, including a gift of the city of Venice to the emperor in Constantinople, finally gained him the recognition he wanted. But it was not until the year 812 that the Byzantine emperor hailed Charles as an equal, as Emperor of the West.

Charles' fame spread and he even opened negotiations with the great Moslem ruler, Harun al-Rashid, who lived in Baghdad. Concerned about Christian pilgrims who journeyed to the holy city of Jerusalem in the heart of Moslem territory, Charles sent costly gifts to Harun to cement friendship and ensure protection of the Christians. The wealthy and sophisticated Moslem sent back even costlier gifts, among which was an elephant named Abul-Abbas, the like of which had never been seen by the Franks; it was a source of curiosity and delight and henceforth accompanied Charles everywhere, even on his military campaigns. Another gift which enchanted Charles was a water clock of skilled workmanship. Out of twelve little windows that opened and shut twelve miniature knights appeared at the striking of each hour.

When Charles' conquests were finished he turned his attention to problems of reform within his own realm. His laws, known as capitularies, covered a wide range of subjects, from reforms of church singing and incorrect grammar to broader ideas of justice. Sometimes these capitularies were short sermons on how to behave in church, how to keep the Sabbath, and how to keep clean. (Charles was obsessed with cleanliness and, unlike most medieval men, took a bath every day.) He thought of himself as a Biblical king who preached as well as ruled.

To check the growing abuses of wealthy and corrupt feudal counts and bishops, Charles sent picked messengers, called "missi," throughout his realm. The missi traveled in pairs, one a layman, one a churchman, inspecting conditions and reporting back abuses or injustices.

They checked on the conduct of monks and priests. They investigated the rich counts and bishops who were in charge of counties and dioceses to see that they did not extract unfair payment and undue service from the people.

Though Charles allowed his different subjects to live by their own codes of law he tried to improve some of them. The old custom of "wergeld," a fine imposed on a murderer to be paid to the family of the victim, had been devised to curb revenge and blood feuds by substituting a payment for vengeance. The amount of the wergeld was determined by the victim's importance, a noble's being three times as much as a peasant's. But blood feuds still existed in Charles' day; he determined to stop them and insisted that wergelds be paid promptly and that the victim's family, under no circumstances, seek revenge. He added a new touch to the old law, that the Church mete out a penance for the murderer. So began the theory that murder was a crime against the community rather than just an offense against a family or clan. Although Charles used men under oath to help decide landownership disputes, he often resorted to the quicker method of "ordeal of the cross," for he felt it showed the judgment of God and could not be wrong. When a violent dispute between a bishop and an abbot over the ownership of a monastery could not be settled, Charles ordered the use of this ordeal. In the royal chapel each stood with arms outstretched in the form of a cross. The bishop's arms dropped first and the abbot won the dispute. Few doubted the truth of divine judgment.

Charles was so interested in farming that he renamed the months of the year according to their seasonal activities, calling June, Brachmanoth, break ground month; July, Heuvimanoth, haying month; November, Herbistomanoth, harvest month, and so forth. He issued detailed capitularies about the management of large estates, which were his chief source of wealth, with their cattle and horses, grain, vegetables, and fruit, and their own mills, forges, and breweries. All estates were ordered to have artisans, even armorers to equip their warriors.

Charles also insisted that peasants give their due service, three days of work a week for their overlord tilling the land, tending cattle, or

Medieval peasants plowing.
From a fifteenth-century
manuscript.

harvesting wheat. They could work their own little plot of land the other days but from it they must give their lord presents of eggs, cheese, meat, and wool. These peasants were freer than household slaves but they were bound to the land they lived on; if the land was given to a new lord, they were transferred along with the cattle, fields, and orchards.

Towards the end of his life Charles tried to lighten the military burdens of his subjects. All freemen, owning at least thirty acres of land, were liable for military service. Charles realized that many could not afford to equip themselves with proper armor. He decreed that only those owning a hundred acres need answer the summons to war, that those owning less could combine with other small land-owners and provide equipment for one knight. This allowed more men to stay on farms and yet provided one well-equipped knight who was more valuable than several ill-armed men. Charles' sense of responsibility for his subjects was rare for a man of his time.

Only towards the end of his life did he realize the value of a fleet and then it was too late. In 810 the Danes launched an attack on his northern coastline, sending two hundred ships to harass harbors and

69

river towns. It was rumored that the Danish king even planned to attack Aachen. For the first time in his life Charles could not decide how to cope with an enemy. He knew his few crude, flat river boats were no match for the long dragon-prowed Danish ships and, for once, the great warrior moved slowly and indecisively. There is a tale that, gazing out of a window, he saw a flash of Viking sails upon the horizon and began to weep. "Do you know why I weep so bitterly? I am torn by a great sorrow because I forsee what evil things they will do to my empire." As he marched north and approached Verden, scene of the horrible massacre of thirty years before, Abul-Abbas, his elephant, died. As he waited for his host to assemble, he got word that his favorite daughter and his son, the King of Italy, had died of the plague. Heavy of heart, Charles seemed incapable of action. Fortunately, the Danes did not attack and the threat from the north subsided for the moment. But this was only a brief calm before the storm which was soon to break. The terror of the north seas had begun and no one, not even Charles, could stop it.

Evil omens were abroad. As Charles journeyed home, a meteor flashed across the heavens. Charles' horse shied and fell, throwing him to the ground with such force that his sword belt was shattered and his javelin flung twenty feet away. That the great warrior king, who had spent his life in the saddle, could be thrown from his horse and maimed—he limped for the rest of his life—was indeed an evil sign.

After this expedition Charles returned to Aachen where he spent his last sad and lonely years. His wife and his beloved scholar friend, Alcuin, had both died and the crowning blow was the death of his favorite son, Charles, whom he had trained to take over his rule. Charles consoled himself with religion, preaching, and dictating sermons to his people. He hesitated a long time before he summoned his only remaining and least capable son, Louis, to Aachen. He did his best to instruct his heir in how to rule, to be firm yet understanding, to be ruthless only when necessary. Unfortunately, Charles did not pass on his robust and energetic personality to this weak son.

On a Sunday in the fall of 813 Charles, now seventy-one, put on the imperial robes he so seldom wore and, leaning on his son's arm,

A medieval artist's conception of an elephant.

limped to the altar of his chapel where a new gold crown lay sparkling. After kneeling in prayer, Charles arose and addressed his son, admonishing him to rule wisely. He then placed the crown on Louis' head. No Pope or bishop was called to officiate. As the ruler of Western Christendom, Charles felt no need to call upon the Pope. He alone would confer upon his son the divine right and power over his empire. It was his last public act.

Late in November, when the cold wind blew from the forests across the misty valley to Aachen, Charles went hunting. He had been suffering from gout but, headstrong as ever, he disappeared into the woods for nearly a month. In January he contracted a severe fever and pain in his side. Always mistrustful of doctors and their remedies, he doctored himself. He who had always scorned fasting, now ate sparingly, denying himself the great roasts he so loved. People knew that his end was near for more strange things happened. Inside his chapel dome the huge letters of Charles' name began to fade, his great wooden bridge over the Rhine burned, and the colonnade between his palace and chapel collapsed. On January 21, 814, he received Holy Communion and, as he closed his eyes, he uttered the Biblical words, "Into thy hands, O Lord, I commend my spirit." He was seventy-two years old and had reigned for forty-six of them.

This great warrior Christian king had halted the decline of civilization in the Dark Ages and had united the Christians of the West, both Romans and barbarians. Though his weak descendants let power slip away and plunged the empire into anarchy and could not stem the Viking invasions, things were rarely as bad as before. The common culture of the Christian faith, which had been Charles' most cherished goal, persisted throughout the Middle Ages. His high ideals, his desire for reform, and his love of learning survived in men's minds. He remained the model of the perfect ruler and he is "Charles the Great" in many languages. He is claimed especially by the two great countries which were once united under him, France and Germany. There is still a legend that he will return one day to reunite the peoples of Europe.

In the twelfth century, more than three hundred years after his death, Charles was made a saint and his empire called the Holy Roman Empire. Myths and legends about the great king grew; he became not only a saintly leader but a worker of miracles, a hero whose deeds of prowess could never be surpassed. He has been called, "The supreme example in human history of the Christian King. Men recognized that in him kingship had reached a higher level, and through the long centuries his memory remained, transmuted into an immortal figure of strength and wisdom."

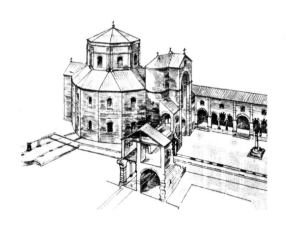

Charlemagne's chapel.

THE END OF THE DARK AGES

Northmen landing.

After Charlemagne's death his great Christian empire, which reached from Spain to the Elbe, gradually broke up into many kingdoms. His lands went first to his only remaining son, Louis; but after Louis' death, according to the old Frankish custom, they were divided among Louis' sons—and then their sons. None of them had Charlemagne's fighting skill or his dream of unity.

Of all the divisions of land after Charlemagne's death, that between the East and West Franks was the most lasting. Charlemagne had been able to hold these two parts of his empire together, but by the time of his grandsons this tie was impossible. They were obviously becoming two different peoples. The East Franks kept the old language of the Germanic forest people, and their cousins the West Franks adopted the various Latin dialects of the old Roman provinces they had overrun. The West Franks were to become the French, and the East Franks, Germans.

Just seventy-five years after Charlemagne's death there were seven kingdoms where there had been one empire—and many dukedoms and counties as powerful as the kingdoms. Though the dream of a unified Christian empire persisted with the German rulers who were often crowned emperors, Charlemagne's original empire was now lost in a jumble of small states constantly changing boundaries through wars, marriage dowries, and deaths.

This political chaos set back for another hundred and fifty years the civilizing process that Charlemagne had started. Enemies outside the boundaries of his old empire took advantage of the squabbles of his heirs and harassed the divided lands. From three directions came marauders: Moslems from the south, Hungarians from the east, and Vikings from the north.

It became impossible for the weak kings of Europe to defend their kingdoms on so many frontiers. Defense had to be left to local warlords. Peasants fled to these lords and took refuge in their strongholds, surrendering their freedom and their small plots of land in return for protection. A nearby baron in a fortress was more useful than a faraway king. Minor knights with little more than their mail shirts, horses, and swords could not survive without becoming vassals to more powerful overlords. Thus the feudal system, in which the less strong owed service to the strong, increased its grip on society.

The Moslem fleets from their bases in Spain and Africa darted from port to port in southern France and Italy, raiding as they went. There was no navy—not even a fishing fleet—to oppose them. At one time (846) raiding Moslems even reached Rome and sacked St. Peter's, the great basilica outside the city walls where Pope Gregory had preached and Charlemagne had been crowned.

From the east, Hungarian warriors threatened the weak German states. They were as mobile on their horses as the Moslems in their ships; carrying rolled-up tents, they rode swiftly to rob monasteries, orchards, and fields, and even to capture helpless families for the profitable slave trade. It was not until the middle of the tenth century that a German emperor, Otto the Great, rid his land of them and sent them back for good to Hungary.

74

A ninth-century fortified church.

But the most destructive raiders of all, with the most lasting effects upon Europe, were the Vikings, sailing from the Scandinavian fjords in slim, dragon-prowed ships. Ignorant and pagan, they destroyed everything in their path. Year by year their raids grew more intense and lasted longer. In 881 they stabled their horses in Charlemagne's old chapel in Aachen; far to the west they invaded Ireland and destroyed the monasteries and brilliant manuscripts of the Irish monks.

Every spring along the northern coasts of Europe the inhabitants caught the glimpse of shining shields and axeblades reflected low over the waves, and watched the long ships beach and the tall blond warriors in their scarlet cloaks and jeweled bracelets jump out with flaming torches and swinging axes. When the local lords gathered their forces to fall upon the pirates, the Northmen would swoop away to another river mouth. Coastal towns soon shrank to mere fishing villages, and the few trade routes leading to them dried up; merchants feared that their pack-trains would meet the dreaded Vikings on a desolate road or that their barges would meet a dragon-ship around some riverbend. So great was the fear of the Northmen that their name was added to the prayers of trembling monks whose churches and abbeys were gradually being destroyed:

"A furore Normanorum libera nos, Domine!"
("From the fury of the Northmen, free us, O God")

In 843 to the dismay of the French, a group of Vikings decided not to depart in the fall as was their usual custom. They stayed on in northern France, spending the winters hunting, trapping, repairing their ships, hanging their striped sails to dry under church roofs. In 885 seven hundred of their shallow boats sailed easily up the unprotected river Seine and besieged Paris until given a pound of silver for each ship by a desperate King of France, Charles the Fat.

Viking strongholds in the north of France grew bigger and became permanent, and gradually enterprising Frenchmen offered to sell them goods and food. Over the years the strongholds became market towns, and the Northmen became traders and farmers instead of pirates. Their settlements around the river Seine, including the big town of Rouen, came to be called Normandy—land of the Northmen. In 911 the King of France, Charles the Simple, who now had only a small kingdom, realized that he had better come to terms with the powerful Normans. In return for their pledge not to plunder his kingdom he officially gave them Normandy and made their chieftain Rollo—a man so huge no horse could carry him—his vassal duke. Rollo became a Christian; Benedictine monks became clerks and advisors to the man whose people had destroyed every monastery in Normandy. Within another generation, the rough Normans lost their Scandinavian language and spoke French. Their leaders forsook their uncouth ways, became nobles of France, and enjoyed the benefits and power of the French feudal system. They began to rebuild the monasteries which their grandfathers had destroyed. Soon they were on their way to becoming the most powerful feudal dukedom in Europe.

The Viking conquests took another form in Anglo-Saxon England. While in France the Northmen became feudal Frenchmen, in England it was easier for them to keep their own wild customs and language. The many little Anglo-Saxon kingdoms which the Vikings attacked were ruled by chieftains very much like the Viking leaders —fighting with axes, hunting, banqueting and drinking for days on end in their tall timbered halls, handing out booty generously to their followers. Although the Anglo-Saxons had been Christians since the days of Pope Gregory I, and although some of the monks who lived among them had been great scholars like Alcuin, not much learning had rubbed off on the Anglo-Saxon population.

The Vikings came to England every spring and in 851 spent their first winter there. Within a few years a huge force destroyed the north of England and sacked its famous monasteries. Then more Vikings overran the middle Anglo-Saxon kingdoms. Only the bravery of Alfred the Great, king of the small southern kingdom of Wessex, at the end of the ninth century prevented southern England, by a series of desperate fights, from also becoming a Viking settlement.

Alfred's son, grandson and great-grandson gradually won back England from the Viking invaders. During the tenth century these splendid Anglo-Saxon kings brought brief peace to England. Their treasure-houses bulged with coins and jeweled ornaments. They rebuilt the ruined churches and monasteries, and encouraged learning. The Dark Ages were ending.

Alfred's descendents ruled England well until in 1016 one of them, known as Ethelred the Unready, let England fall once more under Scandinavian power, so much so that two Danish kings, Sweyn Forkbeard and his son Canute, actually became kings of England. Ethelred and his queen fled across the channel with their two sons to the Norman court. For twenty-five years one of these sons, Prince Edward, later to become King Edward the Confessor of England, remained there in exile and grew attached to Norman people and Norman ways. Before his recall to the English throne in 1042 he came to know and admire his distant cousin William—young son of the sixth duke of Normandy and great-great-great-grandson of Rollo the Northman. Years later this friendship would give William a chance to seize the English throne.

WILLIAM THE CONQUEROR

William the Conqueror.

When the sixth duke of Normandy, Robert the Magnificent, was seventeen, he fell in love with Herlève, the daughter of a man who tanned hides by the river that flowed below the ducal fortress. Their son William was born in 1027.

A few people prophesied great things for the baby. An old legend tells that one day when a nurse put him down to play, he seized some of the white oat-straw that covered the cold stone floor. His strong grasp so impressed the watchers that they said he would never let go anything he set his hand upon and would be a mighty conqueror.

The barons and bishops of the duchy would have laughed at such a prophecy. They arranged a grand marriage for Duke Robert with a Danish princess, expecting that he would soon forget the tanner's daughter and that the illegitimate young William would be pushed into the background by other, higher-born brothers. But Duke Robert rejected the Danish princess, and brought Herlève and the child to live at his court at Rouen.

William grew strong and handsome. His young father doted on him, and the retainers of the household treated him with affection. The ducal court at Rouen was a bustling, important place, full of ambassadors, high-ranking churchmen, armed knights, foreign merchants on their way upriver to Paris, and pilgrims on their way to Rome. There was also the English Prince Edward, a cousin of the duke, who had been exiled in Normandy so long that he had almost forgotten English ways.

When William was only seven years old his father decided to go on a pilgrimage to Jerusalem, and he announced to his counselors that William would be left in charge of the duchy. They pleaded with him to change his mind, for they feared the turbulent barons and the chaos that would occur if Robert should not come back.

Duke Robert could not be dissuaded. He appointed guardians and tutors for William; he sent the child to do homage to his overlord, the King of France, and asked the king to keep an eye on his young vassal. Then he assembled the great men of his land, presenting William to them as their lord. All knelt before the seven-year-old boy in an impressive feudal ceremony and put their hands between his small ones, swearing to be his "man" and to be faithful unto death. But many of the kneeling barons were enraged and insulted to have a child chosen to rule them.

The news that everyone had feared came the following year, 1035: Duke Robert had died of the fever as he was returning from Jerusalem. A huge number of vassals immediately renounced their vows to William, the new eight-year-old Duke of Normandy, and left his court in a hurry. Taking advantage of William's extreme youth and inexperience, the barons joined in a game of raid and counter-raid, "devastating each other's lands by iron and fire," each seeking to expand his power. Some of the barons, fortifying their houses with ditches and palisades, added a square central tower of stone, called a "donjon" or "keep," with walls many feet thick and no windows on the first floors. These were the ancestors of the magnificent Norman castles of the next centuries.

Ambitious lords conspired to remove William's guardians. Once, when murderers killed one of them in his bed, they overlooked the young duke, hiding in the bloody blankets. Assassins soon killed all his protectors and tutors. Sometimes William's humble relatives from his mother's side of the family saved his life by taking him secretly to the huts of their friends, the peasants and woodcutters of the deep forests.

Fortunately there were other violent barons who decided to throw in their lot with the young duke. As William grew older he became tall and muscular; he was an excellent horseman and so skillful with lance and sword that he was able to hold his own with much older warriors. The men who remained loyal to him observed his extraordinary bravery, his dignity, and his confidence that God would help him in all his endeavors. They realized that, young as he was, he was a born ruler—if he could manage to survive.

In 1047, when he was twenty, Duke William asked his overlord, the French king, to help him subdue a revolt of powerful barons. Together they faced the barons near a small market town called Val-ès-Dunes. The knights on both sides drew up their horses in formation; there were no archers or infantry—just horsemen charging each other with lance and sword.

It was William's first pitched battle, and in it William showed the bravery and good fortune for which he was to become so famous. Alone or with few followers he galloped into the thickest ranks of the enemy, showing an early genius for being in the right place at the right time.

An old French poem describes his charge against the most famous warrior of the opposition, Hardez of Bayeux:

Williame verz li s'eslessa,	William launched himself against him,
Un glaive tint, bien l'avisa;	Held a sword and aimed it well
Parmi li cors lez le menton	Between the body and the chin,
Entre la gorge et le gotron	Between the throat and the gullet,
Li fist passer le fer trenchant.	He sliced with biting iron.

This terrifying performance started a rout of the rebel warriors. They fled into the marshes and stumbled into the river Orne; their horses ran wild over the plain. So many of them drowned that the millwheels were clogged with bodies and could not turn.

This was a decisive day in William's life, but more rebellions were to come. Not only did he have to fight his barons but also the changeable King of France who several times invaded Normandy. He set about methodically destroying the power of his barons, besieging and burning their new castles until they surrendered. Then he won their loyalty by his generosity in victory.

Although William had a reputation for mercy, he could be brutal. During a small border war he approached a wooden bridge that protected a rebel town. As the defenders covered the bridge's timbers with wet leather hides to protect them against fire, they drummed on the skins and yelled, "Hides! Hides! Hides for the tanner!" William, a tanner's illegitimate grandson, grew pale with rage at this reference to his birth and swore to cut off the limbs of the taunting citizens like the pruning of a tree. Ordering the ditch under the bridge to be filled with wood and brush, he set it on fire. When the bridge and its defenders collapsed, William kept his oath. Thirty-two defenders of the bridge were brought before him and their hands and feet were cut off and thrown over the walls of the town.

Gradually few were left who dared conspire against the duke. As peace came to Normandy, knights were able to stay home and oversee their properties; serfs were able to plow without losing their oxen to raiders; the land began to prosper again.

During this time William was married to Matilda, daughter of the Count of Flanders, a neighboring country of rising wealth and power. Matilda was a brilliant catch for any lord; she was the niece of the King of France and she was also beautiful, intelligent, and rich. William loved her deeply and sought her counsel during all his complicated and dangerous career.

Pope Leo IX did not approve the marriage, for he feared the mighty combination of Flanders and Normandy. It was only after years of negotiation that his successor, Pope Nicholas II, approved of it and ordered the couple, as penance for marrying without papal blessing, to build a monastery and a nunnery. Year after year in the Norman town of Caen rose the massive walls and thick, round columns of the abbey churches of William and Matilda. High, thin walls and big windows would have to wait for French architects of the next century, but these Norman churches had grandeur and beauty. Small, round-arched windows let rays of light into the deep shadows and corners of the vast, dark interiors. Workmen decorated the walls, wooden ceilings, and altars with bright paint; banners, tapestries, and embroideries were hung everywhere. William and Matilda came often to supervise the buildings and bring gifts.

Carpenters and stonecutters building a church.

In addition, William built at least twenty other abbeys. He appointed abbots and bishops of vigor and education. Though he was completely illiterate, William sought their company, saying that from them he learned the maxims of wisdom and truth. William, like so many bloodthirsty warriors of the Middle Ages, was a deeply religious man. Feeling that he owed his successes to God's will, he tried always to repay his debt to God. He took a leading part in all the important councils of the Norman church and in a short time had its loyal and powerful support.

Across the channel, King Edward the Confessor, who during his twenty-five years of exile in the Norman Court had come to prefer the Normans to the English, was filling his court with Norman knights and priests, appointing Norman sheriffs to tax the people and Norman clerks to interpret English laws. He even succeeded in banishing the two most powerful English lords, Earl Godwin of Wessex and his son Harold, who had vehemently opposed the King's Norman favorites. During the year of their banishment in 1051 the childless King Edward secretly invited the Norman Duke William, his distant cousin, to be his heir.

The offer was a well-kept secret for many years. William first had to be sure of his own strength in Normandy before he dared announce such an agreement. And if King Edward had any intention of making it official, he was unable to do so, for the banished English earls swept back into power and threw out King Edward's Norman favorites. Great English nobles, among them Harold who had inherited the earldom of Wessex, once more took their places around the throne of the weak King Edward. They obviously would never allow William, a hated Norman, to become King of England.

By the year 1064 William was in his thirties and seemed at the height of his power. He was at the top of a great pyramid of churchmen and warriors, all under his control. He was famous throughout Europe for his warlike deeds and riches. His appearance was magnificent. He was tall, with long arms and legs and enormous shoulders made muscular by years of hunting and fighting. His eyes were dark, his chin bold, his hair cut close to his head in the Norman fashion. He wore rich clothes embroidered in gold and ornamented with fur. Restless, surrounded by other restless and strong men, he looked for something to occupy his tremendous energy. But he did not plan to follow his father's example and go on a pilgrimage; he had a bigger goal—the English throne.

William's spies now reported that King Edward, old and doddering, was increasingly under Earl Harold's thumb; in fact, the English were calling Harold "Under-King" and expected him to be the king's heir. Duke William looked for an opportunity to persuade Harold that he was wasting his time if he had designs on the English throne. With the astounding luck that attended William's entire career, the opportunity soon came.

One windy day in 1064 the English Earl Harold, his blond hair cut low on his neck, his blond moustache sweeping across his cheeks, waded barelegged to a ship in a southern English port. He carried his favorite hound under one arm and his falcon on the other. He wore a simple tunic; his servants carried aboard a warm cloak and his sword and shield, but no other armor.

Maybe Harold intended merely to sail along the English shore and stop somewhere for hunting; maybe he wanted to cross to Flanders. Perhaps on sudden impulse—for Harold was an impulsive man—he decided to hunt in Normandy. Whatever his intent, it is probable that a sudden storm drove the English hunting party unexpectedly to the shores of Count Guy of Ponthieu, a vassal of William's, where Harold was recognized, disarmed, and made prisoner. William, seizing this opportunity to have Harold in his power, ordered Count Guy to release Harold to him.

With a band of armed cavalry, William rode to receive Harold. Disguising his true purpose, he set out to charm the English earl. He gave him rich clothes, horses, and weapons; he entertained him lavishly with feats of arms, good hunting, and feasts in one ducal estate after another. The two noblemen had many things in common: both loved sport and battle; both had great properties and wealth; both had attractive manners and devoted followers. They seemed to become great friends.

William persuaded Harold to go with him on a military campaign into the neighboring province of Brittany where they had some fine fighting side by side. Each admired the other's courage and strength. But as the Brittany campaign progressed, Harold found himself caught in a net which was to get tighter and tighter.

The two warriors shared the same tent and meals, and one day in this friendly atmosphere, William mentioned the promise that King Edward had made to him thirteen years before—to leave him the throne of England. He then asked Harold to help him achieve this goal at the death of King Edward.

Earl Harold had no authority to promise the English throne. But as William's guest—and in a way, his prisoner—he seemed to agree. Undoubtedly he thought that once home and out of William's reach, he could forget the whole conversation. But he underestimated the guile of his adversary, who soon tightened the net some more. At the end of a day of battle, he knighted Harold in a formal feudal ceremony, putting his hand on Harold's head and giving him weapons. According to the feudal laws of the Middle Ages, Harold now became William's "man," to serve him in battle and call him his lord.

This may not have meant much to the English Harold, for his people did not have these feudal customs. Perhaps he looked upon it simply as a foreign ceremony of honor. But it meant one thing to William: that from now on, Harold owed him allegiance. To make sure that Harold realized it, too, William assembled his most important barons and churchmen, and summoned Harold to stand before them. Seated in splendid robes on his ducal throne and carrying his great sword of state, William pointed to two ornate caskets on tables draped in rich cloths; in the caskets were the bones of the most revered saints in Normandy. He asked Harold to place his hands on these caskets and promise that he would aid William to inherit the throne of England.

Harold was in an impossible position. If he had thought that his private conversations with William were not binding, he now found out how wrong he had been. As a man of honor, he could not back out before this magnificent, forbidding assembly. With his hands on the sacred caskets he promised before witnesses—who in turn told all of Europe—that he would recognize and aid William's claim to the English throne. "Let God be our Aid!" roared the Norman barons. Harold had ensured his own doom.

Harold was now allowed to return home, laden with gifts. With bent head and guilty face he told King Edward of his foolish oath. The ailing king, vague and ineffective though he was, realized the danger his foremost earl had brought to their country. Though Edward had indeed promised William the throne in 1051, now he was dominated by Anglo-Saxon nobles, and it would no longer be possible to turn the throne over to a foreigner. Yet Harold had sworn an oath on sacred saints' bones; God's terrible punishment would surely come to him and to his country if he broke such an oath. Harold knew this well.

King Edward's health began to fail rapidly. England was in a real predicament. She was not a united country under one will like Normandy, but was weakened by a combination of jealous earls who secretly felt they had just as much right to the English throne as Harold. The north and central parts of England were particularly uncooperative, even rebellious. Harold desperately tried to bring some sort of unity to the unstable kingdom and to strengthen its defenses.

The powerful Norwegian king, Harold Hardraada was threatening to invade England from the north and to take the throne for himself. William, the Norman duke, was waiting across the Channel for the same throne to be handed to him. Harold saw nothing but enemies around him.

As the year of 1066 opened, King Edward lay on his deathbed. Surrounded by the queen, the Archbishop of Canterbury, and Earl Harold, he bequeathed his throne to Harold, and then died.

The Witan (the king's assembly of lords and churchmen) agreed to King Edward's last wishes and acclaimed Harold as their king. On the very day of King Edward's funeral, Harold was crowned in Westminster Abbey. The feeling of danger was increased by a comet which appeared for days and was thought to be an omen of disaster.

When Duke William heard that Harold had broken his oath and taken the crown of England for himself, his wrath was terrible. Pacing up and down in his palace at Rouen, he laced and unlaced his cloak; then he sat on a bench in the great hall, leaned against a pillar, and hid his frowning face from his courtiers, who did not dare come near. In those hours of wrathful preoccupation he began to plan the invasion of England, a plan that for political and military brilliance has seldom been equalled.

First, William determined to line up other countries on his side. In a triumph of diplomacy he persuaded the Pope, Alexander II, to declare to the world that Harold had broken his sacred oath and that William had been wronged. Pope Alexander, hoping that William in return would strengthen papal control of the English Church, gave him a banner, a costly ring containing one of the hairs of St. Peter, and his blessing on the invasion. Thus Europe was persuaded that William's proposed invasion of England was not only right, but even holy.

William was then able to call for foreign volunteers to join his holy war under the Pope's banners. Knights swarmed from the rest of France, Flanders, Italy, and the German Empire. Some of their motives may have been holy, but the joy of battle lured many and plunder lured more. William was known to be a good paymaster and England was known to have many treasures.

William's own Norman barons at first objected bitterly—the whole venture would be impossible; enough ships could never be built to transport thousands of warriors, horses, and supplies to a hostile shore; and paying for such an enterprise would ruin them all. But William softened each one with promises of lands, treasure, and titles in England.

One after another agreed to provide manned ships: one hundred ships, eighty ships, sixty—and so on down to a certain monk who pledged one ship and twenty fighting men (and who later was rewarded with a bishopric in England). Duchess Matilda pledged a flagship for her husband, the most beautiful and swift of them all, painted with gay colors and with a dragon-like beast carved on its prow. William's scribes wrote down all the pledges carefully and put the duke's great seal on them so that there would be no backing out.

In an amazingly short time—the six months of the spring and summer of 1066—a huge invasion fleet was completed. No one knows how big William's fleet was, but he must have needed many hundreds of ships to carry an estimated four thousand knights and their horses; two thousand infantrymen and archers; the sailors, priests, grooms, armor-repairers, cooks, wine-carriers, ditch-diggers, and handymen; spears and shields, pots and pans, and even planks to build three small wooden forts. There was no space for oarsmen to row the ships if the winds should fail. Many of the ships were overloaded and unmaneuverable. If King Harold had any sort of navy, he could send William's heavy ships to the bottom of the channel.

But King Harold had no navy, and the few English ships that patrolled the shores during the summer of 1066 were called back to London in September. As for Harold's army, it was old-fashioned; except for the king's own bodyguard—the famous Anglo-Danish "housecarls" with their huge double-edged axes—the defense of England depended on local men recruited by local lords for short periods. These militiamen had been guarding the coast since the spring, but when the September harvest-time came, they went home to their farms. Although Harold knew from his spies that William's fleet was growing daily, he could only hope that it would not be ready before rough winter set in. His spies also told him that the Norwegian king's fleet was assembling in Norwegian fjords and was almost ready to sail. Harold could not be in both north and south at once, and so moved back with his housecarls to London, ready to march in either direction to repel whichever invasion came first.

England's southern coast was now undefended. Duke William assembled his men and ships in the mouth of the Somme River and prepared to sail. For a time, however, William's luck seemed to desert him; rains came, and the north winds blew against him.

For two weeks William's ships were beached and his armies huddled in dripping tents on the muddy banks. His men muttered, "The man is mad who seeks to seize the land of another." William constantly went among them to keep up their spirits. Every day he looked anxiously at the weathervane of the local monastery of St. Valery which pointed into the unwelcome northwinds. He and his men brought gifts to the monastery and prayed before the sacred bones of its patron saint that the storm might cease and the winds reverse themselves.

William's prayers were answered in a way he could not have anticipated. The same winds which were keeping him on his own shores brought the fleet of the Norwegian king across the North Sea to land in the north of England on September 18. His army routed the English earls of the north and took the important city of York.

King Harold had no choice but to meet this danger. Thus while Duke William was chafing at the delay which kept him from crossing to England, the unfortunate Harold was racing northward from London with his brothers and other lords, his army of housecarls, and any local troops he could find along the way. So great was Harold's speed that he succeeded in surprising the Scandinavian army on September 25, 1066, and after a tremendous battle the invading king and most of his men lay dead on English fields. But Harold's victory was costly. He had barely time to bury his dead before a rider brought him the terrible news he had hoped never to hear: William's army had landed in the south of England.

Only two days after Harold's victory in the north (which William knew nothing about) the winds had shifted. The day of September 27 dawned clear and bright, with a steady wind blowing toward England. William lost no time. Trumpets sounded, church bells rang, tents were rolled up, sails flapped dry in the sun, casks of wine and wagonloads of spears were brought to the boats. Servants put lances through the empty sleeves of their masters' heavy mail shirts and carried them to the ships. The horses were urged on board, sometimes ten or more to a boat; then the soldiers clambered in and sat wherever they could among animals and gear. Finally as the sun disappeared, the steersmen, sailmen, and lookouts took their places. Lanterns flickered on every mast, anchors were pulled up, and with Duke William's flagship in the lead, the fleet started on its way.

Ships carrying horses.

William's flagship.

Throughout the night the ships moved slowly northwest. In the morning the wide flat beach of Pevensey lay ahead. No army, no soldiers, no peasants were there to oppose the Normans. Only a local knight watched with horror from the shelter of the woods as the invading ships with their dragon prows and striped sails rode in on the gentle waves to shore. He saw the barelegged grooms drag horses on to the beach and the Norman knights ride off to reconnoiter the countryside. He saw foragers butcher oxen and sheep, and carpenters unload planks and start to build a hasty fort among some ancient Roman ruins. Then waiting no longer, the English watcher rode at top speed day and night to warn his king, who was resting in York two hundred and sixty miles away.

Harold tried to collect an army from the northern earls to replace his fallen men, but the earls delayed. Their jealousy of Harold was stronger than their concern for England's danger. So when Harold returned to London on October 6 he did not know whether the earls would send a man to help him—and they never did. In his haste to return he could not collect enough horses to carry all his archers and infantry with him on his swift march, so left them behind to straggle back as best they could.

King Harold spent five days in London recruiting men from nearby loyal counties to replace his losses. Meanwhile reports poured in that William's army was devastating Harold's own beloved southern earldom.

Harold's mother, wife, and brothers urged him to rest. Other advisors counseled him to wait until the country sent enough reinforcements to outnumber William's army. Others suggested that he draw William near London and then cut him off from his supply lines. But Harold's impatience got the better of him. With half an army, tired from two long marches and a wild battle in between, he marched again.

On October 11, two weeks after William's landing, Harold started southward on the great Roman road through the thick woods that lay between him and Hastings, William's base camp. He sent messengers ahead, asking local troops to assemble on Senlac Hill at the gray gnarled apple tree, a well-known landmark. Harold knew that this rendezvous lay directly across William's only path to London. With troops exhausted from a sixty-mile march in two days, he arrived there late the evening of October 13.

When William's scouts reported that the English were gathering on a hill five miles to the north, William quickly decided to attack early the following morning, October 14, before any more English reinforcements could arrive. With his knights trained to move on horseback rapidly around a battlefield and to strike in many places, and with his superiority in the number of archers, William felt he had an advantage over the English foot soldiers.

When the stars began to fade and the half moon disappeared in the southern sky, William's army started to move north towards the hill where Harold's army blocked its path. William, wearing around his neck the saints' bones on which Harold had sworn his oath, led the column of marchers, riders, and chanting priests which stretched three miles along the old trackway from the coast. At about seven in the morning, the head of the column paused, and William ordered his knights to halt and put on their armor. Over their bright padded tunics went their long mailed shirts; over their short hair and shaved faces went their cone-shaped helmets with long nose-pieces.

Then, riding over the top of a small rise, they saw the English as thick as bees on a long low hill across a sloping valley. The mighty housecarls stood in the front with their three-foot limewood shields and their Danish pole-axes that could cut down a horse and man with one blow. Their long hair and moustaches distinguished them from the Normans; otherwise they wore the same kind of armor. Behind these guardians standing like a wall were the troops of the countryside. Few had armor; most wore leather shirts and caps, and their weapons were the kind they hunted or farmed with—javelins, scythes, axes, hammers, and slings. King Harold himself stood on the highest central point. His two brothers, Gyrth and Leofwine, stood near him. Harold's two great flags, the Dragon of Wessex and the Fighting Man, a banner with an armed warrior embroidered in gold and precious stones, waved at his side.

William spread his army across the base of the gently sloping hill: the Bretons on the left, the French and Flemish on the right, the

Norman cavalry charging the housecarls.

Normans in the center. William's command post was directly opposite the man he had last seen two years before in Normandy—now his implacable enemy.

William's archers then let loose their arrows. They twanged through the morning haze and rattled against the firm great shields. The few English archers sent back answering arrows. Stones, hatchets, and javelins were hurled by both sides. William's infantrymen ran shouting up the slope. The English, on high ground, had the advantage; their close shields and vicious axes were an effective combination against both Norman archers and infantrymen. Then William sent his dreaded Norman knights from the rear, spurring their war-horses and roaring their piercing battle cry *"Diex-Aie!"* (Let God Aid Us!) Charging uphill toward the fierce moustached English who waited with their battle-axes, they did no better than the archers and the infantry; the shields of the housecarls were as as steady as a stone wall and their axes were deadly against horse and man. Harold's old Saxon tactics seemed to be superior—as long as his line of defense stood firm and did not break.

Willam's knights from Brittany fared the worst. From his command post William saw them falter, then retreat. Some English pursued them downhill, breaking Harold's command to hold the line. There was a mix-up on low ground, with hand-to-hand combats, and horses and men falling together. William galloped instantly into the middle of the furious fighting. He was unhorsed, and the rumor spread that he was dead. Then even William's Norman center began to panic. Seeing his own knights retreat, William grabbed a horse from another knight. Pushing his helmet back from his face to show that he was alive, drawing his sword, and getting in the way of his fleeing men, he shouted: "Look at me! Look at me! What madness persuades you to flee? I live and I will conquer, by God's grace!" His half-brother Bishop Odo, swinging his mace, rallied another group of fugitives. Together the brothers organized a counter-attack. Wheeling and charging, they surrounded the part of the English army that had left the crown of the hill and now stood in the marshy valley. Against the circling Norman horsemen the English were helpless and were soon cut down. William could not fail to observe that if more English could be enticed to leave the protection of the line of shields on the hill, it would be easy to surround them and repeat this successful maneuver.

The sun was high and both armies paused before the next attack. Wine-bearers and water-carriers ran through the ranks; men collected arrows and weapons from the grass and redistributed them; others stripped valuable armor from the dead. Then the battle resumed.

William dominated the battlefield. When horses were killed under him, he fought on foot, hacking and hewing with a broken sword until someone brought him a fresh horse and weapons. Still the assault failed to overwhelm the English line. But William's other plan —to tempt parts of the enemy to leave their line—was gradually successful. Several times groups of English, impatient of standing still, broke out to pursue William's knights who had been ordered to feign flight. The Norman horsemen then wheeled, surrounded and destroyed them.

Gradually Harold's army was cut to pieces. His flanks had been so weakened by William's cavalry that they had to draw in nearer the center. King Harold's two younger brothers fell and the English began to despair. But as long as King Harold stood firmly in the center with his bright banners waving proudly above his head, they fought desperately.

The sun began to sink behind the treetops and the shadows of the exhausted fighters lengthened. One more tactic was left to William. He ordered his archers to aim their arrows high in the air so that they would fall behind the front line of shields, upon the heads and faces of the English. One such arrow sped in a high fateful arc to where King Harold stood, tall and defiant. Falling swiftly from the sky, it pierced the King's eye. Harold, in agony, wrenched it out and fell to his knees. Reports of his fall caused confusion and despair among his troops. Now Norman, French, and Flemish knights rode up both ends of the ridge and attacked the small bodyguard still standing around the dying English king. Four Norman knights succeeded in reaching Harold; they hacked at him and killed him. Thus the great battle ended.

Harold's army is cut to pieces.

By six o'clock darkness had fallen and torches blazed on Senlac Hill among the thousands of dead and dying men and horses. William walked among the corpses to Harold's body, lying among his bloody, dusty banners. He knelt down to give a prayer of thanksgiving and vowed to build an abbey on that very spot.

William returned to Hastings and waited there for five days, expecting that delegations of the English would come to offer terms. But England was now in complete disorder. Lords, bishops, and citizens met in London again and again in uncertainty and confusion. No one had the strength or purpose to unite England and oppose William.

William moved slowly, letting rumors precede him which told the countryside of his ferocity to anyone who resisted and of his mercy to anyone who surrendered. He was in no hurry to attack London, his main objective, and waste his men needlessly, but instead started on a huge S-curve around it. Turning eastward, he marched along the coast. Port after port fell into his hands. Then he turned inland and continued his conquest. At last the only city of any consequence that remained was London, protected to the south by a river and one solitary wooden bridge. William passed the city, forded the river some miles to the west, and turned slowly back, devastating the countryside. Reports of his ruthlessness poured into London.

Finally, a delegation of all the people of importance—including the northern earls who had not helped Harold—came out of the city's gates. William, surrounded by his barons and bishops, graciously accepted their offer to make him their king.

Before William entered London to be crowned, he sent ahead Norman carpenters and stoneworkers to make a fortress-dwelling within the city. Soon on the banks of the Thames rose the earliest part of a famous building—the Tower of London. While it was being built, William spent his days hunting in the thick forests near the city.

On Christmas Day, 1066, William rode to Westminster Abbey and was crowned King of England by the same archbishop who in the previous January had placed a crown on Harold's head. Before the assembled Norman and English clergy and nobility, William swore to protect the Church, to govern his people with justice and to wipe out lawlessness.

William now had tremendous riches to dispose of, for all of Harold's royal domains, his brothers' earldoms, and other properties and treasures of those who fell at Hastings were declared forfeit to the Crown. In addition he received quantities of gold from cities, churches, and monasteries—all hoping for merciful treatment. He rewarded his barons—about two hundred in all—with the spoils of the conquered: a county here, a town there; a port and harbor with its shipping revenues; forests, mills, and farms with their produce, laborers, and animals. These nobles in turn parceled out portions of their new estates to the knights of their households. In return for their holdings, all pledged service to William as king. Even the religious houses, receiving enormous grants of land, had to promise to provide men for William's army—sometimes as many as sixty knights from one abbey, a huge expense. Serf to earl in a fixed feudal scale became vassals of the Crown.

In this way William increased, rather than divided, his power. He was guaranteed an army of trained and equipped knights any time he needed them—a much better system than Harold's with his disobedient earls and militia who disbanded when their short terms of service ended. And William was careful not to make any lord too powerful, or give him too much land.

Eventually not a single great English lord or bishop retained his lands or his rank; all were held by Normans or French. By introducing the French feudal system and a completely new French-speaking ruling class, William made a revolutionary change in England.

In 1067 William went back to Normandy and in triumph displayed his treasures, trophies, and hostages. Then he returned to England, leaving his trusted wife Matilda to administer Normandy. The following year he summoned her to join him in England for he wanted her to share his honors equally, and in May she was crowned Queen at Westminster.

Rumors of English revolt in outlying districts began to reach London. In the next three years, William crushed the men of north and central England who, had they been united in 1066, could have pushed him back into the sea. He ordered Norman castles to be built

A motte and bailey.

A Norman castle.
Rochester, England.

in every conquered town. Raised in a hurry, at first each was a simple fortress-house on a mound of earth (motte) with a wooden stockade around it, and a courtyard (bailey) below, protected by another stockade and a ditch (moat). Gradually they were rebuilt in massive stone and increased in size. Staffed with William's toughest barons and looming above the small wooden towns, they played an essential part in William's campaigns to intimidate the English. By the end of the eleventh century there were almost a hundred of them in England.

Using the ruined northern city of York as his base, William ranged in fury with sword and torch over an area a hundred miles wide. Later he reminisced, "I fell on the English of the north counties like a raving lion. I commanded houses and stores with all their implements and furniture to be burnt, and large herds of cattle and beasts of burden to be butchered." People starved in the wintry forests; wolves lurked in the streets of uninhabited towns; fields could not be tilled. Even seventeen years later when an inventory of the kingdom was made, the Yorkshire properties again and again were reported as wilderness.

Lesser revolts in both England and Normandy occupied William the rest of his life. He had to campaign from the Scottish border to the southern borders of Normandy where the French King Philip ceaselessly urged his lords to invade Normandy and check William's power.

William was a great statesman as well as a warrior. Having conquered England completely with sword and torch, he could have continued a harsh and bitter program. Instead, he took care to continue the traditions of the common people and to see that the old laws were respected. In each shire of England, William found courts of justice which had been accustomed to decide local squabbles. William did not destroy the rights of these ancient courts, but sent his sheriffs and commissioners to them, along with the local representatives; all were answerable to the king. Such was William's concern with the law that it was said in his time that a man might go unmolested from one end of his kingdom to the other with his purse full of gold, and "no man durst slay another."

William and his Norman bishops interfered so much with the English church that the Pope objected. He felt that the King of England had no right to control the Church and demanded that William swear an oath of fealty to him. This William refused to do. But because he respected the Church, and also recognized that he owed much of his conquest of England to papal support, he ordered a large sum of money (called St. Peter's pence) to be sent yearly to Rome. It was left to later medieval Popes and English kings to argue the bitter question of which one was supreme in the English church.

Three times a year William assembled the great men of his realm in full and solemn council, and listened to complaints and settled disputes that had not been settled in the smaller courts. He needed interpreters to understand his new subjects, for although he tried to learn their language, its gutteral sounds were too much for him. None of his barons spoke English either, and for three hundred years French was the language of anyone of importance in England.

At the king's magnificent Christmas court in 1085 there were many complaints about unfair taxation. William had realized for a long time that it was difficult to tax the kingdom justly, since the ownership of land and wealth had been so shifted about since the Conquest. Where did the wealth lie now? William ordered a "Description of

All England," not only as it had been in the last days of King Edward's reign, but as it was now, twenty years later. Four commissioners were sent into every shire of the land to find out how many water mills there were, how many acres of plowland, how much woodland, how many fishponds on each estate from which money could be collected for the coffers of the king. Were some barons hiding their wealth? Were they sending him all the knights they could afford from each manor? How many men labored in England—freeman, serf, or even slave?

So thorough was the king's survey that a monk complained "there was not a single yard of land nor indeed one ox or one cow or one pig left out, that was not put down in his record." Landholders compared the parchment rolls of the king's commissioners to God's record book at the Day of Judgment, or Doom; and they called the survey "Domesday Book," the name that has persisted in history. This famous book, copied from the rolls in Latin by the king's clerks, can still be seen; it is one of England's greatest treasures and the greatest record of any medieval kingdom. In less than a year this amazing survey was finished—an extraordinary achievement for an age of slow communication.

William's last years of accomplishment did not bring him happiness. Queen Matilda and most of the companions of his youth were dead. He quarreled constantly with his oldest son Robert who was arrogant and irresponsible. Robert demanded his inheritance, the Duchy of Normandy, while his father was alive, but William refused, knowing that Robert would not be able to control it; Robert then conspired with the French king against his father. William's half-brother Odo, who had helped turn the tide at Hastings, was involved in a conspiracy and thrown into prison. William grew harsh and melancholy. His fits of anger and depression became frequent. He grew fat and rode heavily in his saddle. Only the Archbishop of Canterbury, Lanfranc, could break into his moods and talk frankly to him.

At the end of 1086 William crossed to Normandy, leaving the archbishop in charge of the kingdom. England was never to see him again.

The following year he had a border dispute with the King of

France, and during the negotiations the French king joked about William's weight. When William heard of it, one of his furious rages took hold of him. Determined to teach the King of France a lesson, William ordered the disputed territory to be put to the sword. Brooding and fierce, he rode through the narrow cobbled streets of the burning town of Mantes, only thirty miles from Paris. His great stallion stumbled on a flaming ember and threw him hard against the iron pommel of his saddle. In agony William slid off his horse. His dismayed followers unlaced his helmet, removed his chain shirt and helped him to a litter. Slowly in the summer heat the suffering king was carried back to Rouen, seat of his Norman duchy, through lines of wailing peasants and grief-stricken passersby. His two doctors, both churchmen, saw at once that he was dying.

William knew this, too. He could not stand the creaks and shouts of street and river traffic, the hammering of the stonemasons and the ringing of the bells, and asked to be carried to a quiet priory on a hill outside the city walls. There in great pain, but with the determination he had shown all his life, he arranged the affairs of his kingdom and duchy. Dictating his will, he left to his treacherous son Robert the Duchy of Normandy, although he foresaw that this splitting of his possessions would start trouble; his second son William Rufus (the Red-faced) would be King of England; his third son Henry (eventually the great King Henry I) was given a large sum of money but no land. He distributed treasures to the churches and the poor. Clerks recorded his wishes carefully. Memories and regrets rose to torment the dying king, and he prayed for forgiveness for the many deeds of cruelty and bloodshed he had committed in the fifty years since his father had left him the Duchy of Normandy. On the ninth of September, 1087, he died. His body was carried by boat and wagon to Caen and buried in the abbey church he had built long before at the Pope's request.

So ended the extraordinary career of William the Conqueror, one of the most famous of all the medieval kings. Starting with only a feeble hold on a rebellious duchy, he managed to conquer the kingdom of England and turn it into a strong feudal monarchy which henceforth would take a leading part in the drama of the Middle Ages in Europe.

PART III

THE PEAK OF
THE MIDDLE AGES

Pope Urban preaching the First Crusade.

Less than ten years after William the Conqueror's death, a vast new undertaking captured the imagination of the Christians of the West. This was an even bigger enterprise than William's conquest of England—a holy war against the Moslem infidels who occupied the Holy Land in Syria.

A holy war was bound to appeal to the Christians of the West in the eleventh century for never before had there been such an upsurge of religious fervor. Never had there been such crowds of pilgrims traveling to distant shrines of saints and martyrs. By the latter part of the century, bands of adventurous knights set out every spring on the dusty roads to Spain where the nearest infidels, the Spanish Moslems, lived. Filing through the pass of Roncesvalles and singing as they went the songs of Charlemagne and brave Roland who long ago fought the infidels there, they helped the tiny Christian kingdoms in the north of Spain push the Moslems further south. Restless Norman knights also had the blessings of the church when they captured Sicily from the Moslems and set up a Christian kingdom.

But the Holy Land was to be the real battleground. In 1095, when Pope Urban received an urgent plea from the Byzantine Empire to send help against a new horde of infidels, the Seljuk Turks, he was eager to respond. The Turks, a warlike and nomadic tribe from the steppes of Asia, had been rapidly expanding westward. They had taken over not only some of the Byzantine land in Asia Minor but also the Holy Land and the sacred city of Jerusalem from the Arab Moslems. The Turks had become Moslems themselves but, unlike the Arab Moslems who had occupied the Holy Land for centuries and had treated Christians with respect, they were intolerant and threatened the safety of Christian pilgrims.

Pope Urban, a Frenchman, made his appeal to the Christians of the West in the little French town of Clermont. He urged his listeners to rise up, take the cross and join in a crusade to recover the Holy Land. He told the knights to forget their petty quarrels, to unite in this righteous cause and win everlasting glory in the Kingdom of Heaven. God would be the leader of this holy war and those who joined would be true Christian soldiers. Their sign would be a red cross on their tunics.

Shouts of "God wills it" arose from the crowd who pressed forward in a wave of exultation and enthusiasm. Many fell on their knees then and there and confessed their sins. Pope Urban made a sign of absolution and promised forgiveness to all who took the cross.

The Byzantine emperor had hoped for a few bands of warring knights from the West to help his own armies drive the Turks out

Crusaders attacking Moslems.

of his territory. More concerned about his own lands than the Holy Land, he was dismayed at the huge host of Western knights and their peasant followers that descended upon his empire like locusts, consuming everything in sight. Horrified at the crudity and boorishness of the Westerners, the more refined and cultivated Byzantines gave the crusaders a chilly reception. The Western knights were equally appalled by the Byzantines, whom they thought soft and effete. Mutual distrust increased between the East and West.

The Byzantine emperor, however, did his best to feed the Western armies and placate his people. Eventually the great host moved on to Palestine and in 1099 wrested the Holy Land from the Moslems and set up a Christian Kingdom of Jerusalem. Many leading knights carved out feudal states for themselves and settled there for life.

When the twelfth century dawned, Pope and Church were more powerful than ever before. Since Charlemagne's day kings and em-

103

perors had assumed the right to defend Christendom and to fight the pagans and infidels, but when Pope Urban had preached and organized the First Crusade, no one had questioned his right to do so. People now looked to the Pope rather than the Holy Roman Emperor for leadership. The Holy Roman Empire, now only a collection of German states and northern Italy, had lost its influence on peoples west of the Rhine River.

New forces and new interests were at work which were to make the twelfth century the greatest and most exciting time of the Middle Ages. For, along with the religious zeal and desire to crusade beyond the seas, there arose an interest in learning. Through pilgrimages and the First Crusade itself, contact with the higher Moslem civilization aroused men's curiosity. Though the Church continued to dominate man's thoughts, scholars, clerks, and monks began to translate into Latin Arabic works, which the Arabs had translated from the ancient Greek. Works on science and mathematics, Euclid's geometry, Aristotle's writings on logic and reason traveled along the pilgrim highways to the north of Europe. Trade was opened up with the East and life in the West became more prosperous and a little more civilized.

The center of this new interest in learning was the royal domain of France, known as the Ile de France, a small territory surrounding Paris. Here, in the early part of the twelfth century, a wise and sensible king, Louis the Fat, was strengthening his kingdom. Although his domain was smaller than many of the feudal duchies and counties whose lords were his vassals, all of them owed him allegiance. And he had one source of power which his vassals did not have; he was king by the grace of God, anointed by the church. He owed allegiance to no man.

In spite of his obesity—it was said he was so fat that he could not bend over to tie his boots nor mount a horse without help—King Louis was a tireless monarch, riding from one end of his domain to the other, fulfilling his duties and asserting his rights. In 1124, when the Germans threatened his eastern borders, Louis commanded enough respect to rally help not only from vassals within his kingdom but also from vassals in the great counties of Anjou and Flanders and the duchies of Burgundy and Aquitaine. This was the sure sign of the rising power of a feudal monarch. But the growth of the French monarchy was slow and it would be a long time before the French king had the absolute power over all his lands and vassals which William the Conqueror had so quickly achieved in England. In fact, the greatest threat to Louis was the King of England, who was also Duke of Normandy. As Duke he owed King Louis allegiance but as King of England he dared defy the King of France. He was the one important duke who did not respond to Louis' summons for help against the Germans.

Shortly before his death in 1137, King Louis had what seemed like a heaven-sent opportunity to enlarge his little kingdom. One of his wealthiest vassals, the Duke of Aquitaine, died suddenly, leaving his great fief in the hands of a young daughter, Eleanor. If King Louis could arrange to marry her to his heir, Prince Louis, in one swift stroke he would attach his largest and richest fief securely to the crown. The future looked bright for the French royal dynasty. Louis was pleased to think how upset the King of England and the grasping Count of Anjou, whose land lay between the French domain and the Duchy of Aquitaine, would be if his plans succeeded.

Fortunately for Louis, he would not live to know the troubles that would follow in the wake of his son's brilliant marriage, nor that the power of a pretty and tempestuous woman could so easily change the destiny of kings and the boundaries of kingdoms.

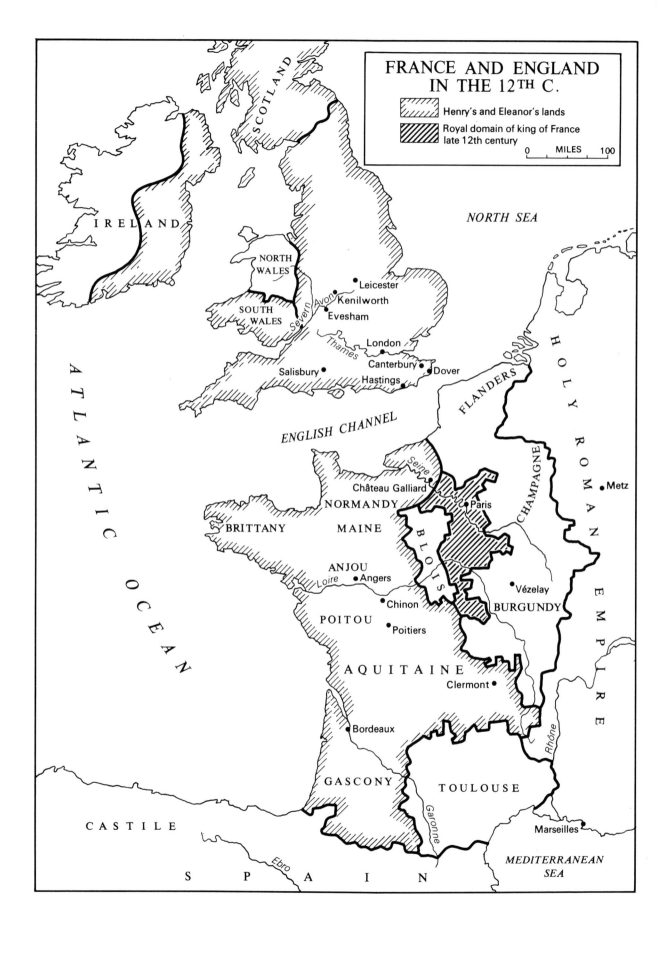

FRANCE AND ENGLAND
IN THE 12TH C.

Henry's and Eleanor's lands

Royal domain of king of France
late 12th century

0   MILES   100

SCOTLAND

IRELAND

NORTH SEA

NORTH
WALES

Leicester

Kenilworth

SOUTH
WALES

Evesham

Severn
Avon

Thames

London

Salisbury

Canterbury

Dover

Hastings

ATLANTIC OCEAN

ENGLISH CHANNEL

FLANDERS

HOLY ROMAN EMPIRE

Seine

Château Galliard

NORMANDY

Paris

Metz

BRITTANY

MAINE

BLOIS

CHAMPAGNE

ANJOU

Loire

Angers

Chinon

Vézelay

POITOU

Poitiers

BURGUNDY

AQUITAINE

Clermont

Bordeaux

Rhône

GASCONY

TOULOUSE

Garonne

CASTILE

Marseilles

S   P   A   I   N

Ebro

MEDITERRANEAN
SEA

ELEANOR OF AQUITAINE

A young noblewoman reading.

The news of the death of Louis' great vassal, the Duke of Aquitaine, had come swiftly and secretly to King Louis the Fat as he lay dying. By feudal law, the duchess, daughter of his vassal, was Louis' to dispose of in marriage; but the king knew that some unruly baron of the south might easily defy the feudal law. In fact it was quite likely that some warrior noble would try to kidnap the duchess and bear her off to his high-walled castle. King Louis immediately made arrangements for his son, the prince, to travel south.

The prize of Aquitaine was a lovely young girl of fifteen. Her long black braids hung below her waist and her deep-set eyes sparkled with gaiety. She knew how to please and was well aware of her charm and wit. Scarcely had the news of her father's death come to Duchess Eleanor in Bordeaux, when messengers galloped into the castle court-yard to tell her that Prince Louis was on his way to claim her as his bride.

King Louis and the Prince knew little of the duchess herself. It was her land, the great fief of Aquitaine, which interested the royal family. Aquitaine stretched from the Loire River to the Pyrenees, from the limestone heights of central France to the Atlantic Ocean. Long ago the Romans had named it Aqua-tania, land of waters, for wide rivers and their many tributaries flowed through its rich, fertile valleys. They had preferred it to the north and the imprint of their art and architecture still lingered there. The land varied from mellow wheat fields, vineyards, and olive groves to flat salt marshes near the coast. High cliffs above the bend of rivers were natural sites for feudal strongholds and behind the hilltop castles stretched cool, dark forests. The Aquitanians, fiercely proud and independent, had always held aloof from the north. Even in Charlemagne's day they had been arrogant and rebellious. "They were quick to anger, violent in battle and hot in the pursuit of love and adventure." They loved gaiety, song and dance, and cultivated a more refined and sophisticated way of life than the more serious northerners.

Eleanor was a true Aquitanian whose grandfather had been one of the first troubadours, composing his own music and verse, as well as a warrior and adventurer. It was said of him, "he was one of the most courteous men in the world . . . valiant in warfare, and bounteous in love and gallantry." Eleanor inherited his love of poetry and adventure. She had many accomplishments; not only could she sing and dance, sew and spin, but she could also read and write, a rarity for a woman of the twelfth century. She had learned much from traveling with her father as he tended to feudal business, visiting monasteries, abbeys, and seasonal fairs in his duchy. Eleanor loved to listen to the wandering minstrels who came often to her family's castle to chant the deeds of Frankish heroes, and to the troubadours, like her grandfather, with their songs of love. From the ducal pavilion she watched exciting feats of arms when knights rushed full tilt at one another in bloody tournaments.

In a worldly way Eleanor was far more educated than her future husband, Prince Louis, who had started life in the somber and austere cloisters of Notre Dame in Paris. Louis had planned to be a monk but his elder brother died, leaving him as heir to the throne of France. He had little training to be a king and inherited little of his father's political wisdom. But he was a handsome prince, tall and slender with long golden locks and mild blue eyes. He was just two years older than Eleanor.

The dying old king provided the prince with an escort of five hundred of the most distinguished knights of his royal domain to guide him through the dangerous and rebellious country south of the Loire River. Traveling by night, the royal cavalcade arrived in five weeks' time at the banks of the Garonne River. They set up their colored tents and pavilions opposite the town of Bordeaux where the square towers of the bishop's palace loomed above the Roman walls. Here Eleanor awaited her prince.

Two weeks of festivities preceded the marriage. Red and white wines flowed freely at feasts which followed water sports on the river, tournaments and dances on the castle's green lawn. On the wedding day the young couple wound their way over the cobblestone streets between gayly decorated houses to the dim old Romanesque church of St. Andrew. Tall tapers lighted the rounded apse and incense filled the air. Louis and Eleanor were married in the presence of their vassals and crowned Duke and Duchess of Aquitaine. The prince was enraptured with his beautiful bride but no one knows what Eleanor thought of her bridegroom.

On their way north to Paris the couple stopped at Poitiers, in the northern part of Aquitaine, where more vassals came to pay them homage. In the midst of the festivities, messengers from Paris galloped over the bridge to tell the prince that his father, King Louis the Fat, was dead. And so it was as King Louis VII and Queen Eleanor of France that the young couple approached the gates of Paris at the end of the summer of 1137.

To get to the heart of Paris, which was then the little island in the Seine River known as the Ile de la Cité, Eleanor and Louis had to pass through the noisy merchant suburb on the right bank and cross a big bridge. They could see barges and wherries unloading fish, salt, and cattle from Normandy, barrels of wine, stacks of grain and hay being pushed up the banks. But once they passed through the tower gatehouse onto the fortified stone bridge they had no view, for its thick crenellated walls rose high above their heads. A little beyond the bridge the king and queen went through the gateway to the old Frankish palace whose towers rose above the roofs of the city. Louis led his young bride up the worn steps of the keep to a large, gloomy hall. The only heat came from a central fireplace, filling the air with smoke. Through narrow slits the river traffic could be heard but barely seen. Kitchens and a chapel were attached to the keep; armorers' and blacksmiths' shops were built against the courtyard wall. A little garden of cypress trees, shrubs and trellised vines ran down to the western tip of the island where the river's currents joined and flowed on their circuitous path towards Normandy and the sea.

Beyond the palace walls were noisy, crowded streets, darkened by overhanging upper stories of ancient wooden dwellings. Swine and goats roamed the dirty roads, vendors shouted out the prices of their wine and pastries. Each street showed its activity—the street of the drapers where cloth was sold, the bakers' and wine merchants' streets, and the street of the Jews where money was lent.

Eleanor found Paris a somber city compared to the gay south where she had been brought up; but Paris was not dull. It was full of intellectual ferment and students flocked there from all over Europe to pursue studies, to hear masters discuss geometry and astronomy, logic and reason, good and evil. Eleanor's quick mind absorbed many of these ideas.

From her garden wall Eleanor could see the little bridge which led to the left bank where most of the students lived. Tall wooden houses projected over the edge of this little bridge in higglety-pigglety fash-

Medieval shops in Paris.

ion. Teachers lived here and held outdoor classes, lecturing from benches between the narrow houses. It was a good place to draw a crowd and the larger the crowd the better the teachers liked it. A radical young monk, Peter Abelard, held students spellbound as he tried to explain Christianity in terms of reason and logic. Eleanor could also see students playing games and dancing on the large open field below the monastery of St. Genevieve, along the river's edge.

111

The queen, of course, could not become involved in any of this life but she wished her court could be livelier than it was. She was disappointed to find that the king preferred the seclusion of the cloisters of Notre Dame to a court life. Meek and pious, Louis took up his religious education again and spent little time in the royal court. But Eleanor had brought a large retinue of southerners, knights, troubadours, and ladies to Paris and she did her best to recreate the gay life of the south, to liven up the dreary old palace. The singing, dancing, and feasting that went on behind the palace walls quite shocked the serious-minded Parisians. Tongues began to wag about the behavior of the queen, who did not seem to take her religion as seriously as did the king, and who laughed and joked a great deal and danced and sang with those elegantly dressed young knights she had imported from Aquitaine.

In spite of his piety Louis could be rash and stubborn. In a quarrel with the Count of Champagne over the appointment of a bishop, he incurred the wrath of the Pope, who finally resorted to the ban of excommunication, the most dreaded of all punishments of the Middle Ages. Excommunication denied the victim all religious sacraments and closed the doors of the Church to him; if he died still under the ban, his soul was damned forever. That the pious Louis should be excommunicated was almost more than he could bear. Angry and humiliated, he blamed all his troubles on his vassal count and, to vindicate his rights as overlord, took up arms and invaded his vassal's fief of Champagne.

His army attacked the poorly defended town of Vitry and set fire to its wooden houses. The townspeople, more than a thousand, fled to the church for safety, but it too caught fire. The roof collapsed and the men, women, and children, trapped inside, were all consumed in flames.

Horrified and stricken by guilt, Louis fell ill. The roar and crackling of the fire at Vitry and the cries of the people haunted him. The Pope, impressed by Louis' remorse, soon lifted the ban of excommunication. But still Louis could not get over his sense of guilt and remained ill and depressed. Even Eleanor could not raise his spirits.

Had the wise old Abbot Suger, who was Louis' advisor, been on

Gothic sculpture over central door-way at St. Denis.

hand he might have prevented this rash and terrible deed. But Suger was so immersed in a project of which he had dreamed for years, the rebuilding of the old abbey church of St. Denis, dedicated to the patron saint of France and long a burial place for French kings, that he neglected everything else, even his care of the young king and queen. As soon as his remodeling of the church was finished he turned his attention to the unhappy Louis.

Suger invited the king and queen to a dedication ceremony and arranged to have Louis play an important role on this occasion, hoping to cure the king's illness. Early in the morning of a feast day in June, 1144, Abbot Suger and King Louis, bearing a casket containing the relics of St. Denis, led the procession of visiting dignitaries. Holy water was sprinkled on the new white stone of the facade before the procession passed through the wide portals. Over the central doorway a majestic statue of Christ, with arms outstretched, looked down as king and queen, white-robed bishops, hooded monks, and wealthy nobles entered the church. Beyond the old nave, the new choir and altar caught their gaze. "The entire sanctuary was pervaded by a wonderful and continuous light entering through the most sacred windows," Suger proudly said. Tiny pieces of colored glass, sparkling like jewels in a rainbow of colors, told the story of the Bible and the salvation of man. The whole eastern end of the church, with its choir

Romanesque walls of stone . . .

and chapels radiating like petals of a flower, was ablaze with light and color.

Suger's church was the first Gothic building and it was a daring experiment. Eager to make it the most splendid house of God on earth, Suger sought above all to let in light which, filtered through pieces of colored glass, would appear to come from Heaven itself. Abandoning the old Romanesque barrel vaulted roofs which required massive walls for support, Suger experimented with a new type of vaulting— intersecting pointed arches whose ribs carried the weight of the roof down onto supporting columns. The space between the columns was mostly filled with glass instead of thick masonry. The delicate appearance of Suger's building was a marked contrast to the earlier, more earthbound churches. Yet this new experiment was far stronger than it looked. When a great storm destroyed many nearby buildings, Suger's delicate pointed arches and thin stone vaulting stood firm. Soon other Gothic cathedrals on an even grander scale arose throughout Europe.

But the dedication ceremony was not a cure for King Louis' sense

...and Gothic walls of glass.

of guilt and could not wash away the sins of Vitry. One of the dignitaries present, the renowned Abbot Bernard of the Order of Cistercian Monks, realized that the king must have a more worthwhile penance. He did not have to wait long. Edessa, a Frankish state in the Holy Land, had fallen to the Turks. What better and more worthwhile penance for King Louis than a second crusade to rescue the now-threatened Kingdom of Jerusalem?

No one favored the idea more than Louis. The Pope, knowing Louis' true piety, favored him above all others to lead the crusade. Eleanor was just as eager for a crusade as the king but not for the same reason. She longed for adventure, to get away from Paris, and to see more of the world. Bored by a husband who spent so much of his time in the cloisters, Eleanor could not wait for the glorious adventure of a crusade.

At Easter time in the spring of 1146, King Louis called an assembly to the little hill town of Vézelay southeast of Paris. News that Abbot Bernard would speak brought such crowds that the church could not hold them. On a platform erected on the hillside below the town the thin, frail abbot addressed the multitude in a thunderous voice. "The earth trembles and is shaken because the King of Heaven has lost his land." He urged the French to take the cross and fly to arms, to let Christendom re-echo with the words of the prophet, "Woe to him who dyeth not his sword in blood." He promised forgiveness of sins to all who took part and everlasting reward in Heaven to those who died in the cause.

"Crosses, crosses, give us crosses," shouted the people. King Louis was the first to take the cross and, overcome by emotion, burst into tears and prostrated himself before the abbot. Eleanor, too, took the cross and knelt before the holy man, offering her vassal knights from Aquitaine. Barons, knights and ladies pressed forward to get crosses, which soon gave out. Abbot Bernard flung off his outer cloak and snipped it into little crosses as more and more people pledged themselves for the crusade.

While Louis prepared for the crusade by pious works, Eleanor journeyed south to gather her own vassals and friends, ladies of the court, troubadours, and minstrels, all kinds of people unsuited for a holy war. Many disapproved of the queen going; her huge train of clothes and finery would be a nuisance. But Louis could not bear to leave her behind. Eleanor, in any case, was determined to go.

In the early summer of 1147 the host assembled at the town of Metz: knights from France, Burgundy, Normandy, and Aquitaine; Eleanor's gay court followers with their hounds and falcons, peasants and paupers. The huge army of crusaders, traveling ten to twenty miles a day through Germany and the plains of Hungary, took three months to get to Constantinople.

In the glorious city of Constantinople Eleanor and Louis were housed in one of the emperor's palaces overlooking the harbor where the golden domes of churches were reflected in the waters below. Eleanor was enchanted with the elegance and refinement of Byzantine court life. She and Louis were lavishly entertained; served by well disciplined slaves, they feasted on rare delicacies and wines, cooled in snow from the mountains. They listened to strange harmonies of eastern music and watched sinuous dancers and acrobats while nearby fountains jetted perfumed waters.

To Louis the pomp and glitter of the emperor's court seemed exaggerated and even distasteful. After visiting innumerable churches and their sacred shrines, he was anxious to be on his way to join his German allies who were already in Asia Minor.

Their trip from Constantinople over the narrow mountain passes of Asia Minor to the Holy Land was full of hazards and disasters. It was difficult to get the heavily armed crusaders with their cumbersome baggage train up the tortuous mountain paths; they were an easy prey to sudden attacks by the Turks. Eleanor and the ladies, however, were well protected and, when tired of jogging on horseback, were carried in litters or covered wagons. At night they slept in painted beds set up in tents or pavilions. But the loss of men and equipment was considerable and it was a sadly depleted army which arrived in the spring at Antioch where Eleanor's uncle, Prince Raymond, ruled.

In Antioch Eleanor and Louis, revived from the toils of their journey, again were feasted and entertained. Eleanor delighted in this gay, foreign metropolis with its exotic architecture and colorful bazaars, where caravans unloaded ivories, bright-colored silks, and spices from the Far East to be put on cargo ships bound for western Mediterranean ports.

Eleanor especially enjoyed the company of her uncle, who came from Aquitaine and spoke her native tongue. She agreed with his sensible plan for the crusaders to launch an attack on the Turks immediately. But Louis insisted that he must go first to Jerusalem, still in the hands of Christians, and do his penance there before he took up arms against the infidels. He was annoyed that Eleanor was having such a good time that she did not want to leave Antioch. Eleanor had begun to feel young again, free to laugh, to sing and make jokes with her own countryman. The gayer Eleanor became, the gloomier Louis was. Finally, he told her that she must prepare to leave for Jerusalem right away. At this Eleanor flew into a rage—Louis could go on alone but under no circumstances would she leave this delightful city.

And then she blurted out what had probably been on her mind a long time, that she wanted to divorce him! She reminded Louis that they were cousins in the fourth degree, too closely related to be lawfully married in the eyes of the Church. The king was stunned and horrified. He knew of their kinship, which had been waived by the Church at the time of their marriage. He began to brood. Maybe their marriage was cursed, for the queen had produced no male heir, only one daughter. In despair Louis consulted his chaplain and magnates. And then to everybody's surprise the indecisive Louis acted quickly and decisively. In the middle of the night he and his knights seized Eleanor, slipped out of Antioch, and sped on towards Jerusalem. Such humiliation for the proud queen did not help heal the breach between them.

Within the Holy City, Louis at last did penance for his sins as he prostrated himself in prayer before the holiest of all holy altars. This was King Louis' only consolation of the Second Crusade, which ended in failure before the unyielding walls of Damascus.

In July, 1149, two years after the crusaders had set out with such high hopes and ambition, the sad and humiliated king embarked for home, stopping in Italy where Eleanor, who had followed in a separate vessel, joined him. Here the king and queen paused to have an audience with the Pope, who tried to patch up their differences.

Late in November the royal couple arrived in Paris. The winter of 1149 was cold and severe and Eleanor was depressed, feeling her youth slipping away as she remained a captive queen. When she gave birth to a second daughter, she thought her marriage must surely be cursed. She began to hope for means of separation. Abbot Suger, ever mindful of the good of the realm, managed to keep the rift between the king and queen from widening but when he died in 1151, Louis was no longer able to combat the discontent of Eleanor which increased day by day.

In the summer following Suger's death, the great grandson of William the Conqueror, Henry, Duke of Normandy and heir to the throne of England, appeared in Paris to pay homage to his overlord, the King of France. As Henry knelt in homage for his fief, Eleanor noticed that this young man was very different from King Louis. She immediately fell in love with him, though he was only eighteen, eleven years her junior. Not handsome, for he was squarely built with massive shoulders, a thick neck and a large round head, Henry nevertheless had a winning personality. His lively face and clear gray eyes

Medieval castle.

were framed by tawny hair—some said it was a lion's face. Bold and overflowing with energy, he was also courteous, educated, and well spoken. But from his father's family, the Counts of Anjou, his inheritance was dark and violent. "From the devil they came, to the devil they will go," was the current saying about the Counts of Anjou.

Henry must have been impressed with Eleanor's beauty, charm, and lively mind and he knew that she was duchess of the largest and fairest fief in France. Whatever words passed between the two were kept a secret.

In less than a year King Louis, backed by the Church and Abbot Bernard, who had never approved of the Queen, granted Eleanor a divorce on the grounds of too close kinship. He generously gave her back her Duchy of Aquitaine on condition she remain a loyal vassal.

Once free, Eleanor wasted no time. Mounting her palfrey and followed by an escort of her vassals, she headed south to her ancestral home of Poitiers. She was a prize for any ambitious knight to kidnap; only with the greatest difficulty did she outwit and escape two attempts to capture her. In Poitiers she was safe amid her friends and vassals.

In the month of May of 1152—just eight weeks after her divorce—young Henry, Duke of Normandy, and now also Count of Anjou, came riding over the drawbridge to Eleanor's castle. He had a falcon

119

tied to his wrist and a sprig of broom plant, *plantagenesta,* stuck in his cap and so earned the nickname of Plantagenet. The two were married quietly. Eleanor had cast aside a "dull king for a bold young knight," Louis' greatest potential enemy.

The news broke like a thunderbolt in Paris. Eleanor and Henry were both vassals of the King of France and had no right to marry without his consent. It was a grave affront to their overlord and a terrible threat to the royal domain of France. With Normandy, Anjou, and Aquitaine, Eleanor and Henry now held the largest and fairest fiefs of France.

King Louis demanded that his vassal Henry appear before him to answer for his treason. But Henry, master of far more land than his overlord the king, felt safe enough to ignore the summons. Louis had no recourse except war. He charged into Normandy but found he was no match for Henry. Getting the worst of it and falling ill, he soon gave up and retired to his palace by the Seine.

Henry and Eleanor were now free to ride south through their vast provinces. Henry was pleased with his charming bride but more pleased with his wealthy lands. He cast his practical eyes over the lush vineyards, the olive groves, and plump grazing sheep, the well-bred horses and supply of ships at Bordeaux. Then he traveled north and set sail for England to press his claim to the English throne.

He left Eleanor in Anjou, where his red flintstone castle rose above a river and looked down on soft, green meadows and beyond to rolling, vineclad hills. This was more pleasing to Eleanor than the cold, bleak palace in Paris and it was far from the critical eye of Abbot Bernard or the conscience of King Louis.

With her wide knowledge of Constantinople, Antioch, and other eastern places, Eleanor was well equipped to be the center of a refined and cultivated court. From the East she had brought back ideas of courtesy, elegance, and culture. She now opened her court to the poets and knights of Anjou and Aquitaine. Here troubadours and wandering minstrels found a ready ear for their songs of love and chivalry. The songs of a young troubadour, Bernart de Ventadour, enchanted her and she welcomed him at her court. He soon fell in love with her but knowing he should not seek so high, contented himself with pouring out his love in verse.

Thirteenth-century musicians.

Domma, per vostr' amor   Sweet lady, for your love,
Jonh las mas et ador   With clasped hands I bless
Gens cors ab frescha color,   Your radiance, high above
Gran mal me faitz traire.   My deep unhappiness.

Ordinarily the noblewoman of the Christian West commanded little respect and had no rights at all; she was usually married off for the sake of her land and to produce a family of sons. But Eleanor kept striving to elevate the position of women. She sought to add ideals of courtesy towards women to the old knightly ideals of skill at arms, courage, and loyalty. At the same time the worship of the Virgin Mary was spreading within the churches. God, the Supreme Judge, had been remote from men; Mary, the Mother of God, seemed closer and more human. Men looked to her for forgiveness and mercy. With the cult of Mary and with Eleanor's ideals of chivalry, the virtues of women began to be extolled and to shed a softening influence on society.

Thirteenth-century Virgin and Child.

Eleanor also fulfilled her role as a traditional feudal woman and gave birth to a son, the first of eight children she was to bear to Henry. To King Louis this was another ominous sign of the rising glory of his enemy, Duke Henry, and of the waning of the French royal power.

The crowning blow to Louis came soon when Henry's cousin, King Stephen of England, died and Henry was proclaimed his successor. Henry, only twenty-one, was now King of England, Duke of Normandy and Aquitaine, Count of Anjou and the neighboring lands of Maine and Touraine. His realm stretched from Scotland to the Pyrenees. Louis feared his little kingdom might be swallowed up.

In December, 1154, defying stormy seas and howling gales, Henry, Eleanor, and their infant son sailed across the choppy channel to

England. On the Sunday before Christmas the two were crowned King and Queen of England at Westminster Abbey. Henry, usually careless of his dress and looks, bore himself regally. He wore a short French mantle, unlike the long English style, and looked ready to defy any danger and spring into action quickly.

Eleanor was dressed in the latest style of a long, tight-fitting gown over which a loose robe, with full sleeves tapering to a point and almost touching the ground, trailed out in back. It was made of the finest silk brought back from the East and lined with costly ermine and sable. Over her dark hair she wore a wimple which was held in place by a gold coronet. From her ears hung long pendants set with precious stones; jeweled bracelets adorned her arms.

Eleanor and Henry first stayed across the Thames from the Tower of London. The river was a busy thoroughfare and London a prosperous city, as full of merchants as Paris was of students. The royal couple did not stay settled for long, for Henry had much to attend to. The countryside was deeply scarred by the ravages of civil wars which had devastated England during King Stephen's weak reign. Taking their entire household with them, Henry and Eleanor went on tiring journeys over narrow muddy lanes through the rough countryside. Ruined farms and castles, deserted villages, and forests full of lawless poachers confronted them. Even so, Eleanor sometimes followed Henry into the woods to hunt the wild stag. She sat with him at sessions of the courts of justice which he held at whatever great castle he stayed in. Passionately interested in law, Henry was determined to end the lawlessness and anarchy in his new kingdom. Eleanor's quick mind absorbed the problems of justice and government as she traveled with her husband.

When the royal couple moved to the recently remodeled palace of Westminster, Eleanor began to liven up the English court. Knowing her interest and generosity, poets and minstrels from the continent sought her out. One poet wrote of her,

> The sweet young Queen
> Draws the thoughts of all upon her
> As sirens lure the witless mariners
> Upon the reefs.

Dancers, acrobats, and mummers entertained the court when it was not on the move.

But Henry usually was on the move, dashing back and forth between England and his French provinces. When Eleanor stayed behind she managed the kingdom as though she were a king. She was also rapidly increasing her family. Between the years of 1153 and 1166 she had five sons and three daughters. Two of her sons would live to be kings, her favorite, Richard the Lion Heart, and her youngest and least loved, John, nicknamed Lackland for his lack of lands and titles.

Both Queen Eleanor and King Henry preferred their native French lands to England, though Henry never neglected his English kingdom and was one of its greatest medieval kings; he brought it order, peace, and justice. In France he had difficulty with the Aquitanians who resented him. Only Eleanor, their beloved duchess, who knew and understood them well, could control these fiercely independent vassals.

Henry's ambitions were boundless. He dreamed of a time when his house would hold two crowns, the English and the French. At first he and Eleanor aimed to gain their ends by marriage alliances. While their children were still in their infancy, they were betrothed to other royal houses in France, Germany, Spain, and Sicily.

The first decade of Henry's and Eleanor's reign was prosperous and successful. They expanded the frontiers of their huge empire by conquest and marriage alliances, built up its wealth, and spread learning and art to its far corners. Fortune smiled on them while the royal house of France looked out on a bleak, feudal world surrounded by Henry's strong castles where his lion banners floated defiantly from the towers.

But Eleanor's and Henry's first happy and successful years were not to last. In spite of their common interests and ambitions each was used to having his own way. Eleanor could not manage Henry as she had her docile King Louis; she found his will as strong as her own. Even before the birth of their last son, John, Henry had begun to neglect Eleanor and seek the companionship of younger women. Their affection for each other began to cool and Eleanor grew bitter.

At this same time Henry became involved in a quarrel with his

Murder of Thomas à Becket.

former friend, Thomas à Becket, whom he had made Archbishop of Canterbury. As Eleanor could not manage Henry, so Henry could not manage his archbishop, who upheld the rights of the Church against Henry's interference. After years of strife, the quarrel ended disastrously in the murder of Archbishop Thomas by four of Henry's loyal knights in the cathedral of Canterbury. But Thomas dead became more powerful than alive and his tomb became a shrine of pilgrimage. This tragedy plunged Henry into utter despair and lost him considerable prestige. It was an ill omen for his remaining years, when trouble after trouble began to overwhelm him.

Another event which threatened Henry's future power and ambitions and gave new hope to the French was the birth to King Louis and his new queen of the longed-for male heir, Prince Philip. Bonfires were lit and bells tolled out the glad tidings. A prophetic shout went up, "There is born to us, in Paris tonight, a prince who shall be a scourge to the English."

But Queen Eleanor was to be the greatest threat of all to Henry.

The Queen had stayed aloof from the Becket quarrel. She and Henry saw little of each other at this time and she was growing to hate the king, who made no secret of his devotion to a fair young girl, Rosamond. Eleanor was not the sort of woman to suffer public neglect and insult. Inflamed with jealousy, she vowed vengeance on the king and she knew how to strike where it would hurt him most. She loved her sons; they loved and admired her—they would be her tools against the king, their father.

It was easy to incite the older sons, now at the age of knighthood, against their father, for though he had given them fine-sounding titles, he gave them no power. Henry meant to keep power in his own hands as long as he lived. But Eleanor knew the grasping nature of her sons. She would goad them on to claim the rights their titles seemed to give them. She could use to her advantage the feudal relationship between her sons and the French king. She aimed to make her sons' allegiance to their overlord more important than their obedience to their father. She knew that her ex-husband, King Louis, in spite of his bitterness towards her, would take her sons' side if it would hurt his rival, Henry.

Asserting her independence, Eleanor took her favorite son, Richard, and withdrew to her Duchy of Aquitaine. Though a neglected queen, she was still Duchess of Aquitaine in her own right, and her vassals rejoiced to have their mistress back. Eleanor cancelled some of Henry's oppressive laws, recalled rebellious barons he had banished, and pleased her subjects by reviving old customs and ceremonies. At the city of Limoges she had her handsome Richard, aged fifteen, crowned Duke of Aquitaine with as much ritual as a royal coronation. She paraded him everywhere and saw that her vassals paid homage to their future duke. After this goodwill tour, she set up her court at Poitiers. Here she would train Richard for his future role and here she would conspire against King Henry.

She settled in the old castle of her ancestors, recently remodeled to suit her tastes. Henry, although somewhat disgraced by the Becket affair, was by no means subdued and was far away conquering Ireland. Eleanor alone was in charge of most of his continental lands. Her court swarmed with young people, for not only her own handsome sons and beautiful daughters but also her daughters-in-law and future daughters-in-law now came to Poitiers. It was an odd household, with children of her two estranged husbands mingling together as well as other highborn young men and women who flocked to her court to learn the arts of chivalry and good manners. To the consternation of their elders, many of the young men were affecting long hair and shoes with pointed toes and the young ladies dragged after them such long trains that they raised clouds of dust. Eleanor soon found that she needed help in training the youth at her court. Strangely enough the person who came to help her was her own first child, the daughter born to her and Louis long ago. Marie, now Countess of Champagne, had been well educated in the strict schooling of Paris. Under her mother's influence she now blossomed in the more lenient traditions of the south and responded eagerly to its lyric poetry and music.

Eleanor and Marie together set about to school the boisterous young knights in courtly behavior and, especially, manners towards women. Abandoned by Henry, Eleanor sought more than ever to gain respect for her sex. She preferred the tales of King Arthur and his knights who performed deeds of valor for the love and admiration of a lady to the heroic songs of Charlemagne where women did not count. As the feudal code required homage to a lord, so Eleanor's court required that her knights give homage and pledge their service to a damsel of their choice.

> Lady, I am and will always be
> Your faithful servant, I guarantee.
> I am your vassal pledged and sworn
> And evermore henceforth shall be.

Eleanor's court became known as a "court of love" where she and Marie passed judgment on how a knight should behave in wooing a lady. Sitting on a raised dais at the end of her long arcaded hall, Eleanor and Marie conducted a sort of mock trial. They listened to the young men present their cases and then handed down decisions on rules of conduct; a suitor must prove his worth by quests of dangerous adventures and years of pining before he could expect even a smile from his lady. In Eleanor's court the usual rules of feudal society were turned upside down and women reigned supreme. Even if these ideals were not lived up to in real life, they were the basis of a new code of chivalry and romantic love. Eleanor's ideal knight was the model for the courteous gentleman of later times.

When the serious business of the court was finished, knights and ladies adjourned to the courtyard for dancing and gossip. The favorite and most absorbing topic was rebellion and conspiracy. The young Plantagenets—the unstable oldest son, Prince Henry, bold and dashing Richard, and ruthless Geoffrey—listened to their mother pour out her venom against their father, King Henry. Other adventurous young knights, always eager to rebel, lent a ready ear.

Even in far-off Ireland Henry heard rumors of conspiracy. Fearing trouble, he left for France in a hurry. Unlike King Louis, Henry always made up his mind quickly. "Now in Ireland, now in England, now in Anjou, the King of the English seems rather to come on wings than by horse or boat," Louis remarked of his enemy. Though Henry was worried about his sons, especially Prince Henry who clamored for his independence and the right to rule his fiefs, he hoped to appease them.

But Eleanor's machinations were more powerful than Henry realized, and were beginning to work. Henry's last years were embittered as each one of his sons turned against him. On his castle wall at Winchester a fresco depicted a huge eagle, beset by four young eaglets, clawing and pecking at its eyes and wings. Henry told a friend that the eagle was himself, the fierce eaglets his four sons, and he added, "thus will they pursue me till I die."

In the summer of 1173 the rebellion broke. Prince Henry and the French king attacked Normandy and plotted an invasion of England, but Henry still had enough power and loyal knights to put down this revolt. He sent sharp messages to Eleanor, telling her to stop fomenting trouble and to cease turning their sons against him. Getting no reply, he flew into a rage and started for Poitiers, storming castles and laying waste the vineyards and farms. He captured many rebels and sent them to his dark dungeons in Normandy. He sought the queen in Poitiers but Eleanor, disguised as a man and astride a horse, was fleeing towards Paris where her three older sons had gone to join the King of France. While Henry's men were ravaging the countryside,

A troubadour sings to his lady.

some spied a small convoy of knights heading north. Eleanor was recognized and conducted, a prisoner, to the English king.

Before he dealt with Eleanor, Henry returned to Poitiers to rout out the rest of the rebels and sweep away all vestiges of Eleanor's court. The great hall where Eleanor laid down the rules of love and chivalry was emptied. Marie of Champagne went home, the troubadours dispersed, the music stopped, and gloom descended on the once gay city.

Eleanor was put aboard a ship which carried her across the stormy channel to England and the confinement of strong castles, far from the seat of treachery and sedition. Eleanor's sons resented their mother's imprisonment and her vassals of Aquitaine demanded her release. Poets of the south cried out in plaintive verse that the wicked king of the north had stolen their mistress.

After King Henry had extinguished the last fires of rebellion, he tried to make peace with his sons. On their insistence, he softened Eleanor's imprisonment. Though always under guard, she sometimes was allowed to move from castle to castle and to join certain family gatherings. Henry wanted to divorce her but he dared not press this idea too far. His sons would never agree to it and Eleanor's faithful vassals would rebel again; he might lose his valuable southern lands.

In fact, strife and revolt started soon again, partly kept alive by the troubadours of the south, who hated Henry's harsh rule and longed for Eleanor's return, and by the French who kept seeking to break the power of the English king by siding with the young Plantagenets.

In 1183 young Prince Henry died suddenly and Eleanor's favorite, Richard, took his place as heir to the throne of England, at the same time adding the prince's titles of Duke of Normandy and Count of Anjou to his own title of Duke of Aquitaine. King Henry feared that Richard, fearless and intelligent, would be far more difficult to deal with than his unstable oldest son had been and he also felt that Richard had more than his share of lands. He asked him to give Aquitaine to his youngest brother, John. When Richard refused, Henry was driven to call upon his captive queen to help rearrange their sons' inheritance.

Eleanor had been in captivity ten years when she emerged to meet her estranged husband and their sons at Windsor Castle. She was sixty-two. Her braids, no longer black, were hidden beneath her wimple, her graceful figure had grown heavier, and her laughing eyes more serious but her mind and purpose had not been dulled by her long imprisonment and she was still able to exert her political influence. She flatly refused to let John replace Richard as Duke of Aquitaine and she insisted upon holding to the feudal oaths already pledged. Her two older sons and other nobles of the realm supported her and agreed that Richard should keep the title of Duke of Aquitaine and rule it for her, until, if ever free, she could return to power there herself.

Back in her thick-walled castle, Eleanor soon learned of the death of another son, Geoffrey, killed in a tournament. Of her five sons only Richard and John, who now became the hope and darling of his father as Richard was of his mother, were left to battle for their inheritance. She had also heard of the death of her ex-husband, the gentle King Louis, whose son, Philip, became the King of France and, as predicted, an instrument for Henry's downfall. As determined and ambitious as Henry, Philip aimed to win back bit by bit the lands he felt belonged to France. He saw that he could play upon the discontent of Richard, ever suspicious that King Henry planned to disinherit him in favor of John. Eleanor must have been pleased to hear the tales which trickled back to her of Philip's and Richard's machinations against Henry.

But in 1187 dreadful news from the Holy Land interrupted the bickerings between the French and English. The Moslems, now united under one strong ruler, Saladin, had captured many of the Christian states in Syria. Even Jerusalem and the True Cross were now in their hands. For a moment Henry and Philip forgot their quarrels, exchanged the kiss of peace and pledged themselves to a third crusade. They both promised to observe the Truce of God, a ban on fighting set up by the Church.

The Truce of God was short lived. While Henry prepared for the crusade in England he heard that fighting had broken out again in France. Determined to stop this, he hastily made ready to cross the channel, pausing briefly at Salisbury castle where Eleanor was still a prisoner. As he set sail, his island and his queen were blotted out by a tempest of wind and rain.

Back in France the enmity between Henry and Philip flared up. The crusade had to wait while the Christian kings settled their own war and the money raised for overseas was squandered on the local battlefields.

Richard, though already pledged and more eager than anyone for the crusade, now caused further trouble and delay. Convinced that

Henry meant to disinherit him in favor of John, he definitely broke with his father and became King Philip's liege man. Many knights deserted Henry, thinking their future lay with young Richard. Only John and a few followers remained faithful to Henry who now realized that his son, Richard, meant to hound him to death. He shut himself up in his old Norman castle at Le Mans, thinking that Richard and Philip would not attack his person. But the demon that was in Henry was in Richard, too. He and Philip did try to capture King Henry, who escaped with difficulty and fled, worn out and humiliated, to his castle of Chinon. An old leg sore had festered, spreading pain and fever through his body. It was clear he did not have long to live, but in spite of pain and fever, he answered Philip's summons to a last parley. He was so weak that he could hardly keep his saddle. Yet, as was his custom at parley, he insisted on staying astride his horse to listen to Philip's harsh terms of unconditional surrender. When ordered to give his son the kiss of peace, Henry whispered fiercely as Richard approached, "God grant I may not die before I have had my revenge on you."

Soon Henry was dying in Chinon. He asked to see the list of names of those who had deserted him. When he found that his beloved John was one, he turned his face to the wall. "It is enough," he said. "I care no more for myself or for the world." He could be heard muttering, "Shame, shame, shame on a conquered king." Eleanor's terrible vengeance had done its work and the king who had forged an empire died, deserted by his friends and family.

As soon as the news of Henry's death reached England, Eleanor was free. Though sixty-eight years old, her mind and energy were as good as ever and she emerged from prison a wiser and more understanding woman. Her old age was to be her most magnificent.

No one objected when she assumed the responsibilities of government until Richard could be crowned. In fact she was immediately recognized as "Eleanor, by the grace of God, Queen of England." She hastened to London and gathered the important nobles and churchmen to swear oaths of fealty to her son, the new king, while he finished business in Normandy. Eleanor then set out on a trip to important English towns and castle strongholds, receiving more oaths of allegiance to Richard. She presided at courts of justice and set her own seal upon decisions. She released prisoners who had languished long in dungeons, waiting for the king's justice. She pardoned criminals and trespassers against Henry's harsh forest laws and did her best to remove all grievances and mete out justice. She had learned a great deal about government and justice from Henry. But where Henry had been admired and feared, Eleanor was admired and loved. She tried to build up enthusiasm for Richard, who, though born in England, had lived most of his life in France and was little known to the English.

Eleanor prepared England for the most splendid coronation it had ever witnessed, setting the fashion for all future crownings of English kings down to the present time. She knew that Richard, unlike his father, would enjoy the pageantry she arranged.

The coronation took place on September 3, 1189. The procession to Westminster was led by church dignitaries bearing a gold cross and holy water. Other magnates carried the royal cap, the golden spurs, the sceptre, and sword of state. Then came Richard, the most regal-looking monarch since William the Conqueror. Tall and shapely, he had the figure of a warrior and his handsome face with its fine features was framed with amber-gold hair. He impressed all by his knightly bearing and courteous manners and people thrilled to see that he already wore the crusader cross upon his royal robes. He walked beneath a canopy supported by four lances held aloft by his barons. At the crossing of the transept of the great abbey, Richard was formally acclaimed King and took the threefold coronation oath, swearing on the Gospels and relics of saints to maintain the Church and people in peace, to suppress wrongdoing and to temper justice with mercy. He was anointed with holy oil, armed with the spurs and sword of state, and crowned by the archbishop. He was now King Richard I of England by the grace of God.

This great spectacle was almost the last view the English had of their new king. Richard was anxious to be off on the Third Crusade which interested him far more than ruling his kingdom. To raise money he put up for sale everything he could think of—castles, manors, even public offices. "I would sell all London if I could find a buyer for it," he said. Within three months he and Eleanor had set the government of England in order, collected men, money, and a fleet, and set sail across the wintry channel.

Though a regency was set up to rule England during Richard's absence on crusade, Eleanor was the key figure and real ruler of the vast Plantagenet realm. Like Henry before her she had to divide her time between England and her continental domains.

Eleanor's first concern was Richard and the future of the realm. Should Richard die on crusade the whole empire would fall to John, who was vicious and cruel and not to be trusted. She knew his eyes were on the crown and that he was waiting for Richard's absence on crusade to plot his devious course. Richard must have a wife and heir. While attending to government affairs and keeping a watchful eye on John, Eleanor began to search for a suitable bride—one with a worthwhile dowry of wealth and lands.

Eleanor's wisdom and skill in making decisions continued to be a marvel to all. A contemporary called her, "a matchless woman, beautiful and eloquent . . . indefatigable for every undertaking . . . the admiration of her age." She was too busy to feel old and she still had twelve fruitful years ahead of her.

RICHARD THE LION HEART

Richard the Lion Heart.

In his ten-year reign Richard was to spend only six months in his English kingdom. He was not a great English king like his father; but what mattered more to men and women of the twelfth century, he was a great crusader whose deeds of courage and prowess in arms, whose courtesy and skill in poetry, made him the perfect chivalrous knight. Though the English paid heavily for his adventures overseas, they were proud of his fame as the greatest knight in Christendom.

King Richard, King Philip of France, and the Holy Roman Emperor Frederick Barbarossa were the leaders of the Third Crusade. The emperor, a gallant old man nearing seventy, had already started on the crusade with an enormous host of Germans, expecting the other two armies to join him shortly.

No one was more devoted to the crusade than Richard, who was determined to take along the best equipment. Always interested in the strategy of war, he assembled parts of siege engines, huge catapults, movable towers and battering rams. His weapons were much the same as those used in William the Conqueror's time except for the new crossbow, which shot iron-tipped bolts released by a trigger mechanism. It was deadly and accurate, in fact so deadly that the Church had banned its use except against the infidels. Richard and his knights had chain mail which covered them from head to foot.

Man with crossbow.

Over this they wore knee-length, sleeveless tunics to shade the metal from the sun. Their helmets were no longer conical headpieces with nose-guards, but pot-shaped, covering the whole face except for eye-slits and holes for breathing. Richard's had a crest, showing a lion and a sprig of broom plant. This was his personal device for being recognized in battle.

In July, 1190, Richard and Philip assembled their hosts at Vézelay, where Eleanor and Louis had heard Abbot Bernard preach the Second Crusade. Eleanor would not be going on this adventure for there were to be no women tagging along this time, but she could be proud of her son to whom all turned their gaze. "He far surpassed other men in the courtesy of his manners and the vastness of his strength." Richard was thirty-three, ten years older than Philip, and already had the reputation of a fearless warrior and chivalrous knight. As King of France, Philip was Richard's overlord but he suffered in comparison; he was not a very knightly figure. Now that their common enemy, Henry, was dead, their friendship had ceased and they distrusted each other.

The two great armies—the French with red, the English with white crosses on their tunics—started south along the dusty roads. Bright banners fluttered, new armor glistened in the sun, and the heavy tread of marching men and war-horses brought forth villagers to wave and cheer them on to the Holy War against the enemies of Christ. In the south of France the armies separated, Philip's to travel by land and Richard's by sea. They were to meet in Sicily and sail together to the Holy Land.

Philip arrived unostentatiously in Sicily in early September, and a week later Richard sailed into the harbor with pennons flying from the masts amid a great blowing of horns and trumpets. He had gathered ships from England, Normandy and Aquitaine, one hundred and fourteen in all. Some of these were large cargo vessels, high-pooped with castles fore and aft. They were loaded with "abundance of gold, silver, rich furs, precious vestments, arms, and supplies of bacon, cheese, and wines," for even on crusade Richard expected to live in style. Others were the Mediterranean type of low war-galley with two rows of oars and a single mast with a triangular, lateen sail. Each

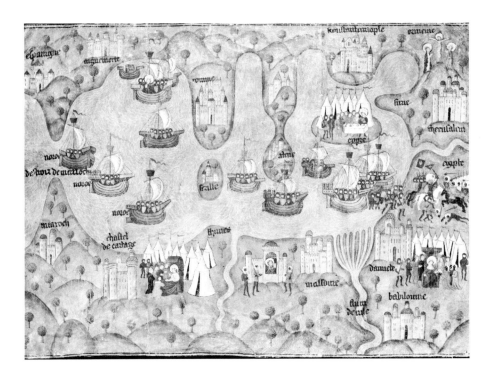

A crusader map.

could carry forty knights with their gear and horses and forty foot soldiers besides the crew. Richard's own great warship had red sails emblazoned with lions and a huge iron-beaked prow for ramming enemy ship. At its stern was a covered pavilion.

Richard always managed to steal the show from Philip, whose jealousy and resentment of his more knightly companion in arms grew more bitter every day. Quarrels broke out between the kings and they spent a winter of uneasy peace waiting for spring weather before sailing. During the winter they learned that the Emperor Frederick Barbarossa had been drowned as he neared the Holy Land and that only a small force of Germans had continued on the crusade.

In the meantime Queen Eleanor had found a bride for Richard— the docile young Princess Berengaria of Navarre. In the middle of winter the indefatigable old queen set out on horseback with her charge. Over the Alps, through the plains of Lombardy, over the

138

Apennines, on down to the tip of Italy they journeyed through the rain and mud of early spring.

When Philip heard that Queen Eleanor was on her way with a bride for Richard, he angrily reminded the English king that he had long ago promised to wed Philip's sister, the French princess. Richard, however, preferred his mother's choice and rudely broke his pledge to Philip, who had to swallow this insult to the honor of his royal family. Henceforth he hated Richard more than ever.

On the very day that Philip set sail for the Holy Land, Eleanor arrived with Princess Berengaria. She dared not linger long, fearing that John might cause trouble in her absence. After four days of discussing affairs of state with her beloved son, she retraced her steps to Normandy to take up her post of watching and waiting for Richard's return.

Richard at last set sail in April, 1191, taking his future bride with him, contrary to the agreement that no women should accompany the crusade. In spite of precautions to keep his fleet together—his trumpet blast by day and a huge candle burning in the lantern atop his mast at night—storms scattered his ships. Finding some at the island of Cyprus, Richard decided to capture it. This proved a worthwhile delay for Cyprus was rich in grain, wine, and sheep and became the main base of supplies for this and later crusades. Before he left the island Richard celebrated his marriage to Princess Berengaria and had her crowned Queen of England. By June he was on the last stretch of his voyage to the Kingdom of Jerusalem, where the French and German crusaders awaited him impatiently.

Only a few coastal cities of the kingdom remained in Christian hands—even the Holy City of Jerusalem had fallen to the Moslems (more often called Saracens by the crusaders) who were united under the leadership of the great and powerful Sultan of Egypt and Syria, Saladin. Saladin was a man of honor, as chivalrous as King Richard but considerably more tolerant and merciful. He had little respect for the knights of the West, with whom he had had unpleasant dealings, and he intended to get rid of the "vile Christian dogs" who had brought such dishonor to his Moslem country.

The crusaders had been trickling into the Holy Land ever since

Saladin's capture of Jerusalem and for over a year had been laying siege to the important seaport of Acre, held by the flower of Saladin's army. Saladin and the rest of his army were camped in the hills behind the city, so that the besiegers of Acre were themselves besieged.

Jutting out into the Mediterranean Sea on an L-shaped promontory, Acre was a far stronger fortress than any in Europe. Disease and lack of food harassed both the crusaders and the Saracens within the walled town. It was difficult to make any large scale assault on the citadel. Whenever the crusaders attacked, the Saracens within raised a terrible din, beating on basins and shouting to the skies to alert Saladin's army, which swooped down from the hills to the crusaders' camp. The crusaders then had to return to defend their camp below the city's walls.

As Richard's fleet sailed into the harbor of Acre, he could see Saladin's colored tents and his army swarming on the hills behind the high-walled city. The sight of Richard's approaching fleet gave new hope to the despairing crusaders. The crowds on the shore went wild

A crusader warship such as Richard's.

In the midst of the siege.

with rejoicing. When Richard landed, bonfires were lit, trumpets and clarions blared and the night was spent in revelry.

The crusaders now looked to Richard for leadership rather than to Philip, and Richard did everything he could to assure his own popularity; he immediately offered higher pay than Philip to any who would enter his service.

The crusader camp was full of rotting corpses of men and horses; most newcomers collapsed with fevers in the disease-ridden area. Both kings fell ill with a strange fever which caused their nails and hair to drop out. While Richard was ill he tried to negotiate with Saladin, but the reply came back, "Warring kings should not have speech with each other until terms of peace between them have been arranged." However, the courteous Saladin did send fruits, cooled in snow from nearby mountains, to refresh the invalid kings.

When Philip recovered, the French began an assault on the citadel. They set up their huge catapult, known as the "Evil Neighbor," and began pounding away at the "Accursed Tower," the strongest of the towers of Acre; its enormous height and thick walls seemed to defy the attackers below. A huge ditch surrounding the walls made it difficult to get close. Some crusaders spent their time filling up the ditch with stones and even corpses of men and horses, exposing themselves to a rain of arrows and "Greek fire," the deadly combustible which the Saracens hurled down in pots to set fire to the wooden siege engines.

Philip ordered a movable shed, or penthouse, to approach the walls. Under its cover, crossbowmen protected a huge battering ram. Close behind followed a high movable tower concealing hundreds of archers who planned to rush onto the walls from its top level and attack the defenders with crossbow bolts and swords. Both engines lumbered slowly forward, pushed on rollers. Suddenly a heap of dry logs sailed from the walls and crashed into them. Like fire-breathing dragons, pots of Greek fire flew swiftly after. Both penthouse and tower burst into flames, burning the men inside.

But stone-casting machines kept up a steady barrage, hurling great rocks day and night at the walls and towers. One of Richard's great mangonels hurled a huge rock—which he had brought all the way from Sicily—with such force that it killed twelve men at once. The Saracens were so impressed that they kept the stone to show to Saladin.

Richard was impatient to end the siege. He knew that the Saracens must be near starvation; the crusaders now controlled the harbor and no supplies could get to the besieged. Though still sick, Richard had himself carried on silken cushions, under cover of a penthouse, towards the Accursed Tower. Here he supervised his sappers digging

Two stone-casting machines, a trébu-chet and mangonel.

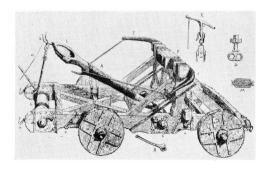

tunnels to undermine and set fire to the tower's base. From his cush-ioned seat protected by his crossbowmen and using his own crossbow, the king shot at the enemy on the walls. When his sappers had a big enough tunnel, they carried in logs and combustibles and fired them under the tower which lurched but did not fall. Then Richard of-fered high rewards to any of his men who could loosen stones from the walls near the tower. At the sight of gold pieces, many brave men leaped forward with picks and axes despite the rain of arrows and stones from above. Their work, combined with the sappers' tunnel underground and the constant barrage of catapults, at last had its effect. With a great roar of stones and rubble, the Accursed Tower finally fell. When the smoke and dust cleared away there was a huge breach in the wall.

Sappers undermine wall while a battering ram cracks it.

The final assault now began. Some rushed through the breach, others climbed scaling ladders, and archers leapt onto the walls from the tops of movable towers. The battle cry of "Christ and the Holy Sepulchre" rang out as the crusaders poured into Acre, hacking at the Saracens with their long swords. The enemy, though starving and desperate, put up a valiant resistance. Cascades of Greek fire met the crusaders scaling the ladders; when the fire penetrated the knights' armor, it burned the flesh. Many, shrieking with pain, tore off their mail hauberks, only to be pierced by arrows.

The Saracens within the citadel were soon ready to sue for peace. On July 12 they pledged themselves in Saladin's name to give up Acre, return the True Cross and fifteen hundred Christian prisoners, and pay 200,000 gold pieces. Until these terms were fulfilled, Richard would keep the Saracens left in Acre as prisoners of war.

Saladin, who had not been consulted, was angered at the terms of surrender. He was about to dispatch a message, refusing to agree, when he noticed crusader banners flying above the battered walls of Acre. It was too late; the treaty had been made in his name and, as a man of honor, he would abide by it.

Quarrels arose among the crusaders as soon as they took over Acre. Richard, who set himself up in the palace of the kings, was incensed to see the German banner flying next to his. In a rage he had it pulled down and thrown into a muddy ditch. Duke Leopold, head of the German crusaders since the death of the emperor, soon removed his Germans and left for home, bearing a lasting hatred for the English king.

Richard was more incensed when he heard that Philip, who had fallen ill again, wanted to return to France. But he finally agreed to Philip's departure on condition he leave most of his knights behind and that he promise not to molest any of Richard's lands. Philip gave his oath and set sail from Acre at the end of July, 1191. Richard was now in full command of the crusade. He had made enemies of the French and German leaders but the lesser knights and foot soldiers worshipped him.

Richard had agreed that Saladin could fulfill the terms of surrender in three installments but when the first arrived it was not complete—the specified Christian prisoners of noble rank and the True Cross were missing. Richard felt that Saladin was playing with him and had broken his bargain. According to the rights of war he resorted to brutal reprisals. Leading the twenty-six hundred Saracen prisoners of Acre, men, women, and children bound by ropes, to the plain below Saladin's camp, he had them all killed except the strongest and most important who were saved for slave labor and future ransom.

No one at the time, neither Moslem nor Christian, was shocked at this cold-blooded massacre. The crusaders felt it due vengeance for Christians killed in the siege of Acre and for Saladin's not fulfilling the terms of surrender on time. But after this Saladin, who had treated Christians with considerable mercy, killed them all except those worth a ransom. He kept the True Cross.

Richard left the ruined battlements of Acre and led his army south, along the coast, towards Jaffa, which he wanted as a base for his attack on Jerusalem. He organized his men carefully so that they could withstand attacks from Saladin's army, which was moving in a parallel course in the hills. Richard's fleet kept pace with his army, which he divided into three columns: the baggage train of supplies nearest the coast, the knights and their valuable war-horses in the middle. The third column of foot soldiers shielded the knights and faced the hills.

The lightly armed Saracens on their swift horses began to harass the crusaders. Galloping towards the tightly packed columns, they let loose their arrows and iron-tipped reed spears, then wheeled and sped away. They were surprised to see Richard's foot soldiers continue marching, undisturbed by arrows sticking in their thick quilted jackets; they looked like porcupines. The road became more and more impassable with knifelike reeds and thorny scrub. The sun beat down unmercifully on the iron helmets and mail coats, but the crusaders bore themselves manfully, singing, "Help us, O Sepulchre," to lift up their spirits. Richard occasionally left his battle standard to ride up and down, encouraging his men.

Saladin was saving the real strength of his army to force a battle when the crusaders emerged onto the plain, just north of their objective, Jaffa. He lined up his cavalry on the plain and hid his reserves in the nearby forest of Arsuf. Richard knew a battle was imminent and commanded his men to keep their places until his trumpets gave the signal to charge.

Early in the morning the Saracens began to attack, sending in wave after wave of Negro and Bedouin foot soldiers, yelling and howling and shooting arrows. They harassed the rear guard so much that the knights had to march backwards, fighting to hold them at bay. Then came Saladin's Turkish cavalry, whirling their scimitars and spiked maces. "On steeds swifter than eagles they thundered down upon us, till the whirling dust raised by their rapid flight blackened the very air," said an eyewitness. Some, employed just to make a din, clashed cymbals and gongs, beat drums and blew trumpets. The louder their noise the fiercer they fought. Above the din could sometimes be heard, "There is no God but Allah and Mahomet is his prophet."

Suddenly two knights took matters into their own hands and started to charge before the signal was given. Others followed and galloped after, shouting, "St. George, St. George." Richard saw what was happening and ordered the trumpets to sound. Setting spurs to his war-horse, he thundered down the line to take the lead. His English-Norman knights wheeled and galloped after him. Slashing to right and left with his two-edged sword, Richard pressed through the Turks, leaving a lane of dead. Terrified by the charge of the ironclad knights, the Turks fled to the forest; some panicked and rode their horses into the sea. The battle of Arsuf was a great moral victory for the crusaders and a humiliating defeat for the larger forces of the Saracens. Saladin was greatly impressed by Richard's tactics and personal bravery. Unlike the English king, the sultan never fought in person; though he often saw Richard from a distance, he never came face to face with him.

The Christian host continued its march to Jaffa. Richard wanted to rest his men and secure supplies before attacking Jerusalem. He would have to lead his men over unknown mountainous terrain with Saracen troops harassing him all the way. He needed men, money, and equipment, all of which were running short. He asked for a parley with Saladin who, though he still refused to meet Richard, allowed his brother Saphadin to talk with the English king. The two had several meetings and even went hunting together. They became good friends and exchanged costly gifts but Richard's negotiations for peace came to nothing. He always made the same demand—surrender of the True Cross and the entire Kingdom of Jerusalem. Saladin sent back word that Jerusalem was just as holy to the Moslems as it was to the Christians, but he encouraged his brother to string out his talks with Richard. Reinforcements were on their way and he needed time.

It was not until late in November that Richard started slowly inland. The terrible winter weather had already set in; torrential rains came down, cold winds blew in from the sea, and the mountain passes turned to muddy streams. High gales uprooted the tents, rain soaked and rotted the food and rusted armor. Though the crusaders were almost within twelve miles of Jerusalem, a council of war advised retreat.

On the dreary climb down through sleet and slithery mud, quarrels broke out. The French blamed the English, the English blamed the French and Germans, and many deserted. Troubles now came thick and fast to Richard. When the German Conrad, Lord of the crusader state of Tyre, was mysteriously murdered, the disgruntled French and Germans accused Richard. Then came the worst possible news. A small fishing smack arrived bearing a letter from Queen Eleanor, reporting that John and Philip were conspiring to set John on the throne of England and to invade Richard's Duchy of Normandy. Eleanor urged Richard to hurry home. Richard was incensed and talked of abandoning the crusade but when one of his vassal knights knelt before him, with tears streaming down his face, and begged the king to finish the crusade, Richard could not let his men down.

The crusaders decided to make another attempt to take Jerusalem and set forth once more in early June. Again they got within twelve miles of the Holy City. Spirits revived and quarrels ceased. While the crusaders assembled the engines of war, Richard pondered the problem of the difficult siege. One day, at dawn, he rode forth on a scouting expedition into the Judean hills. Looking up suddenly, he saw

Jerusalem on the Judean hills.

the white walls, the high towers and slender minarets of the Holy
City rising in the distance. He quickly covered his face with his shield
and cried out, "Fair Lord, I pray Thee not to let me see Thy Holy
City if so it be I may not deliver it out of the hands of Thine enemies." He soon discovered that Saladin had poisoned all the wells,
destroyed the cisterns, and blocked up the springs in the neighbor-
hood. There would be no water for men or horses and all would die
of thirst in the scorching summer heat on the dry Judean hills if they
tried an assault now. Another council of war was held and again the
order to retreat was given.

At this second retreat the Christian army fell apart. The French
refused to pitch their tents near the English and hurled jeers and
insults at Richard. Many more crusaders sought passage for home.
Richard, leaving his sick and wounded with a small guard in Jaffa,
went on to Acre, determined to sail for home, peace or no peace.

But the war was not over yet. While Richard was preparing for his
journey home, a messenger appeared, saying that Saladin had at-

148

tacked and captured Jaffa in his absence. The desperate defenders had retreated to the fortified central tower and had agreed to surrender if help did not come quickly. "God yet lives," cried Richard, "and with His guidance I will do what I can." Collecting as many knights as he could, he set off by sea towards Jaffa.

The crusaders in Jaffa had just agreed to surrender when they spotted Richard's galley with its great red sail emblazoned with lions. Richard saw the Saracen banners flying from the towers of the town and thought he was too late. As he waited for his other ships, he noticed a man scramble down the walls, plunge into the sea and swim towards his boat. The swimmer reported that a few Christians still held out within the citadel. At this Richard leapt into the water shouting, "Shame on him who lags behind now." Richard and his men cut their way into the town, completely surprising the Saracens who, fearing that a huge Christian host followed the English king, panicked and fled.

Richard had only fifty-four knights and fifteen horses, four hundred bowmen and fifteen hundred spearmen. They were outnumbered by more than three to one. Since Jaffa was full of corpses, the crusaders camped outside. At dawn one of Richard's men who was scouting, heard the neighing of horses and the distant tramp of soldiers. He rushed back to arouse Richard, asleep in his tent. The king jumped up, threw on his mail coat and sprang onto a horse. He prepared to withstand the attack as best he could. Behind a palisade of sharp stakes to trip the onrushing enemy horses he placed a solid wall of kneeling spearmen, each protected by his shield and each holding his lance firmly at an angle to impale the Saracen cavalry. In the second line crossbowmen worked in pairs, one to load and one to discharge the arrow. Richard warned his men that flight would mean certain death.

Saladin's men were in seven divisions of a thousand each. When the first wave of Saracen horsemen charged, they were checked by the sharp stakes and bristling spears. Richard was delighted and shouted, "We have only to stand firm against every fresh attempt till by God's help the victory is ours." Five or six times the enemy charged, only to be repelled as their horses reared and crossbow bolts

The king seemed to be every-where.

penetrated the lightly armed riders. By mid-afternoon Richard, full of confidence, led a counterattack. Under cover of his archers, who now discharged all their bolts at the oncoming enemy, Richard charged forward with his fifteen mounted knights followed by his spearmen. The king seemed to be everywhere at once, his long arm wielding his sword so skillfully that he cut his way right through the enemy.

Saladin, watching from his tent, was lost in angry admiration at the bravery and prowess of his adversary. Seeing Richard's horse fall beneath him, the chivalrous sultan sent forth a groom, leading two swift Arabian steeds as a gift, in token of his esteem for the English king. Saladin could not get his men to attack again. By late afternoon the Saracens were in full retreat.

This was Richard's final and greatest victory in the Holy Land. His superb tactics and his bravery had won the day and also won him immortal fame and the name of Richard the Lion Heart. But Richard could not follow up this victory. Jaffa and the land around it festered in the summer heat, which spread sickness; Richard now came down with typhus. His forces had dwindled to almost nothing and he was too sick to fight. By September a peace was concluded which allowed the crusaders to keep their coastal cities from Tyre to Jaffa. Christian and Moslem pilgrims would be free to come and go to Jerusalem and worship at their separate shrines. The peace was to last five years, at the end of which time Richard threatened to return to liberate the Kingdom of Jerusalem from Saladin's rule. To this the gallant sultan replied that if he had to lose Jerusalem he would rather lose it to Richard than any other prince in the world.

Richard sailed from Acre early in October, 1192, a little more than a year after his arrival. He left behind such fear of himself that, for years, Moslem women silenced their children with the words, "Be quiet, the King of England is coming."

Though the Third Crusade was not completely successful, it kept the few Christian lands in Syria secure for another century. But never again would such a galaxy of princely warriors journey together to the Holy Land and perform such deeds of daring and chivalry. Its two great opponents, Richard and Saladin, cast a special luster on the Third Crusade, when the chivalry of the twelfth century was at its height.

Richard's voyage home was full of adventure, shipwreck, and narrow escapes. All the princes of the West were aroused against him; each had his own grudge against the crusader king and each now sought his ruin. Richard was warned that he would be seized if he landed in France. So, seeking secret ways among the islands and avoiding open seas, he came to Corfu, where he hired a pirate vessel and headed north. Driven by furious gales to the head of the Adriatic, his ship foundered, casting him and his few companions on the shore near Venice. The land belonged to relatives of Conrad, of whose murder Richard had been accused, and to vassals of the Duke

Richard leaves the Holy Land.

of Austria, whose banner Richard had thrown in the ditch at Acre.

Richard was aware of the peril. Disguising himself as a merchant, he and his friends somehow found horses and sped north in the middle of the night. But word had spread that the King of England had landed in German territory and spies were on the lookout. A Norman knight, employed in a German household, was dispatched to search every pilgrim inn, to try to discover Richard by speech or any other sign. The Norman finally found the king, but instead of revealing him he gave Richard his horse and urged him to fly for his life.

Accompanied now by only one knight and a boy who could speak German, the king rode for three days and nights without stopping to eat or sleep to the environs of Vienna, in the heart of Duke Leopold's land. He had ridden one hundred and fifty miles at great speed and, still not fully recovered from his typhus, he collapsed from hunger and exhaustion. While he lay sick in a tavern, the young boy, seeking food for his master, aroused suspicion by stupidly appearing in the marketplace wearing Richard's gloves in his belt. He was quickly seized and threatened with having his tongue torn out if he did not immediately divulge the king's whereabouts. Duke Leopold was summoned and, guided by the boy, rode to the tavern. Hearing the hubbub outside, Richard dashed to the kitchen, threw on a kitchen boy's smock and busied himself with the large spit of roasting capons. But the king could not pass himself off as a kitchen boy— his regal bearing and, some said, his great ruby ring gave him away. Richard knew the game was up but refused to surrender to anyone except the duke himself. To him he surrendered honorably, handing over his sword. He was led away to Durenstein, a remote fortress high above the Danube River.

Queen Eleanor and the English had been baffled as to Richard's whereabouts. Crusaders had been straggling home all during the fall of 1192, expecting to find their king already there. John tried to convince the English that Richard was dead, in hope of seizing the throne immediately. King Philip, of course, was helping him—he saw in John a weaker man than Richard and hoped to use him to get back the lands he felt belonged to France. Only Eleanor and the barons, still loyal to Richard, had kept the two in check and managed to hold on to most of Richard's possessions.

The German Emperor, Henry VI, was delighted to learn of the capture of Richard and helped Duke Leopold draw up a long list of charges against him, accusing the English king of the murder of the German Conrad, of dishonoring the German banner in Acre, and of outrageous conduct towards the king of France. They painted his crimes as black as possible and demanded a huge ransom of one thousand marks of silver, more than two years' taxes to the Crown of England.

When Richard appeared before them to answer for his crimes, he stood forth boldly and spoke eloquently in his own defense. The courtly manners taught him long ago by his mother were useful to him now. He answered every charge with such sincerity and good reason, such grace and humility, that he aroused the sympathy of all his listeners, even his accusers, and many burst into tears and applause as he finished. The emperor himself was moved to pity and gave Richard the kiss of peace. For a while the royal prisoner was treated as an honored guest and was hopeful of a quick release.

But King Philip, greatly fearing this, bribed the emperor, who then sent Richard off to the imperial dungeon in a mountain castle and put him under heavy guard. While the English king languished, King Philip, with John's connivance, invaded Normandy.

As soon as the news of Richard's capture reached England, Queen Eleanor quickly summoned the magnates of the realm and dispatched two abbots to Germany to seek out her son. When they finally located Richard, he was able to send a message to his mother, requesting that she collect the ransom money as soon as possible and deliver it in person—she was the only person he really trusted. He also wrote a poem lamenting that his friends did nothing to help him while his enemy, King Philip, contrary to his oath, ravaged his lands.

> No prisoner can tell his honest thought
> Unless he speaks as one who suffers wrong;
> But for his comfort he may make a song.
> My friends are many, but their gifts are naught.
> Shame will be theirs, if, for my ransom, here
>   I lie another year.

153

What marvel that my heart is sad and sore
When my own lord torments my helpless lands!
Well do I know that, if he held his hands,
Remembering the common oath we swore,
I should not here imprisoned with my song,
      Remain a prisoner long.

Queen Eleanor poured out her anguish in letters to the Pope, up-braiding him for not coming to the aid of her son. Signing herself, "Eleanor, by the wrath of God, Queen of England," she wrote, "The kings and princes of the earth have conspired against my son, the anointed of the Lord. One keeps him in chains while another ravages his lands; . . . And while this goes on the sword of St. Peter reposes in its scabbard . . . Justice, the fear of God, faith and honor have dispersed. Arise, Seigneur, why do you sleep?"

The Pope gave Eleanor little help except to urge the English to raise the ransom for Richard's release. Eleanor lost no time in trying to collect the huge amount. Though it was the duty of every royal vassal to contribute to a king's ransom, it was no easy job to meet the emperor's terms. The country had already been bled for the crusade but Eleanor used every art she could to raise the sum. Taxes fell on poor as well as rich, churchmen and laymen. Churches and monas-teries yielded up their treasure of golden reliquaries, jeweled chal-ices, and even crosses from the altars. The austere Cistercian monks, having no valuable treasure, gave a year's crop of their wool. As the ransom trickled in—it seemed far too slowly to the impatient queen —Eleanor placed her seal upon it and stowed it away in St. Paul's Ca-thedral for safety.

In the winter of 1194, more than a year after Richard had left the Holy Land, the emperor finally agreed to release his prisoner as soon as the ransom arrived. Philip, hearing this, warned John that, "the Devil is unchained."

By mid-winter Eleanor, then seventy-three years old, had collected the ransom and set off across the wintry channel and made her way through snow and ice to the valley of the Rhine. When the sacks of money were handed over, Richard was free. His mother, worn out by her worries and labors, fell weeping into his arms. The onlookers dissolved into tears, too, at the sight of the aged queen embracing her beloved son.

When Richard returned to London, he was hailed as the great hero of the crusade, the champion who had, almost singlehanded, checked the might of the infidel foe and had then been betrayed by his Christian allies. But Richard was impatient to be off to France where he knew he must at last come to grips with his greatest enemy, King Philip. In less than two months he and Eleanor left England, never to return.

In Normandy, John appeared, humble and full of remorse. Fearing his brother, he sought his mother first that she might intercede in his behalf. But Richard was generous to this brother who had betrayed him, saying, "John mistakes me if he is afraid. After all he is my brother." He put out his arms to raise John, who lay weeping at his feet. John was easily persuaded to help Richard retrieve the castles which he and Philip had captured in the king's absence.

The struggle between Richard and Philip that ensued lasted for five years, interspersed with truces, during which time each side raised more men and money. Richard resorted to reviving bloody tournaments, though banned by the Church, and made money by extracting entrance fees from every knight who entered. He also sold charters of freedom to towns; wealthy merchants were glad to pay him for the privilege of running local government themselves. Richard's need for money had at least this one benefit—it aided the growth of local town government.

The Duchy of Normandy was the main bone of contention between the kings. Philip had been nibbling away at Richard's Norman frontiers, hoping to get to the Norman capital of Rouen, which of all places Richard wanted to prevent the French from taking. If he could block the Seine River and the road beside it—the only feasible approach—he could check the French advance. Beyond Philip's border castles the Seine took a large loop, on one side of which rose high chalky cliffs. Upon the highest of these, known as the Rock of Andelys, Richard built a castle which surpassed anything yet seen in Europe. The site was perfect, for the Rock rose precipitously from the river to an unassailable height; its land side was joined to the

Château Gaillard under siege.

hills behind by only a narrow ridge and its summit commanded an excellent view of the whole borderland.

Richard was his own architect and supervised every detail. He first blockaded the river at the foot of the great rock with a double stockade, and then built fortifications and a huge tower on the river side of the cliff. Underground passages led from this outer tower to the main citadel on the summit where the massive round keep rose to an even greater height. Richard built all his towers round like those in Acre for they withstood attack better than square ones. Running along the top of the keep were machicolations or galleries with openings for shooting arrows, dropping stones or burning pitch. Its thick walls splayed out at the base and were twenty feet wide at the angles. The keep and its courtyard were surrounded by a circular wall whose only entrance was a portcullis and drawbridge over a deep moat hewn out of the Rock. A second wall with flanking towers, rising out of the Rock itself, further protected the citadel. A third triangular section,

156

separated from the main part, faced the hills where attack was most likely.

Richard's castle was an extraordinary and unique engineering feat; he had cleverly fitted his masonry to the natural rocky foundations and made it not only superbly functional and impregnable but also beautiful. It was built with great speed and was almost complete in a year. "Behold," cried Richard proudly, "how fair is my one-year-old daughter." He named his fortress, "Château Gaillard," or Saucy Castle, in defiance of the French. When Philip saw the finished castle he was dismayed but cried out in bravado, "If its walls were made of iron, yet would I take them." To which Richard gaily retorted, "By God's throat, if its walls were made of butter, yet would I hold them."

The lofty castle kept the French from getting to the heart of Normandy but it did not stop the war. Richard was more desperate than ever for money. In the spring of 1199 he went to his royal treasure castle of Chinon, only to find the coffers empty. While there, as if in answer to his prayers, he heard that a great treasure trove of gold had been unearthed by a poor farmer near the castle of Châlus. The owner of the castle had surrendered part of the treasure to his overlord, who in turn had offered it to his overlord, Richard. But Richard wanted it all and set off immediately to secure it by besieging Châlus.

This was no impregnable fortress like Château Gaillard but a small castle, standing on a low hill. Its owner fled at Richard's approach; only about forty peasants and their families were left to defend it. Richard surrounded the castle and set up siege engines while the defenders did the best they could by hurling down stones and shooting arrows. One evening Richard, unarmed except for a helmet, was reconnoitering to see how to make an assault on the tower. Suddenly he noticed a man on top of the tower. The man had been parrying blows all day with a frying pan and firing back missiles he collected from the besiegers. As Richard went closer the man let loose a crossbow bolt which whistled through the air, hitting the king below the neck and embedding itself in his left shoulder. With a sharp cry of pain, Richard rushed for shelter and tried to withdraw the bolt. But the wooden shaft broke off and left the iron barb in the wound. A surgeon was called and, by the light of a lantern, dug deeply into Richard's shoulder and finally cut out the metal barb. But the wound was large and deep, close to the spine; gangrene soon set in. Richard knew that he would not recover and sent for his mother, who was at the Abbey of Fontevrault, a hundred miles to the north. Traveling day and night, Eleanor was soon at her son's side.

As Richard lay dying he bequeathed the English throne, all his lands and castles to his faithless brother John, and what treasure he had to the poor for the repose of his soul. Then he called in the man who had shot him and asked, "What harm have I done you that you have killed me?" The peasant answered boldly, "You slew my father and brothers and you meant to kill me. Therefore take what revenge you think fit, for I will endure the greatest tortures you can devise as long as you have met your end." Touched by the man's courage, the king replied, "Go hence in peace, I forgive you my death and will exact no revenge." He ordered the man to be unshackled and gave him a gift in token of his full mercy.

Richard then confessed his sins and asked to be buried at his father's feet in the Abbey of Fontevrault. He died in April, 1199, at the age of forty-two. The grief-stricken queen had Richard's body dressed in his coronation robes of pale blue, green, and rose. Jeweled gloves were placed on his hands and golden sandals on his feet. According to the royal custom, Richard was buried in three places, his body in Fontevrault, his heart in Rouen, his brain in Poitiers.

Eleanor felt she had lost "the staff of her age, the light of her eyes" when Richard died. Of all her sons, only he had fulfilled her ideals of chivalry—a fearless warrior, a poet, and courteous knight whose great exploits would echo through the centuries and proclaim him the greatest knight of the Middle Ages.

In spite of her grief Eleanor knew she must once more set the realm in order and do her best to gain support for her only remaining son, John, the least dependable and most ruthless of her brood. In Aquitaine she made another goodwill tour as she had done with Richard long ago. Despite her age—she was now seventy-nine—and the scorching heat of summer, Eleanor went from town to town, granting charters of liberty. Ever since her own imprisonment she had felt concern for oppressed people and victims of unfair laws. She earned the devotion of merchants and artisans, monks and nuns, as well as her own wealthy vassals.

Then the old queen went on to Tours, where King Philip was holding court. She knew that she must pay homage to her overlord so that there would be no question that she was still Duchess of Aquitaine, and that upon her death, John would be its duke. It was painful to Eleanor to kneel before the man who had betrayed her son, Richard, and even now, was trying to prevent John, the rightful heir, from being crowned King of England. But she knew the value of a vassal's oath and gracefully did her duty.

She had one more mission to complete the settlement of the realm, the arrangement of the marriage of a granddaughter, pledged some time before to Philip's son, Prince Louis. At the age of eighty she set out for Spain and arrived at the court of Castile where her daughter, another Eleanor, presided over a court as brilliant as her own former one at Poitiers. The old queen was asked to choose among her beautiful granddaughters a suitable wife for the French prince. She chose the lovely Blanche, destined to be the mother of a famous king and saint, Louis IX. On their way back they paused to rest at Bordeaux, whence Eleanor had been summoned to the throne of France so many years before. The queen was weary and did not accompany Blanche to the wedding festivities; instead she retired to the quiet Abbey of Fontevrault where she hoped to end her days in peace. But she soon heard that war had started again, that castles and towns were rapidly falling to the French as her unstable son, John, let power slip away. When she learned that the French were laying siege to Richard's great castle, Château Gaillard, while John retreated like a coward, she bitterly realized that she could do nothing more, that Philip, as predicted, was indeed a scourge to the English, the only one able to finish off the great Plantagenet empire.

Queen Eleanor died in March, 1204, at the age of eighty-three but was spared the news that Richard's Rock castle had fallen to the French three weeks before. She was buried in the crypt of Fontevrault

159

between King Henry and her favorite son, Richard. Amid the crashing of castle walls, as fortress after fortress fell to the French, little attention was paid to the death of the great queen. But the nuns who knew her best in her last magnificent years wrote, "She enhanced the grandeur of her birth by the honesty of her life . . . she surpassed almost all the queens of the world."

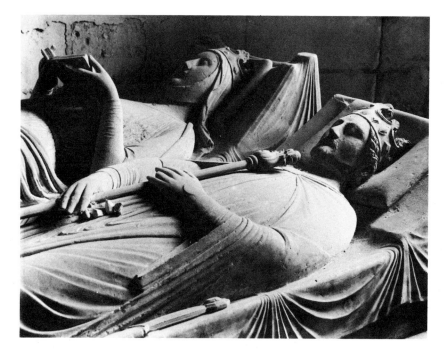

Effigies of Richard and Eleanor.

FRANCIS OF ASSISI

St. Francis. Statue by Della Robbia.

In 1182, when Queen Eleanor was in prison in England and Richard was fighting as usual against his father in France, Francis Bernardone was born in Assisi, a small walled town on the side of a mountain in the middle of Italy. The houses and churches of the town were squeezed along steep narrow streets which rose in layers up the mountain.

Life had not advanced as swiftly in this little inland town as it had in the great Italian seaports like Venice and Genoa. The nobles lived off the produce of their fields, orchards, and vineyards in the big valley below. Some of the merchants, trading with larger Italian cities, were as wealthy as these nobles.

Pietro Bernardone was one of these successful merchants—rich from his trade in cloth which he took north annually in a heavily guarded mule train to the great fairs of southern France. On one of his journeys he met a French girl, married her, and brought her back with him. Pietro, rough and uneducated, was proud of his wife whom he always called the "Lady" Pica. She brought the French language into Pietro's household and sang French troubadour songs of love and chivalry.

Their son was born in the summer of 1182 while Pietro was away on his usual business trip to France. His wife had the boy christened John, but this name did not satisfy Pietro. In a burst of fondness for the land his wife had come from, he changed his son's name to Francesco, which was the Italian way of saying "the little Frenchman."

The boy Francis charmed everyone with his dark, sparkling eyes, his smiling face and friendly nature. Even when very young, he avoided hurting anyone's feelings. His parents put him in a school run by the priests of San Georgio, a church near their house. He had a sketchy education, typical of the merchant class of the day. The priests taught him enough reading and writing to get by and enough Latin so that he could understand the daily church services.

His education ended while he was still very young, and his father took him into his shop. Francis was so courteous to the customers and learned so quickly how to sell rolls of wool, silk, or linen cloth, that his proud father hoped he would carry the family business to great heights.

As Francis grew into a young man he was included by the young nobles of the town in their festivities. Assisi though a small town had a little feudal court which tried to copy the fashionable court life of France, holding tournaments and banquets and inviting troubadours to entertain them with songs of brave knights. There was still a sharp distinction between a man of noble blood and the son of a

Assisi.

merchant whose ancestors might have been runaway serfs, but Francis was a welcome addition to the life of the young nobles. With his fond father's wealth at his disposal, he was probably richer than any of them, and with his generous nature treated them to lavish parties. He was small in stature but his charm and gaiety made up for his lack of physical strength. He wore soft flowing robes of the finest cloth in his father's shop, and dreamed of glory and chivalric deeds. His father was pleased to have Francis behave like a prince's son and even let him out of tending shop to join his noble friends.

Soon Francis became their leader. He was called "the flower of the young people of Assisi," and all predicted great things for him.

For many years he lived a frivolous life. He loved to lead his friends at night through the moonlit narrow streets, singing in his beautiful voice the French songs his mother had taught him, while the rest accompanied him with lutes and horns. They amused themselves in taverns until dawn; then, as peasants from the valley appeared with their donkeys laden with fruits and vegetables and as bells rang to call people to early Mass, Francis and his friends would fall happily into bed.

But Francis often wanted to escape from his boisterous friends. At these times he would walk alone in the mountains, gazing down on the valley of Umbria. The beauty of the meadows with their flowers, the brooks tumbling down the hills, the groves of oaks and the songs of the birds almost overwhelmed him. He felt that God had created an overpoweringly beautiful world and he began to praise Him increasingly in his heart.

Riding off to war.

Before Francis was twenty-one, war broke out between Assisi and its rival town Perugia within sight across the valley. The knights of Assisi, bored when not in battle, welcomed a chance to fight and armed themselves. In shining mail with painted emblems on their shields and pennants fluttering on their spears, they rode down the hill while peasants watched from the fields. Francis was with them, for though he was not of noble birth, times were changing; a rich merchant's son who could afford the expense of armor, horse, and squire was allowed to join the knights.

Francis was elated, but his dreams of glory were shattered as the Perugian knights galloped down from their hilltop, routed the attackers, and threw them into a dungeon. The knights of Assisi were gloomy as the prison days trickled on, but it was not in Francis' nature to be sad. He "made merry in his chains" and cheered the sulky nobles.

Messengers went back and forth between the two cities and finally, although it took a whole year, Assisi raised enough ransom money to release Francis and the knights. Francis went back to his parents' house and peace was restored to the valley.

Although outwardly Francis' life seemed to go on as before, he was deeply troubled. He became a great almsgiver; he could not hear the plea "for the love of God" without emptying his pockets. He fell sick and hovered between life and death. His long recovery gave him time to think about himself. He was over twenty-one and what had he accomplished? Had there been any point to his selfish, spendthrift life? He began to despise himself and the things that had given him pleasure.

Before he could decide what kind of life he really wanted, there came a second opportunity to prove himself in battle—this time for a religious cause. The great Pope Innocent III, tired of being threatened by the German emperor, saw his chance upon the emperor's death to separate southern Italy and Sicily from German control. He sent out a call to battle and many Italian knights eagerly responded. When an Assisan knight began collecting his troops and horses, Francis asked to be his squire, hoping that this war might be the answer to his questionings. The glorious tales of the Crusades seemed to demonstrate that it was a Christian duty to fight for the Church's cause.

Francis' father gave him a fine suit of armor, weapons and a horse, but as he rode around proudly trying them out, he passed a poor knight who had lost all his property and now sat like a beggar in the

Meeting a beggar.

streets. Without hesitation Francis gave him his own brilliant outfit, including the horse, saying that it was given freely for Christ's sake. What his father thought of this performance can be imagined, but he bought Francis new equipment and sent him off with his blessing, perhaps thinking that Francis might be knighted on the battlefield and bring distinction to the family name.

The colorful troop with banners and trumpets assembled in the town square in front of the ancient Roman temple of Minerva and its successor, the Cathedral. Francis, excited and emotional, announced to his parents and friends that he would become a great prince. As the townsfolk cheered, the horsemen trotted through the gate on the dusty road which twisted down the steep hillside. Then they rode southward on the straight Roman road through fields lined by poplar trees and willows.

The troop stopped for the night not many miles along the way to Rome. Darkness fell, campfires were lit, and Francis lay down in his tent to sleep.

The old chronicles say that the voice of God came to him in a dream and asked him what his intentions were. When Francis explained that he was going to fight for the Pope's cause in southern Italy, the voice asked sternly why he wanted to serve a mere servant of the Lord when he could serve the Lord better directly. Francis, perplexed, said, "Lord, what wilt thou have me do?" The voice replied, "Go back to the place of thy birth."

Francis tossed and turned. Was it really the Lord's voice? If he gave up all his hopes of being a glorious knight, how was he meant to serve the Lord better at home? And how could he explain this to his scoffing friends?

By morning light he had made his decision. It took courage, but he rode back to Assisi. Soon the town was gossiping that Pietro Bernardone's son had deserted the Pope's campaign for some strange idea of serving God at home. The friends who had not gone off to war welcomed him back and Francis continued to be their leader, but his heart was not in it. He spent much time alone in meditation, working things out in his mind.

During one evening's gaiety, as the laughing and shouting group ran through the sleeping streets, Francis gradually fell back and withdrew unnoticed in the uproar.

Suddenly he stood motionless. A light seemed to fill the darkness around him, and a feeling of closeness to God flowed through him; he said later that if someone had torn him to pieces, he would have felt nothing. He now was convinced that he must devote his life to God and that a way of doing this would soon be shown him. He spent more and more time in his lonely haunts in the ravines and hills behind Assisi. His parents tried to overlook his strange behavior, hoping it would end soon. Often Francis would rush from the dinner table to give his plate of food to a beggar. He persuaded his mother to put extra heaps of bread on the table—and these soon disappeared. He not only tried to feed every beggar, but gave money and linens to the priests of Assisi's poorer churches.

When Francis asked permission to go on a pilgrimage to Rome, his father sent him off in new fine clothes to show the Romans how richly a merchant from Assisi could dress his son. As soon as Francis reached Rome, he went to the old basilica of St. Peter. Running up the steps past peddlers, pilgrims, and beggars, he pushed his way through the crowded courtyard and entered the shadowy nave brightened by torchlight and candles. He stood in awe at the tomb of St. Peter ornamented by beautiful spiral marble columns that a Roman emperor had put there nine hundred years before, and covered by a canopy on silver pillars which Pope Gregory the Great had added; there was a grille by the tomb into which pilgrims could throw gifts. Francis was mortified to see how small the pilgrim offerings were. To the astonishment of the crowd, he took a fistful of money and hurled it with a clatter through the grille.

After praying, Francis came out through the big courtyard to the steps where many beggars, hoping that pilgrims would remember Christ's commands to give to the poor, were clustered. Impetuously Francis exchanged his fine clothes for the dirty rags of a beggar, then squatted on the steps among the diseased and filthy group. As he begged for alms he felt happy and free.

After his return home he spent much of his time at prayer, asking God what to do, and a voice repeatedly told him, "If you wish to

A medieval crucifix.

know my will, you must scorn the things you have loved in the world and you must enjoy what was unbearable." Francis vowed to love the thing that was most repulsive to him.

A chance to fulfill this vow came soon. As Francis rode near Assisi a leper whose eyelids drooped hideously and whose nose had rotted away, was crouched on the roadside, ringing a bell to warn passersby of his presence. Previously, Francis would have made a detour to avoid this wretched figure; in fact, he used to hold his nose when riding past the leper hospital. But now, although filled with disgust, he forced himself to dismount and approach the leper, who held out his hand for alms. Francis took hold of the deformed hand, put money in the stumpy fingers—and then kissed them humbly. Suddenly a feeling of God's love came over him. He knew at last that he could love all God's creatures equally without considering his own feelings. From this moment his life as a saint is said to have begun. He was twenty-three years old.

On a lonely spot in the midst of an olive grove there stood an old church tended only by an aged priest. Its bell tower had fallen and blocks of stone lay in the courtyard; birds were flying through shutterless windows in the crumbling walls and flowers were growing through cracked steps. Not long after his experience with the leper Francis entered this church and knelt in the half-light before a pale, sad Christ painted on a cross above the altar. The figure seemed to move its lips and say, "Francis, go repair my house which, as thou seest, is wholly falling into ruin."

Francis trembled with amazement. He gave all the money he had with him to the priest to buy a lamp and oil to burn before the crucifix. Then he ran home, grabbed rolls of scarlet cloth from his father's shelves, rode to a nearby town and sold the cloth—and also his horse. Ordering stones to be carted to the little church, he walked back to the startled priest, begging to be allowed to stay with him and repair his church. The old man at first thought Francis was playing a trick on him. Finally, he agreed to let Francis live with him but refused to take any money, for he feared the wrath of Francis' short-tempered father. Francis cast a handful of coins carelessly on the windowsill, then began to lift heavy fallen stones back into place. He was happy at last, for now God had given him something special to do.

His parents soon found out where he was and that he was working like a common laborer. This was too much for his proud father. For many months he had watched Francis' strange behavior, but now he feared that he was becoming a religious fanatic and would never carry on the family business. Collecting some of his friends, he rode in a rage to fetch his son. Francis saw them coming and fled to a mountain cave. A month later he returned to Assisi, ragged, thin, and tearstained from desperate prayer and fasting. The peasants returning from their melon fields, the shopkeepers at their doorways, the young girls getting water at the well, and his former friends sitting at the tavern tables, looked at him in astonishment. Dogs barked at him, children threw rocks and mud. Mocking noises and guffaws brought Pietro Bernardone to his door. When he saw his ragged son walking calmly among the jeering crowds, he sprang upon him, dragged him into the house and shut the heavy door on the curious faces outside. He whipped and threatened Francis and locked him up in a dark room; but Francis was deaf to it all. It was as if other voices were talking to him.

As soon as Pietro left on a business trip, Francis' pious mother, convinced that God was talking to her son, unbolted the door to his room and let him go back to the little church. Pietro on his return upbraided his wife, then again rode to where his son was laboring. This time Francis faced him with quiet courage. Nothing would induce him to go back to his old life.

Pietro grabbed the coins that Francis had tossed long before on the windowsill, roaring that they belonged to him and that Francis was a thief; then he left to appeal to the Bishop of Assisi to make his son return. The bishop agreed to be the judge of this unusual case. He set a day for father and son to appear before him.

A mass of inquisitive people assembled in the bishop's courtyard as Francis and Pietro faced each other before the bishop's throne. Pietro argued bitterly that he had always given Francis the best of everything—clothes, money, banquets, horses—and that he had hoped in return to have a respected, successful son; but now his son had forgotten his duty to his father and was leading a miserable, crazy life. Surely, Pietro continued, he had a right to get some work out of his son and not have him disgrace the family name.

Francis stepped forward and took off, one by one, the clothes given him by his father. The merchant faced his naked son with stunned embarrassment. Utterly defeated, he picked up the clothes from the palace floor and left the court. The old bishop, startled but impressed by Francis' action, rose from his throne, gave him his own mantle, and embraced him. From that moment the bishop encouraged Francis in the hard life he had chosen.

Francis went back to the little church. When the priest tried to feed him, Francis refused even the poor bits the old man cooked for him, for he decided it was not right to be waited on by anyone. He made up his mind that to be truly one of the poor, he must beg for his food. To the town's amazement and his father's disgust he appeared with his begging bowl in the town square, dressed in a hermit's robe with leather belt and shoes. He begged for food for himself and stones for his church, and sang praises of God. At first the food that people tossed him filled him with loathing—old crusts, wrinkled olives, cabbage leaves, dregs of wine; then he conquered his feelings. He forced himself to go to the houses of his former friends; hearing the sounds of their gay banqueting, he would hesitate, but then make himself enter and beg. As his father went to Mass in his fine velvets and warm cape trimmed with fur, and saw his ragged son shivering with cold in the early autumn mornings, he cursed him. But though his own family and strangers mocked him, Francis en-

Francis renounces his father at the bishop's court. Fresco by
Giotto.

dured every insult—even mud and stones—and grew more steadfast.

For two years Francis lived this way. He finished rebuilding the little church, then found another almost as poor and deserted a few miles from Assisi, in the midst of a sparse wood. Called St. Mary of the Angels, it had only one window, and was the smallest of all the churches belonging to the Benedictine monks of the district. Francis repaired the church and built a little hut where he spent many days and nights in prayer. Legend says that the monks finally gave him the property for an annual rental of a basket of fish.

It was in 1209 as he was begging in the town square that he first became inspired to preach. In a clear and fiery voice, and in simple phrases—for Francis was not an educated person—he urged the by-standers to repent of their sins and to copy Christ's perfect life; then he preached peace—a welcome message to those whose lives were continuously upset by the wars of their lords. People said his words were like "a blazing fire piercing through the inmost heart." They thought that he was gazing on heaven as he spoke to them, and they were filled with wonder.

A rich and respected citizen of Assisi, Bernard of Quintavalle, was so moved by his preaching that he offered to join him. Francis was overjoyed to have a companion after his difficult lonely years. Bernard asked what he should do with his money now that he was going to live in poverty. Together they went into a church and asked the priest to open the Bible at random, resolving to do whatever the first words confronting them said. It fell open to Christ's words: "If you wish to be perfect, sell all you have, give to the poor, and follow me."

"This will be our Rule," Francis said, "for all who wish to join our company." Bernard gave all his property and money to the poor, and the two friends preached and prayed together. More men joined them; they begged from door to door, did common labor, helped the poor and urged all to remember the ten commandments and to re-pent of their sins. Soon there were twelve in all who had given their possessions away and exchanged their clothes—and even their shoes —for rough gray tunics and bare feet. Francis called them his "broth-ers" and taught them to build huts of branches and mud next to his own in the woods by St. Mary of the Angels. They slept on bare ground or on sacks filled with straw.

Francis felt so strongly about not having permanent possessions that when he overheard a brother mentioning "Brother Francis' cell," he vacated it at once and took another. He would not keep even a pot or pan for cooking, but ate his food raw, and if he was given cooked food he spoiled its taste with ashes or cold water.

When asked by the Bishop of Assisi why life had to be so unnecessarily poor, Francis answered that if they had possessions they would have to have arms to defend them; a true statement in the days when churches and monasteries needed thick walls to protect their treasures. Many of the churches of Francis' day had more lands and possessions than did great lords, and many bishops and abbots behaved more like overbearing landlords than religious men. They had lost touch with the oppressed, the sick, and the poor. People spoke fervently of the good old days when the Church was simpler and closer to the hearts of the people. Francis knew this and hoped that by his example of poverty he could reach people far more effectively than if he were well-fed and rich. Time and again, though trembling with cold and fever, he would hand over a warm cloak that had been given him to the first beggar he saw, saying, "This was but loaned to me until someone needed it more."

When Francis urged his companions to go out to preach, they protested that they had no education or experience and did not know what to say. Francis assured them that God would put words into their mouths. Some of their listeners would curse and ridicule them, but others would flock to hear them. So they departed happily to do

A Franciscan friar preaching out-of-doors.

as Francis said. When people asked who they were, they replied, "We are penitents of Assisi."

Francis had never read the writings of the Church-scholars of the past hundreds of years, but knew only the words of Christ—and these were the words he used to draw up a set of rules for his followers to live by. The brothers should not have houses, rooms, or even special places of their own within a hermitage, but should let others—even thieves—take their places. They were not to ride, but to go on foot. They should never touch money, even as reward for labor, "for," wrote Francis, "we ought to value money and coin no more than stones." They must never store up anything, but beg from day to day, and when traveling they must carry nothing—"neither bag, nor purse, nor bread, nor money, nor a staff." They should all work, not as overseers but as laborers in the most menial jobs. They should be gentle and submissive to all, answering softly. They should pray regularly, and preach, and never appear gloomy but be merry and courteous. No one should be called prior, or leader, but all should be called Minor Friars, or "Lesser Brothers."

Though in the fall of 1209 Francis had only eleven disciples, he decided that they should go to Rome and submit their Rule to the Pope. When the ragged little group arrived in the city, they fortunately met their own Bishop of Assisi, who arranged that they come before the great and learned Pope Innocent III.

Pope Innocent had long been worried about the growing worldliness of the Church. He was anxious to spread true Christian faith; his Fourth Crusade had ended in a scandal in Constantinople and people were becoming cynical about the Church. He and his cardinals knew that some sects in Italy and southern France were even suggesting that priests, bishops, and Pope be abolished entirely and that everyone should go back to the first, simple days of Christ and his followers. So when Pope Innocent met Francis and his companions and read their "Franciscan" Rule, he thought that Francis' order with its emphasis on poverty, good works, and preaching might be the answer to the Church's critics, particularly if sponsored by the Pope himself.

When the Pope approved the Rule and gave Francis and the friars his blessing, Francis prostrated himself gratefully before him, thanking God for turning the Pope's heart toward them. Then the little group, chattering excitedly with ambitious plans, took their way north again past rich farms with wheat stacked in the fields, grapes hanging heavily to the ground, figs and olives ripening on the trees. Orioles circled overhead, larks sang in the sky, big white oxen strained at wagons heavy with the harvest. Francis' heart filled with joy as it did long before when he was a boy roaming through the hills. He told his brothers that Nature was a book written for them by God, and that they should always praise and adore God's works.

When the Pope's approval became known, hundreds of men joined the Franciscan Order. They too built primitive huts near St. Mary of the Angels and grew a hedge around the area so that strangers should not disturb them at their prayers. From there Francis sent them out to villages and towns throughout Italy.

The old Bishop of Assisi invited Francis to preach on Sundays in the cathedral. Even that big building was too small to hold the crowds that came to hear him. Nobles, peasants, scholars and ignorant people, priests and Benedictine monks from the mountain monastery, poured in to listen to this man in patched tunic and bare feet as he preached with extravagant gestures, burning eyes, and vibrant voice. His words, they said, were "like the beams of a star shining in the gloom of night." Francis scolded people for their greed, and for forgetting God, and for caring more for their possessions than for their souls. It was true that Italy's new prosperity through her trade with the Crusaders had given many people money, and they were spending it extravagantly. Francis shamed them with his vivid descriptions of the pains of Hell and the rewards of Heaven for true repentance. People shuddered and vowed to mend their ways. A new wave of religious fervor spread to province after province.

People began to think of Francis as a saint. He was not much to look at: he was short, with spindly legs, and small worn feet; his face was long, his neck was thin, his beard was sparse. What made him loved was his manner. One of his companions described him this way:

". . . of gentle disposition, easy in his talk, sweet in temper, fervent in all things, swift to pardon, and slow to be angry. He was of ready wit and had an excellent memory; a man most

175

eloquent, of cheerful countenance, free from cowardice and arrogance; stern to himself, tender to others. He showed all meekness to all men . . ."

His reputation spread until he could not appear on any street without a multitude flocking to him. Villages tried to outdo each other in welcoming him; bells would ring, priests would run out, women and children would clap their hands; sick people, believing he must have miraculous powers, would touch him. People with paralysis or epilepsy or blindness offered him loaves to bless, then ate the loaves to be cured. Other sufferers would snip pieces off his tunic, dip them in water, and drink this water hoping to recover. Francis was embarrassed by his popularity. He would have preferred to go off by himself and pray in solitude instead of preaching to crowds, sometimes in as many as five villages a day. But he felt that it was the will of God that he should spread the word about a good Christian life. His feet gradually became swollen and gnarled, and he grew thinner than ever.

As he walked one morning with a few companions, a huge flock of birds appeared; some settled on the trees, some in the meadows, others circled low. Francis admired their bright feathers, the motions of their necks, their chirps and songs. He told his companions to stay by the roadway, and ran eagerly towards the birds. They preened themselves and stretched their necks and did not move even when his tunic brushed against them. Then he spoke to them, saying that they should be grateful to God for their wings which made them free to soar in the heavens. Finally Francis blessed them with the sign of the cross and gave them permission to fly away. From this day on he often preached to living things—flowers and vineyards and woods—and even to things that were not living—fire, fountains, and wind—asking all to praise the Lord. He rescued sheep and lambs being taken to market; he fed bees honey in the winter to keep them alive. A rabbit followed him about, a pheasant came to his call, a grasshopper left its figtree to sing on his finger. In the warm summer nights, he and a nightingale would exchange melodies. Francis did not want to harm even the simplest creature and would remove a worm from a path so that no one would step on it. He set a little garden plot aside for

St. Francis preaching to the birds. Fresco by Giotto.

sweet-smelling flowers and herbs; he loved their beauty and their perfume. All of nature proved to him the wonderful plan of God.

Although Francis had great influence with people, he was not a good administrator, so that when in 1216 an important cardinal asked if he might be the friars' counselor, the offer was welcome. Cardinal Ugolino had great ability and was a man of influence. Without his protection and wise guidance, the Franciscan Order might have faded away.

Ugolino introduced Francis to the new Pope, Honorius III, who proposed that some of Francis' friars should be made bishops. He thought it would be good for the Church to have bishops dedicated to poverty and service. But Francis, unawed by the Pope on his elaborate throne, was firm in his refusal. "We are dedicated to humility," he said. "Leave us as we are. We call ourselves Lesser Brothers, and lesser we shall remain."

That autumn there was a reunion at Assisi of the friars, who returned from their preaching all over Italy. Cardinal Ugolino, many bishops, and an enormous crowd of visitors attended. Francis proposed to send friars on missions to foreign lands and everyone agreed enthusiastically. Although Francis wanted to go abroad also, the Cardinal persuaded him to stay home for the time being. Friars went to Spain, France, Greece, Roumania, Hungary, and Germany—working in lepers' hospitals, tending the sick, preaching, and begging. Many had a hard time. Shepherds thought they were vagabonds and set dogs on them, storekeepers mistrusted them and ran them out of town. Even the clergy often were against them, thinking that because they were ragged and looked different, they were heretics. Those who got to Spain were welcomed by the Christian Spaniards in the north, but when they daringly tried to convert the Mohammedans in southern Spain, they were deported across the Strait to Morocco. When they tried to preach there the sultan had them rolled in broken glass and cut off their heads himself.

Francis was saddened at the bitter reports of the friars who had gone out so innocently and hopefully. Cardinal Ugolino urged him to ask the Pope and his other cardinals for help. Francis was dismayed to have to plead before such a splendid assembly. "I am nothing and I know nothing," he said. Even Cardinal Ugolino was in an agony of suspense as Francis stood silent, having forgotten the speech he had planned. Then suddenly words poured out. Unable to control himself in his enthusiasm, his hands and feet moved as if he were dancing. Ugolino prayed that the Pope and the other cardinals would not despise Francis, and was relieved to see that they had fallen under his spell. At the end of the audience, the Pope ordered letters of recommendation to be sent abroad to princes, bishops, abbots, and priests, ordering them to welcome and aid the Franciscan friars. With this powerful backing, they became tremendously successful.

At last the lower classes all over Europe had men from a religious order living, working, and preaching among them; this was an important change within the Catholic Church. Up to this time the local priests had merely conducted the Latin ritual which few understood; there had been little preaching. The sermons of the friars were down-to-earth and popular. They inspired the people to pray more and feel more gratitude to God.

At another meeting held in Assisi in 1219, Francis electrified the gathering by announcing that he wished to go to Egypt to convert the sultan to Christianity. The Fifth Crusade had started the previous year in another attempt to recapture Jerusalem; as a first step the Christian armies planned to capture Cairo, the important Mohammedan stronghold where al-Malik al-Kamil, the son of Saladin's great chieftain, was Sultan.

Francis hoped that he could save the Christian armies from the slaughter of battle by convincing al-Kamil to become a Christian. With only two friars as companions he set sail, first to Acre, scene of Richard the Lion Heart's victory twenty-six years before and still in Christian hands, then on to Egypt. Here among the hot, flat fields of the Nile delta where gray water buffalo and mudwalled villages could be seen, Francis found the trenches, tents, and siege-towers of the crusaders.

Knights and infantrymen from Spain to Scandinavia, Cyprus and Syria, looked curiously at Francis, small and insignificant in his worn gray robe. When he asked for permission to go to the sultan's camp some miles away across the hot sands, he was told that the sultan had offered a gold piece for the head of every Christian. Francis was undaunted; martyrdom would send him to heaven that much sooner. Permission was granted and Francis set off, carrying a flag of truce.

At first the sultan's sentries let him pass through, thinking he might be an official messenger from the Christians, but when they realized that he had the impudence to want to preach to their sultan, they brandished their scimitars, pushed him down on the sand and beat him. Seeing that Francis was not afraid of their torments or threats, and deciding that he was not dangerous, but only crazy, they finally dragged him to the sultan's tent. Here the luxurious, warlike al-Kamil received the simple, ragged man of peace and poverty. Francis told the sultan that he came to save him from Hell—to which he would surely go unless he became a Christian. He continued to preach with his usual eartnestness and fervor until the sultan's advisors suggested that the sultan put an end to all this nonsense and chop off Francis' head. But al-Kamil recognized Francis as a truly religious man, quite different from the hard and grasping crusaders, and listened patiently to his appeal. Though he was not swayed in the least by Francis' arguments, he was charmed by him. He offered him many gifts, and bags of silver for his poor, but Francis refused them. Then the sultan gave him an escort back to the Christian lines, where the armies were amazed at his safe return. He was surrounded by admirers eager to hear his story.

Francis spent some days there tending the sick among the tents, but soon became disgusted by the selfish bickering among the Christian soldiers; knight against knight, knight against foot soldiers, all nationalities against each other. When this badly disciplined group finally sacked Damietta on November 5, 1219, Francis was appalled at the wild scenes of drunkenness, looting, burning, and knifing in the bazaars of the city. He prophesized that only disaster could come to the Christian troops, and in this he was right, for a year after he had sailed back to Italy, the Fifth Crusade fell apart in the floods and heat and quarrels before Cairo.

Francis returned to Italy in the spring of 1220, landing in Venice. The terrible Egyptian climate and diet, the long voyage in a small boat pitching over the Mediterranean Sea, had wrecked his health. He was forced to break one of his rigidly held rules and ride a donkey on his journey through central Italy to Assisi. People surrounded him in every town along the way, happy to touch only the hem of his robe.

On his arrival in Assisi, he found that new rules had been made in his absence. A year of trial was now required to stop men joining and leaving the Order when they felt like it. Other rules were added as the Order grew. The thought of being the head of this increasingly complex organization became distasteful to Francis.

At the next big meeting he resigned dramatically as head of the Franciscan Order. "Henceforth I am dead to you," he said. He introduced a loyal brother as his successor and prostrated himself before him, promising obedience. The brothers were stunned. Their wails resounded down the valley but Francis was adamant. From then on, he tried to live as an ordinary preaching friar, but he was so famous that he could not do so. People never left him alone, and the brothers, who loved him devotedly, always wanted to be near him.

A year later Francis' successor, Brother Elias, proposed the establishment of Franciscan schools to train friars to go out into the world and preach. He had been impressed by the clever sermons of the learned friars who had once been scholars at the university of Bologna; they could explain things and answer questions skillfully. Francis, uneducated himself, had felt that God and the words of the Bible would be enough inspiration for his friars, and that the poor and the sick did not need scholars to comfort them. However, many Franciscan schools sprang up throughout Europe. They became famous, particularly in Paris and in Oxford.

This side of the Franciscan movement passed Francis by. He was content to live apart from the competition of the world, to preach against envy, wickedness, and greed, to be one of the poor and to follow God's voice. In the spring of 1224 he went to a distant mountainside where he spent fourteen days fasting and praying in solitude. In his mind he relived the life of Christ, and felt so vividly the agony of Christ on the cross that wounds appeared on his hands and feet as if he, too, had been crucified.

Francis wanted to hide these marks (called stigmata) even from his closest brothers. He covered his feet and hands and would not wash in public. But there was not much privacy in Francis' life, nor in anyone's in the Middle Ages. Everybody lived closely together, eat-

St. Francis receiving the stigmata. Painting by Bellini.

ing, sleeping, washing at wells or by streams. When his brothers took his tunic to shake the dust out of it, and when they scratched him (for saints like everyone else in those days had fleas) the scars were discovered. They believed them to be a sign from God. Word of the miracle spread swiftly. Now people were surer than ever that a saint walked among them.

Francis' years of hardship had been too much for his small frame, and at the age of forty-four his health steadily got worse. Though his devoted brothers urged him to guard what strength he had, he pushed them aside and with bright, feverish eyes shining in his pale face went out to preach. Then he began to go blind. When bloodletting, herbs, and ointments did no good, a famous doctor in Sienna suggested applying a hot iron above Francis' eyes. Though his companions were horrified, Francis agreed, and when the iron was brought he calmly said, "My brother Fire, be kind to me at this hour . . . Pray the great Lord to temper thy heat so that I may be able to bear it." As the brothers fled the room, the surgeon pressed the hissing iron from eyebrow to ear on each side of Francis' unflinching face. When the brothers stole back, Francis called them fainthearted and assured them he felt neither heat nor pain.

For a few months his eyes were better. But as he traveled up and down rugged hills and valleys he found that he had to be carried on a stretcher. One day as he lay exhausted and in pain on a mat, he asked a young brother to play the lute and sing to him, for Francis had never forgotten the songs of his youth and always thanked God for bringing music to the world. After a while Francis took the lute gently, and began to sing a song of praise to the Lord for the beautiful world around him. It was taken down by listening brothers and soon everyone was singing it, for it was not in the customary Latin of hymns, but in the everyday language of the people. It was called "Praises of the Creatures" or, sometimes, "The Canticle of the Sun," the first well-known poem in the Italian language.

> Praise be to Thee, my Lord, with all Thy creatures,
> Especially to the honored Brother Sun
> Who brings us the day, and through whom Thou givest light;
> He is beautiful and radiant with great splendor;
> He signifies Thee to us, Most High One.

Praise be to Thee, my Lord, for Sister Moon and for the stars,
Thou hast formed them in heaven, clear and precious and beautiful.

Praise be to Thee, my Lord, for Brother Wind
And for the air, cloudy and fair, and for every kind of weather.

Praise be to Thee, my Lord, for Sister Water
Who is useful, humble, precious and pure.

Praise be to Thee, my Lord, for Brother Fire
By whom Thou lightest up the night
And he is beautiful, strong and merry.

Praise be to Thee, my Lord, for our sister Mother Earth
Who sustains and keeps us
And brings forth various fruits with grass and bright flowers.

When Francis knew he was not going to live much longer, he added another verse in which he praised Brother Death.

His one desire was to die at Assisi, but to get back there was a problem. The towns through which the dying saint had to pass wanted to have him die within their walls, thinking that his saintly bones would bring them luck and fame. The friars decided to carry his stretcher over a difficult, longer route through the hills. When they drew near to Assisi they sent a message ahead saying that they were afraid of a last-minute assault by the Perugians to capture Francis. Assisan nobles and merchants seized their arms and galloped out to escort their saint to die in his own town.

At twilight on the third of October, 1226, as larks flocked and wheeled in circles in the air above his cell, Francis died. He was forty-four years old.

News of his death spread to the crowds who waited outside. People rushed to gaze upon his body. "He was a saint!" cried the rejoicing crowd. "We have his relics! Praise be to God for giving us so precious a gift." Afraid that his bones might be stolen, they put iron bars around his temporary tomb.

Two years later the Pope came to Assisi to pronounce him a saint, officially. Later a huge church was built for Francis' body on a magnificent site on the hill of Assisi. A Franciscan friar, the famous medieval painter Giotto, painted twenty-eight frescoes on its walls showing episodes in the saint's life. The great medieval poet Dante wrote a verse in his praise.

Although these tributes would have displeased the modest Francis, the people of the Middle Ages wanted to commemorate this saintly man in the best way they could, for Francis had brought them an example of a perfect life amidst all the oppression and warfare of the age.

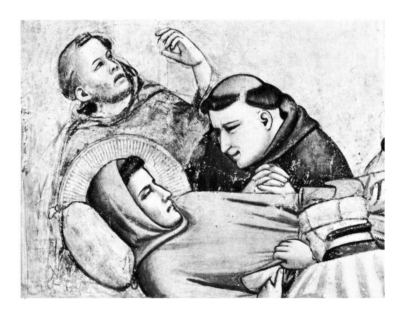

Death of St. Francis. Fresco by Giotto.

BEGINNINGS OF ENGLISH LIBERTIES

King John signs Magna Carta.

Early in the thirteenth century, when St. Francis gave up his worldly life to dedicate himself to pious work, Queen Eleanor's youngest son succeeded to the throne of England. King John was an unstable, cruel man and an unpopular king. His loss of the English possessions in France—Normandy, Anjou, and northern Aquitaine —was a blow to the English, especially to the barons who owned estates on both sides of the channel. In a quarrel with Pope Innocent III John was excommunicated and the whole country laid under interdict. For years people were deprived of church services and sacred burial rites—the whole country suffered from a public shame. Only when the French king and Pope allied against him, did John yield.

In a complete about face, he humbly submitted to the Pope, offering England as a fief and himself and his English subjects as vassals. This was almost as unpopular as the interdict. Though the English revered the Pope, they feared interference in their church. Above all, they feared the taxes they knew would fall on them to swell the riches of the papal court at Rome.

When John was decisively defeated by the French in 1214, his unpopularity reached its peak and his barons began to grumble. John's repeated requests for money and military aid, his oppression and cruelty, caused the barons to unite in an attempt to right their wrongs. Separately the English barons could do little—no one of them was strong enough to force the king to change his ways—but united they could be a powerful force. In 1215 they attempted something which William the Conqueror would never have thought could happen in the strong feudal monarchy which he had set up in England. In the meadow of Runnymede by the Thames River, the barons and high churchmen of the realm, surrounded by their armed retainers, forced King John to place his seal on a long parchment listing their complaints and the means to remedy them. This was the famous document known as Magna Carta, the Great Charter.

Magna Carta was a document in the interest of a feudal society to protect the rights of the king's vassals according to old customs and laws. It was a practical attempt to correct the wrongs of a tyrannical king. Magna Carta stated that the king must consult his barons before demanding financial help beyond the regular feudal dues, such as fees for the knighting of the king's eldest son, the marriage of his daughter, and his ransom in war. This check on the king would lead eventually to the idea of "no taxation without representation." Magna Carta also benefited classes other than the barons. It stated that the Church was free to elect its own leaders and that no freeman was to be imprisoned or put to death without due process of law and it said, "to no one will we sell, deny, or defer justice."

What annoyed John most about Magna Carta was that it showed that the king was subject not just to God but to the law of the land as well, that his power was not absolute, and that the barons had a right to curb him if he broke the law.

Unfortunately, neither barons nor king abided by the charter and civil war broke out. The importance of Magna Carta lay more in the future, when it would be referred to again and again as the basis of English liberty against despotism. For the rest of the thirteenth century a continual struggle was waged to reaffirm it.

In the midst of the civil war John suddenly died and his nine-year-old son, Henry, was hurriedly knighted and crowned while the barons loyal to the royal cause rallied to bring peace and order to the realm. Henry III had the golden hair and handsome features of the Plantagenets. His one defect was a slight droop of the right eye which gave him a shifty look. He was intelligent and observant, especially appreciative of art and beautiful buildings. He was affectionate but bad-tempered, and like his father, easily aroused to suspicion. He was extremely devout and immediately did homage to the Pope for his kingdom of England.

The barons and bishops who ruled during Henry's minority were honest and able and ruled better than Henry ever would; they immediately reaffirmed Magna Carta. Unfortunately, when Henry came of age and began to rule, he proved to be weak and unstatesmanlike. His intellectual and artistic interests made him prefer the French to the English and his and his wife's French relatives poured into England, seeking his friendship and favor. Henry's attempt to rule without the advice of his English barons caused friction and finally another civil war; for the barons, through Magna Carta, had established the right to be consulted.

While France expanded and increased in power during the thirteenth century, England gradually became less involved in continental affairs, turning her attention to her own government of church and state. A feeling of England for the English began to grow. Because of the very weakness of her king which gave the barons a chance to unite and to make themselves heard, England, in the thirteenth century, saw the beginnings of her great parliamentary system of government.

At the same time England's many different local customs and laws were gradually being unified into one system, common to all. England's common law was unique; it was not a written code like the

Roman law, imposed by the central government, but grew slowly from decisions made in courts by traveling justices.

In the beginning of this growth of English law and government a young man, Simon de Montfort, had an important part. Though a Frenchman by birth, he became a leader in the struggle for the rights and liberties of Englishmen during King Henry's long reign of fifty-six years. He was the one Frenchman whom Henry came to hate and fear—not because he was French, for Henry loved the French—but because he became such a zealous English patriot, more English than the English.

SIMON DE MONTFORT

Thirteenth-century knight in homage.

Thirty miles southwest of Paris, near the borders of Normandy, are the ruins of a once great hilltop castle, Montfort L'Amaury. The Montforts, who lived there, were an important noble family, having lands in France, Normandy, England, and the Holy Land. The name Montfort became especially famous in the early thirteenth century when Simon de Montfort, the fourth in line, led a cruel and ruthless crusade against the Albigenses, a group of heretics in southern France, who were causing trouble to the Church. He left behind a fear such as King Richard had left in the Holy Land. But his son, another Simon, was destined to play a very different role, not in his native land of France, but in England where he was long cherished by the people as a martyr for their rights. The spot where this Simon died is marked by a cross which bears the words *Protector Gentis Angliae* (Protector of the English people).

He was born in 1208, the youngest son in the family. He inherited his father's handsome features, his knightly bearing, and his uncompromising character. He received a better education than most nobles' sons and had the usual training for knighthood, being first a page and then a squire. As a page he ran errands in the castle, learned to pass food to his elders in the great hall, to carve roasts of ox or venison. In the field beyond the castle walls, he practiced tilting in preparation for tournaments and war. Bracing his lance, he would race his horse towards the quintain, an armed wooden dummy of a knight attached to a pivot and suspended from a pole. If he hit the dummy's shield squarely all was well but if he made a glancing blow,

Practicing at the quintain.

the dummy swung around and whacked him with its heavy wooden sword.

Simon was only ten years old and still practicing to be a squire when his father was killed in his crusade against the heretics in southern France; his mother and two of his brothers died soon after. Only he and his eldest brother, Amaury, were left and, as had become the custom, the entire family fortune fell to Amaury. Part of the Montfort inheritance was the great Earldom of Leicester in England, but since King John's loss of Normandy to France, it was no longer easy to hold lands on both sides of the channel. A noble now had to choose whether to give allegiance to the English or the French king. Amaury had little interest in his family estate in England. He offered it to Simon, adding that he was welcome to it if he could prove the family claim and manage to get it by himself.

In 1230, at the age of twenty-two, Simon set off for England to seek his fortune. He was ambitious and determined, intelligent and calculating; his dark eyes commanded respect and his magnetic personality won him friends easily. King Henry—just a year older—was immediately attracted to Simon but reluctantly admitted that the Earldom of Leicester had been given away during King John's reign. He promised to see if he could transfer it back to the Montforts. Hopeful of his future now, Simon entered King Henry's service and became his liege man.

Luckily for Simon, the Earl of Leicester agreed that Simon had the better right to the estate, and generously gave up his own claim. For a landless young knight, Simon had done well so far and he rose quickly in the king's favor. The great Earldom of Leicester consisted of several manors, or estates, scattered throughout the country, as well as the castle and old walled town of Leicester, moated by a river and surround by large forests, open fields, and pastures.

Under the feudal system Simon held his earldom from the king and owed him sixty knights' fees, that is, he was responsible for sending sixty knights and horses fully armed and equipped for war when the king needed them. Armor had become so complicated with the addition of metal breastplates and jointed leg plates that it was more expensive than ever to equip a knight. If Simon failed to send his

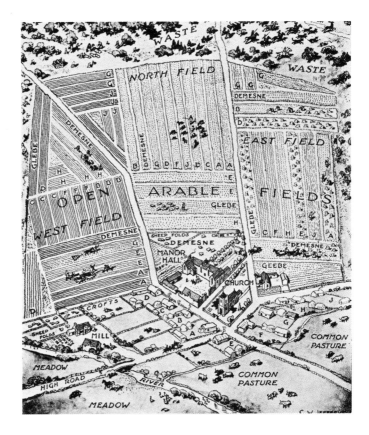

A manor house and lord's domain with fields, meadows, stream and mill.

sixty knights he must send the king a money payment instead.

In turn Simon's peasants and burgesses of the town of Leicester owed him produce from his lands and various other fees. In Leicester Simon had full authority in his manor court, held in the great hall of his castle, and was entitled to the "third penny," which meant that he received a third of all fines collected for offenses. This was profitable, for his peasants were always being brought to the manor court for poaching in his forest, stealing fish from his private fish pond, or letting cattle stray out of bounds.

But Simon knew that it was wise to have the cooperation of his tenants in order to get good service and he not only reaffirmed their old privileges but granted new ones, putting them in writing or charters. Charters were very popular in the thirteenth century, prized by nobles and common folk, for they spelled out clearly just what the privileges were. But they must be paid for in a lump sum or by annual fees. Instead of paying tolls every time they crossed the lord's bridge or ground corn at the lord's mill or pastured cows in his pasture, Simon's peasants could now pay a fixed fee for such privileges forever.

Despite these many fees, Simon often had a hard time making ends meet. Not only did he owe the king a great deal, he also had a huge household to maintain and he found that much of his land was in poor condition. And Simon was not the sole owner of the vast acreage of Leicester. Other distant lords owned parts of it; Robert Grosseteste (Great Head), the Bishop of Lincoln, owned the whole east field, known as St. Margaret's, with its church, farms, and pastures, and received all its produce and fees.

But the friendship that grew up between Simon and Grosseteste was far more valuable than any amount of land. Grosseteste had been chancellor of Oxford University and rector of the Franciscan friars who had recently come to England and settled in Oxford. Unlike their saintly founder, St. Francis, the English Franciscans soon became dedicated scholars, delving into science and mathematics; some were drawn into politics and championed not only the rights of the Church but also the liberties of the common folk. Grosseteste, an inspiration to these friars as he was to all who met him, introduced Simon to many of them who became his friends and supporters. Grosseteste's fine mind and high ideals were the best possible influence on Simon, who was often headstrong and impatient.

As an earl, Simon was one of the great magnates of the realm, occasionally summoned to the king's court to discuss problems of state. Simon's quick rise to prominence and his close friendship with the king was noted jealously by Henry's other foreign favorites. The English barons, fearing that Henry was becoming a mere plaything of his foreign friends, likewise looked askance at this upstart Frenchman who was being especially favored.

To fulfill his ambition, Simon had one more step to take—to marry, if possible, an heiress. King Henry had three sisters, one married to the Holy Roman Emperor, one to the King of Scotland and a young, dark-haired beauty, Eleanor, named for her famous grandmother, Eleanor of Aquitaine. Simon fell in love with Eleanor and she was immediately attracted to the tall knight with dark expressive eyes.

There was one obstacle to this ambitious marriage. Eleanor had been left a widow at the age of sixteen and taken a vow before the Archbishop of Canterbury that she would never marry again—in fact she had promised to become a nun. But Eleanor was not suited for such a role and, after a few years, had cast off her coarse homespun garments and joined the court of her brother, King Henry. Flirtatious, imperious, and extravagant, she captivated young Simon.

Conniving with Henry and disregarding Eleanor's vow to the Church, Simon married the royal princess in the king's private chapel one cold winter night just after the Christmas revels. The only people present in the newly decorated chapel, which was hung with bright tapestries, lighted by huge tapers, and warmed by a brazier of glowing charcoal, were the king, his chaplain, Simon, and Eleanor. The king himself placed Eleanor's hand in Simon's and his chaplain blessed them. Henry had not even consulted the other nobles about the marriage, as was the custom when a king's sister was considering such a step.

Within eight years Simon had risen from a landless young knight to become one of the ten earls of England and had achieved a royal marriage as well. But the English barons, already annoyed at Henry's disregard of their advice and his preference for foreigners, exploded in anger when they heard of the clandestine marriage.

The uproar was greater than Henry or Simon had expected. The barons threatened the bewildered king, who soon realized that he had made a mistake. He in turn became angry and blamed his friend Simon for getting involved in an affair that hurt him more than the earl.

The storm, however, subsided, and Simon, bearing a message from Henry, set off for Rome to have his marriage confirmed and blessed by the Pope. Simon raised what money he could, for the papal court, like all medieval courts, gave speedier, more favorable decisions if plenty of gold was offered. Soon he returned, secure with the papal blessing of his marriage, and joined his wife at the royal castle of Kenilworth in time for the birth of their son, the first of seven children. They named him Henry, for his uncle and godfather, the King.

Simon, in turn, was godfather for King Henry's first son, Prince Edward, and shortly afterwards he and Eleanor were invited to the queen's churching, a traditional purification ceremony following the birth of a child. But as Simon and Eleanor entered the great abbey church of Westminster they were stunned and horrified to be greeted by a torrent of angry words from the king, who ordered them out of his sight. Retreating to their temporary castle, loaned them by the king himself, they found the doors barred. Surprised and humiliated, they returned to beg the king's mercy. This time Henry, who had the terrible temper of his Plantagenet forebears, vilified Simon even more. He accused him of seducing his sister Eleanor, of forcing her to break her vow to the Church and of bribing the Pope to bless their unlawful marriage. And then—in what was probably the real cause of Henry's wrath—he accused Simon of not paying his debts. When the humiliation of being liable for Simon's debts, added to the unpopular marriage, became public, Henry lost his temper and burst out, "You have crowned your vileness by making me against my will, by means of false testimony, the surety of your debts." Smarting under these unexpected insults, the stunned and unhappy couple took a boat down the Thames and crossed the channel to France.

But Henry's childish tantrums never lasted long, and he soon invited Simon and Eleanor to return to England. The quarrel abated but Simon's pride had been stung and he knew he could no longer count on the king's friendship.

Simon, however, was now preparing to join Henry's brother Richard, named for his famous uncle, Richard the Lion Heart, on a crusade to the Holy Land where his own brother, Amaury, was held captive. In need of money, as usual, he sold off part of his great forest of Leicester.

Crusades were no longer glorious expeditions like Richard the Lion Heart's Third Crusade. Many knights preferred to pay their king a sum of money in place of giving service and only small bands of dedicated knights journeyed to the Holy Land. By the time Simon arrived, a truce had been made and his brother released, but Simon made such an impression on the barons of the Kingdom of Jerusalem that he was offered the governorship during the minority of its young king. In spite of his doubts about King Henry, Simon had acquired a loyalty to England and he turned down the glittering offer.

On his return, Simon was summoned to southern France to help Henry, who was conducting an unsuccessful campaign to regain some of the lands his father, King John, had lost to France. It was only through Simon's wisdom and military skill that Henry escaped with his life from the superior French forces. The campaign gained Henry nothing but contempt and heavy debts but it restored Simon to high favor.

Kenilworth Castle with its lake-moat.

He and Eleanor were now given the formidable castle of Kenilworth as a reward for his service. Kenilworth was not a hilltop castle but lay in the gentle rolling midland downs of England. A huge lake moat of one hundred acres, created by damming up streams, surrounded the massive outer walls and rectangular keep, making the castle practically impregnable. Beyond the lake stretched acres and acres of forests and fields. The entrance to the red sandstone keep,

196

with its fourteen-to-twenty-foot thick walls, was on the second floor, opening into the great hall. In two of the massive corner towers were little bedrooms, and at each level recessed in the wall of another tower were stone toilets, over a long chimney-like shaft leading to a ditch below. The fourth tower contained a winding staircase, rising from the ground floor to the great hall and to the battlements above. A deep well with pulley and bucket in one corner of the ground floor supplied water. Henry, far better suited to be an architect than a king, had recently embellished Kenilworth by adding fireplaces and a balcony to one of the tower bedrooms. Simon and Eleanor preferred Kenilworth to all their other castles.

A medieval bath.

Like all noblewomen, Eleanor reigned supreme in running the domestic life of her castle. One of her most important jobs was to see that there was enough food on hand for family, servants, and the many guests who came and went. Visiting nobles and churchmen, with vast numbers of retainers, often descended on Kenilworth with little or no notice, expecting to be well fed and entertained. Hospitality was one of the rules of the Middle Ages which was rarely broken. If Eleanor's supplies ran short she sent to one of her other

A medieval feast.

manors or bought food from a neighboring one. Spices from the East, so valuable that Eleanor kept them locked in a cupboard and handed them sparingly to the cook, were purchased at annual fairs. Wine from Gascony was bought from merchants and carted overland in barrels from the channel ports. Eleanor supervised the brewing of beer which was done right in the castle—it was so flat and insipid that pepper or licorice was added to spice it up.

Eleanor kept a daily record of her household expenses. One account during the fish-eating period of Lent showed that she had one thousand pounds of smoked herring in the castle storerooms, that she dispatched servants to a nearby fish pond to catch fresh fish and that one day a porpoise was delivered to the castle! On the back of her parchment record were lists of wages and gifts to the poor. One item showed three pennies paid to a servant for baths. Servants heated and carried water to a large wooden tub, then scrubbed the lord or lady within it. Nobles of the Middle Ages kept cleaner than nobles of the later Renaissance, who relied heavily on perfume.

Fresh meat was a summer luxury; pastures provided poor fodder in winter and every fall most of the cattle was slaughtered, salted, and put in castle storerooms for the cold months. Venison and boar and all kinds of fowl—even cranes and peacocks whose stringy meat seems inedible to us—were a year round luxury for the privileged who could hunt in the king's forests or their own well-stocked parks.

Simon and Eleanor sat at a table on a raised dais at one end of their long hall while lesser folk occupied side tables. The earl and countess were proud of their few silver serving dishes, goblets, and spoons and their large white tablecloth. A platter, heaped with meat or fish and spicy sauces, was placed between every two persons and served onto their trenchers, which were thick stale pieces of bread used as plates. There were no forks, and spoons were rare, so most people ate with knives and fingers. Dessert was usually dried fruits and nuts. At the end as well as at the beginning of the meal, pageboys appeared with ornate pitchers of scented water and basins for washing greasy fingers.

During these peaceful years at Kenilworth, Simon and Eleanor saw much of their friend, Bishop Grosseteste, and another scholar, the Franciscan Adam Marsh. Better educated than most noblemen of the time, Simon enjoyed discussing all sorts of subjects with these intellectuals. Much of their talk was about the state of the English church and government and stemmed from a growing disappointment with King Henry, especially with his subservience to the Pope and his reliance on foreign friends and relatives, who had recently poured into England. They talked of kingship and agreed that a king was not a king, but a tyrant, when he ruled badly. A king, they said, must rule according to the laws of the land and must uphold the

Aquamanile, a medieval water pitcher.

Great Charter of King John's day. They felt that the powers of an unjust king could be curbed only by insisting that he rule with the advice of his barons in regular council meetings. Simon was intensely interested in the ideas of Grosseteste and Marsh. They, in turn, saw in Simon a man of action, steadfast of purpose, who might be a champion of their ideals.

Simon's peaceful life at Kenilworth was cut short in 1248 when he was commissioned as the king's deputy to go to Gascony, the southern part of Aquitaine, all that was now left to England of Queen Eleanor's great Duchy. Gascony was in a state of turmoil, its nobles involved in family feuds, each trying to seize power. It was important for the English to restore order there, for Gascony supplied England with all its wines in return for English grain and wool.

Simon knew the difficulty of his commission and asked that he have full authority and seven years, if need be, in which to complete his job. He found the situation even worse than he expected and had to use a heavy hand to quell the quarreling Gascons. The Gascons resented Simon's interference and harsh methods, and complaints soon trickled back to King Henry that the earl was unduly severe and, like his father, unnecessarily cruel. The king listened all too readily to charges against his brother-in-law and sent messages rebuking him for his highhanded behavior. Simon replied that the Gascons looked on him with evil eyes because, he said, "I defend your rights and those of the common folk against them." The king was mollified and Simon again brought order to the province.

This only increased complaints against Simon and some of the Gascon leaders slipped off to England to protest to the king. They did their best to undermine Simon's reputation. Simon, believing that he had carried out the king's orders in the only way possible, was incensed. "What, do you lend your ears and your heart to traitors?" he asked the king. "You believe them more than myself who have always remained loyal to you!" The issue became tense and Henry decided to send commissioners of inquiry to Gascony to find out the truth of the complaints. Finally, Simon was summoned to face his accusers before the king and his council.

The king's meeting with his council of great nobles, either to discuss financial aids for war or to try important cases, had now come to be called "parliament" from the French word, *parler,* to talk. In the spring of 1252 Simon appeared at Westminster, in the monks' new refectory, to face his accusers. Though parliament was a high court of justice, Simon's trial was nothing like a dignified court proceeding; it was full of rowdy scenes and angry exchanges. King Henry was the most violent of all, continually interrupting with bursts of temper amid charge and countercharge. At first Simon answered the bitter accusations with restraint and wisdom but finally he, too, lost his temper and shouted back, "Your testimony against me is worthless because you are all liars and traitors."

In the end Simon proved his case and parliament decided in his favor, but within twenty-four hours Henry changed his mind and burst out again, accusing the earl of treachery. Simon, stung to the quick, advanced towards the king, saying, "That word is a lie! Were you not my sovereign an ill hour it would be for you in which you dared utter it." The exasperated king shouted back, "Never have I

A thirteenth-century parliament.

regretted anything so much as the day I allowed you to enter England." Henry finally told Simon to go back to France until he could get there himself, adding the bitter words, "Go back to Gascony, thou lover of strife and reap its rewards like thy father before thee."

Simon was in an impossible situation for none of the Gascon barons now felt any obligation to obey him and, in his absence, Henry's friends did their best to ruin the earl. When Henry appeared in Gascony, Simon retired to Paris. The French welcomed and honored Simon; they even asked him to take over their government while their king, Louis IX, was absent on crusade. But Simon refused this tempting offer as he had the one in the Holy Land. He was still loyal to the land of his adoption and, with some bitterness, to his fickle sovereign, Henry.

In Gascony Henry found out for himself how difficult the situation was. He could not cope with his truculent vassals. In fact they all took advantage of the weak king, who soon realized that he could do nothing without Simon's strong arm. Again he turned to the man he had insulted, and begged for his aid. Simon hesitated, but remembering Grosseteste's advice not to let bitterness determine his actions, dutifully returned to Gascony and once again restored order and saved the king's reputation.

Henry now involved himself and England in the most foolish of all his foolish plans. Not only was he a tool of his foreign friends but, more than any other English king, a tool of the Pope. When Pope Innocent IV, casting around for a rich, pliable ally to wrest the island of Sicily from the Holy Roman Empire, offered the Sicilian crown to Henry's younger son, Edmund, the king was flattered beyond measure, even though the Pope's offer was on condition that Henry supply a huge army of knights and a vast sum of money. The king readily accepted the offer.

Henry had agreed to all this without consulting his nobles in parliament, informing only a few intimate friends and as usual not bothering about the trouble that would follow. Resentment had been mounting daily against the king; the clergy resented being taxed for the Pope's distant wars and the lower classes resented being gouged by the king's sheriffs for his expensive and unsuccessful campaigns and his extravagant new buildings. But the reckless king turned a deaf ear to complaints and relied only on the advice of his foreign favorites instead of openly discussing the problems of the realm in parliament.

By 1257 Henry was in a pitiful state. Pressed by the Pope to pay what he had pledged for the war on Sicily, threatened with excommunication if he failed to do so, and urged by the barons to cut down expenses, the king called a parliament and laid bare his problems. In a pathetic attempt to get his barons' support for the conquest of Sicily, he paraded his little son Edmund in bright Sicilian costume and introduced him as King of Sicily. Instead of being moved to sympathy the barons were horrified. "The faces of all tingled with amazement," as they realized how far their king had committed himself to support the Pope's distant wars when the royal treasury was already empty. And then they heard that Henry's brother Richard, considered the richest man in Europe, had yielded to the flattering prospect of being made King of the Germans and that fifteen boatloads of his riches had gone with him to Germany to buy his election. Anger at the king at last burst out in the words of a monk, "Oh, England! What thy inhabitants produce, strangers plunder and carry away."

Even nature conspired against the king in the winter of 1257-1258, which was cold and severe, followed by floods that ruined crops. Shortage of food turned to famine. The Welsh, taking advantage of the evil times in England, ravaged the borderland and insurgent Scots threatened northern strongholds. When parliament met in the spring of 1258, the country was on the verge of revolution.

Simon, who had returned to England, was no longer thought of as a foreigner but as an honored English noble. He joined the barons in opposition to the king in the April parliament. They frankly told Henry that he had brought the country to the edge of disaster by his foolishness, that he had ignored the Great Charter in not consulting them before committing the kingdom to help the Pope. They refused to give him any financial aid. Simon and seven of the leading barons left parliament to draw up provisions of reform for the good of the realm. Swearing an oath of mutual assistance, they returned to parliament, fully armed. Though they left their swords at the door,

Henry was alarmed. "What is this, my lords? Am I your captive?" he asked. The barons assured the king that he need have no fear if he and Prince Edward would swear to abide by their reforms. The king and prince could do nothing but submit. Parliament was adjourned until June to give the committee time to work out their plan of reform.

On June 11 parliament reassembled at Oxford, which looked more like an armed camp than a university town when Henry arrived. Using the menace of the Welsh as an excuse, the barons had armed again. In reality they wanted to be prepared for any resistance from Henry's unreliable friends and relatives.

This parliament has sometimes been called the "Mad Parliament" but it was anything but mad. The barons were sincerely trying to right the wrong of poor government in the hands of a weak and ineffectual monarch. Known as the Provisions of Oxford, their list of proposed reforms went further than Magna Carta and provided a more effective check on a king who refused to rule according to the law of the land. The Provisions of Oxford stipulated that the king purge his council of foreigners and replace them with responsible Englishmen, that parliament meet regularly three times a year and that abuses of justice be corrected throughout the land. The hated royal sheriffs were to be replaced by loyal and good men chosen in their own shires. A permanent council was set up to advise the king. For a time it would be the ruling power of the country instead of Henry.

Henry's hated French friends and relatives arrogantly refused to agree to such reforms but, outnumbered, they were forced to choose between submission or exile. They chose the latter and soon dispersed to France. A sigh of relief went up at their departure.

The reformers now made the remaining barons, the reluctant king, and Prince Edward swear to uphold the Provisions of Oxford; anyone acting against them was declared a mortal enemy. The king suspected that Simon, the most able and reliable of his opponents, was responsible for uniting the English baronage against him.

One hot summer day following the Oxford parliament, Henry was cooling off in his royal barge on the Thames when a sudden thunder-storm arose, terrifying the king, who quickly put into shore and took refuge in the nearest castle, occupied to his mortification by Simon. The earl greeted his guest cordially, saying, "Fear not, the storm is spent." The king, looking helplessly at Simon and admitting his fear of thunderstorms, added, "But by God's head, I fear thee more than all the thunder and lightning in the world." Simon tried to calm him, "It is not myself, your constant friend, the faithful servant of king and country that you should fear, but your enemies," by which he meant Henry's grasping foreign relatives.

In October a royal proclamation was read aloud in every shire throughout the country announcing the king's oath to uphold the Provisions of Oxford, "for the honor of God and the good of the country." All freemen were also required to take the same oath. The barons then began the difficult task of putting reforms into action, immediately inquiring into complaints of injustice and corruption throughout the land. Responsible men were made sheriffs and the common folk took heart. It seemed that a countrywide reform had started which would reach far down and help even the small land-owners. The clergy, the Franciscans, the scholars at Oxford, and bur-gesses of the towns were fired with enthusiasm.

But the revolutionary enterprise was doomed to failure as selfish-ness and rivalry among the barons bred friction and intrigue. Many lost their enthusiasm when they found that the reforms which they had imposed on the king would curtail their own powers. For seven years, from 1258 to 1265, the struggle for reform—sometimes called the Barons' War—was waged between the king's men and the re-formers while unreliable barons shifted from side to side. Only Simon stood firm in his purpose to uphold the cause of reform.

Simon's strange, magnetic personality drew many to give him un-dying loyalty but his uncomprising nature caused some to hate him passionately. Born to lead, he also aroused jealousies and enmities. He had taken to heart the cause of reform which he had sworn to uphold and he could not tolerate any who went back on their word. When the powerful, conservative Earl of Gloucester, fearing things had gone too far, raised objections, Simon turned on him with scorn: "I care not to live with men so fickle and false as thee. We have all sworn to carry out the business in hand."

Simon's hasty words were a mistake. Earl Gloucester now deserted the reforming barons and became a supporter of the royal cause. King Henry, gaining confidence, secretly communicated with the Pope, asking to be released from his oath to uphold the reforms.

When the time came for the winter parliament of 1260, King Henry was in France. Should parliament meet in the king's absence? Such a thing had never happened before in England but the Provisions of Oxford stipulated that meetings should occur at regular times. It was agreed to postpone parliament for three weeks to await King Henry's return. At the end of three weeks there was still no sign of the king. Simon and Prince Edward, who had fallen under the earl's spell, decided to hold parliament anyway and prepared to march to London.

When this news reached Henry in France he trembled with fear and rage. He quickly sent orders to fortify London and set a date for parliament, summoning only the barons of his own choosing. Simon's name was conspicuously absent from the list. Henry arrived in London with Gloucester and three hundred knights and barred the gates against Simon and Prince Edward. War clouds were gathering.

Prince Edward soon thought better of his alliance with his uncle Simon, and became reconciled with his father. Other barons became lukewarm in the cause of reform and returned to Henry's side. The king was slowly regaining power and began to reappoint his own sheriffs and to recall his unpopular French relatives. Then, in 1261, just three years after his oath to uphold the Provisions of Oxford, the Pope's order, known as a "bull," releasing him from that oath, arrived in England. Gratified by the Pope's backing, Henry felt like a king again and said, "I have resumed royal power."

Simon's support was dwindling rapidly and the disappointed earl brooded as he watched the great ideas of reform slowly dissolve. Finally in despair at what seemed the total collapse of a great cause, he left England, saying that he, "preferred to die without a country than as a perjurer, to desert the truth." The unchangeable Simon had grown to scorn his changeable king, who, in turn, now looked on Simon as an enemy to the crown.

Soldiers looting.

England was unsettled, the people disturbed and restless, let down by the king's party who had dashed their hope of better government. The king's newly appointed sheriffs clashed with those chosen locally under the reform movement. Preachers denounced the royalists, political songs taunted the king and prince. The townspeople, the clergy, and friars rallied to Simon's cause; knights of the shire and lesser landowners clamored for his return. In 1263 he was called back to take the lead against King Henry. Whether Simon wanted it or not, he now became the leader of the people as well as of the few barons still opposing the king.

Unfortunately, the nobles who now supported Simon were mostly young, adventurous knights who had little understanding of government. Simon had lost his hold on the more conservative barons who felt safer in adhering to the king. The townspeople and clergy were little versed in warfare and would be of small use in a crisis. But, despite his shaky position, Simon would not give up his cause.

He met the young nobles secretly in Oxford where the reforming enterprise had begun five years before. They drafted a message to the king, demanding that he reinstate the Provisions of Oxford. When Henry refused, Simon and his followers took matters into their own hands. They attacked and captured many royal castles, securing the Severn valley between England and Wales. Marching east to the channel ports, they took over the great castle of Dover, thus cutting off foreign aid to Henry. The king, the queen, and Prince Edward were safe in the tower of London but London itself was in a turmoil of discord and rioting. Prince Edward, longing for action, escaped to Windsor Castle after recklessly stealing one thousand pounds of silver from London merchants. The London citizens were outraged but soon had their revenge. When the queen took a barge up the Thames to join her son, an excited mob, peering down from the walls as she approached London Bridge, shouted insults and hurled eggs and mud on the royal barge. The queen made a hasty retreat and managed to take refuge in St. Paul's Cathedral. Edward would not forget this insult to his mother.

The war clouds were darker than ever. While Simon and his men were encamped across the river from London, Henry plotted with four London merchants to trap the earl and keep him out of the city where he had such strong support. But a mob of citizens discovered the plot, broke down the gates, and admitted Simon. The mob wanted to kill the merchants but Simon kept them prisoners instead—they would prove useful later.

Simon and the king finally agreed to submit their quarrel to King Louis and both promised to abide by his decision. Henry, a brother-in-law of Louis as he was of Simon, expected a favorable answer. Simon, an admired friend of the French king, was equally hopeful. Henry left for France but Simon was unfortunately prevented by an accident when he fell from his horse and broke his leg. In France Henry was able to build up his cause with tales of the troublemaker Simon and the terrible insults to his queen. Though noted for his fairness, King Louis was after all a king and could hardly be expected to let down another one who was also his brother-in-law. Furthermore, Louis' piety inclined him to agree with the Pope, who backed Henry. In January, 1264, he gave his decision, entirely in favor of King Henry, granting that he should have full power to reign as he pleased with the advice of counselors of his own choosing. He pronounced the Provisions of Oxford null and void as contrary to the sacred rights of kingship. The only loophole he conceded to the reformers was that Henry must observe Magna Carta.

Now the work of five years was swept aside by one pronouncement, and the great peacemaker Louis had brought England, not peace, but war. Simon would not accept the decision. "Though all should forsake me," he said, "I will stand firm with my sons in the just cause to which my faith is pledged! Nor will I fear to risk the fortunes of war."

Henry returned to England, pleased with Louis' decision; but he had not reckoned on the widespread unrest that stirred the lesser folk in every village and town, especially citizens of London, and the clergy and scholars of Oxford who were ready to offer Simon whatever assistance they could. As an admiring chronicler wrote, "So Simon rose to defend the rights and liberties of England."

Finally the war clouds burst. Both sides wanted to secure the channel ports, Henry hoping for reinforcements from France, Simon hoping to prevent them. Above all Simon must keep the king's men from London, the center of the earl's strength. His scouts had been watching Henry's maneuvers in the south and, when the king and prince paused at the little town of Lewes, en route to London, Simon and his small army moved to intercept them. Still recovering from his broken leg, Simon rode in an armored cart. He encamped a few miles north of Lewes where the Weald (wooded hills) offered protection. Archers of the Weald, armed with strong longbows, eagerly joined his forces.

Simon made a last appeal to the king and sent two bishops with the message that, if Henry would abide by the basic principle of the reforms, he would consider certain changes. Henry, with superior forces, and his son Edward and brother Richard beside him, flatly refused.

Sure of victory, the king's men fell into a deep sleep the night of May 14. A few miles north at the edge of the Weald, Simon prepared for battle. Prayers were said and white crosses given out to all his knights. Just before dawn he marched his men to the hilltop facing the town of Lewes, to be ready when the sun rose. Simon made good use of his small army. Now able to mount a horse, he stayed in the rear with reserves to see where he would be most needed. Next to his battle standard he placed his armored cart in full view on the hill— locked inside were the London merchants who had tried to betray him to the king.

Dismounting, Simon addressed his men, "Beloved comrades and followers, we are about to do battle today on behalf of the government of the kingdom, to the honor of God . . . and for the maintenance of our faith." As daylight was breaking, early foragers of the king saw Simon's battle array and rushed to alert the royalists. The king commanded the center, accompanied by his great dragon standard; as it fluttered in the wind its sapphire eyes sparkled and its tongue appeared to shoot forth flames. Henry's brother Richard, King of the Germans, faced Simon's sons and Prince Edward faced the London mob. Edward had been eager for battle and now, filled with a savage energy and thirsting for the blood of the citizens who had insulted his mother, he charged into their midst. The Londoners, poorly armed and mostly on foot, broke ranks and fled. Some fell into the river and drowned while Edward pursued the others mercilessly for miles, thus foolishly removing his support from the king. Seeing this, Simon brought forth his reserves and fell upon the king and quickly captured him. In the meantime Henry's brother Richard did not cover himself with glory. Checked in his advance up the hill, he fled to a nearby windmill and barred himself in. Surrounded by Simon's men who shouted, "Come down, come down, you wretched miller," the proud King of the Germans was forced to surrender. He was a sorry sight, covered with flour and dust, as he emerged from the mill.

When Edward returned from his foolish pursuit, he found the battle almost over but seeing Simon's cart still standing on the hill, he and his knights rushed toward it, angrily shouting, "Come forth, you devil, Simon. Come out, vile traitor!" Not waiting for an answer, his knights broke it down and killed the merchants within—their own royal sympathizers. Edward was captured and joined his father as a prisoner.

The battle was short and almost bloodless; only six hundred were killed and those mostly the ill-armed London citizens. But it was a decisive victory and Simon was able to dictate his terms. Again Henry and Edward had to swear to uphold the reforms of Oxford and to expel the king's evil counselors. The king was used to making promises which he rarely kept but Edward was made of sterner stuff and chafed at this humiliation. Kept as a hostage for his father's good behavior, he secretly plotted and waited for a chance to escape and take his revenge on his uncle Simon.

As Simon marched toward London with his royal captives, townspeople and villagers reveled in the victory of their hero. Political songs in English, French, and Latin sang his praises, such as the Song of Lewes, written by a Franciscan friar:

> Now fair England breathes again, hoping for liberty
> And may the grace of God give her prosperity.
>
> . . . .
>
> He felt that he must fight for truth, or else must truth betray.
> To truth he gave his right hand brave, and trod the rugged way.

Though Simon had won the day, he was in a difficult position. He had to restore the unsettled country to order and defend it against invasion from France where the queen and Henry's relatives were gathering an army. With the help of the new young Earl of Gloucester, son of the earl who had deserted him, and the Bishop of Chichester, Simon set up a temporary government. Step by step, his steadfastness of purpose and the confidence he inspired in his followers had led him to this position. Though he acted in the king's name, Simon had become the real ruler of England.

Simon's aims were now even more liberal than in 1258 in his concern for the interests of the middle classes but he found it almost impossible to rule without the backing of the great landowning barons. For military safety he placed most of the royal castles in the hands of his sons. This was resented by young Gloucester, who began to show signs of jealousy, and by other lords, especially the independent Marcher earls who lived in huge fortified castles near the border of Wales. As Simon took on more and more exceptional powers, he came close to being a dictator. The few nobles who supported him began to fear his power.

The Pope, naturally angry that his vassal, Henry, was again in the clutches of the earl, whom he blamed for England's disturbances, dispatched a cardinal, ordering Henry's restoration to full power; but the cardinal was refused admittance to England. Then the cardinal, angry in turn, dispatched three bishops, armed with a papal bull excommunicating Simon and his party and placing London and other towns supporting him under interdict. When the bishops landed at Dover they were detained and searched. The papal bull was found, torn to bits, and thrown into the sea. The cardinal quickly retaliated and, in a solemn ceremony, excommunicated Simon by bell, book, and candle. The bells of the church rang out, the book of the Bible was closed, and the cardinal and bishops slowly lowered their lighted candles, extinguishing them on the ground. Thus was Simon barred from the Church and, in the eyes of the Church, his soul damned forever.

In January, 1265, Simon called a parliament in the king's name, hoping to make peace in the realm. This parliament known as the Great Parliament has been famous ever since, not for what it did, but for its composition. Needing wider support for his rule, Simon summoned not only the barons and clergy but also two knights from every shire and, for the first time in the history of England, two burgesses—"loyal and good men" from the most important towns. Though these middle-class men—merchants, mayors, and aldermen—were not expected to contribute any ideas and were only to listen and approve, this was a revolutionary step. Simon had started something which would eventually develop into the House of Commons. Though full representation of all classes was a long way off in 1265, Simon has been called the father of the House of Commons because this parliament was a first step towards English representative government, the basis of our American democracy.

Simon was now at the peak of his power and glory. No one, not even he, wanted to do away with England's monarchy but in trying to rule in the king's name, he was in a vulnerable position and his rigorous, radical actions bred jealousy and suspicion. Young Gloucester, like his father before, now deserted Simon and joined the hostile Marcher barons.

In March, Simon was with his wife at their castle of Odiham when

Riding into a medieval town.

news came that one of Henry's French relatives had landed near the Welsh border with 120 knights. Taking his royal captives, Henry and Edward, who accompanied him everywhere, Simon moved west to Hereford castle across the Severn River. Edward, who had given his oath to abide by Simon's government, was only loosely guarded. It was easy for him to get in touch with sympathizers and plot his escape. On the pretence of trying out horses beyond the castle walls, Edward, with the help of his guard, galloped swiftly north where his friends were waiting for him. Once in the safety of the formidable castle of Wigmore, he joined the deserter Gloucester.

With Gloucester's defection and Edward's escape and the Marcher lords united against him, Simon realized that a net was tightening around him. His enemies were just across the Severn River in their strongholds. Simon's wife was still at Odiham castle when she heard the news of Edward's escape. She knew that war had come again and, with her son Simon, moved quickly to help her husband. Traveling through the channel ports, she feasted the citizens of every town, making sure of their support.

Simon was now fifty-seven, worn and thin, longing for a peace he would not compromise to make. Far away and cut off from London and the towns which supported him, he made an alliance with Prince Llywellyn of Wales and sent a message to his son, Simon, to bring reinforcements. Unfortunately, young Simon, unaware of his father's dangerous plight, had leisurely marched to Kenilworth to gather men and supplies. Edward, alerted of young Simon's whereabouts, lost no time in pursuing him. Marching all night long he reached Kenilworth at dawn, surprised and captured many of young Simon's knights and their banners. Young Simon managed to escape in a boat across the lake to safety in the castle keep but Edward had prevented the two Simons from meeting. The earl would get no reinforcements.

Ignorant of this disaster, Earl Simon forded the Severn, heading east in search of his son. His little army and the king were weary and hungry; they paused to rest at the Abbey of Evesham, nestled in a loop of the Avon River. To the north rose a steep hill, to the east one bridge led over the river towards London. Otherwise the river hemmed them in.

Edward had learned exactly where Simon was. Blocking the bridge and placing Gloucester at his right, he led the center, marching behind his knights who carried aloft the captured banners of young Simon de Montfort.

Simon and the king were finishing breakfast when the advancing army was sighted. For a moment Simon was fooled by the banners and thought his son was coming to his rescue. But a barber, watching from the abbey bell tower, detected Edward's own banners with the royal lions in the distance.

"By the arm of St. James, they come on skillfully. It is not from themselves but from us that they have learned that order," exclaimed Simon. He knew that there would be no way out of Evesham and he said to his men, as he quickly armed, "Let us commend our souls to God, because our bodies are theirs." He urged his son Henry to flee but all stood by the earl except some Welsh archers who ran away as the royal army charged forward shouting, "Death to the traitor."

As the enemies neared each other, a huge black cloud blotted out the sun, lightning flashed and heavy drops of rain descended. In the first charge King Henry was wounded and cried out pitifully, "I am Henry of Winchester, your king, do not harm me." A long arm, some said it was Edward's, stretched forth, grabbed the bridle of Henry's horse and led him to safety. The fighting was short and fierce. Simon saw his oldest son killed and cried out, "It is time for me to die." But in a last fury of a well-trained knight he tried to cut his way through Edward's line. His horse fell and he fought on foot, slashing with his two-edged sword until a blow from behind stunned him and he sank to the ground. The bloodthirsty royalists cut off his head and hacked his body to pieces. Of Simon's 160 knights only twelve were left. "Such was the murder of Evesham, for battle it was none," wrote a monk. To add to the horror of this massacre, the Marcher lords impaled Simon's head on a pike and bore it aloft for all to see. Simon the younger, who was at last marching to his father's aid, was greeted by the gruesome sight.

The monks of Evesham tenderly took the mutilated corpse and buried it, but the king's men, feeling that the excommunicated traitor did not deserve a proper burial, unearthed and threw the body in a ditch. They could not, however, still the legend of Simon whom the people now thought of as a saint and martyr. Miracles were soon reported on the spot where he had died. Songs and hymns were composed in his honor.

> Simon of the mountain strong,
> Flower of knightly chivalry,
> Thou who death and deadly wrong,
> Barest, making England free.
>
> .   .   .   .
>
> Feet and head dissevered,
> Pierced corpse and wounded head,
> Flesh and harness stript and torn.
> So with God our champion be
> As our whole defence in thee
> Dying, leaves the world forlorn.

Simon's steadfast devotion to the cause of reform earned him the admiration of the English people. His followers showed their loyalty and held out against the harsh reprisals of the king's party. Ordered to give up their lands and wealth, they became known as the "disinherited" and resisted as best they could, living in the seclusion of forest and glen. Those in Kenilworth surrendered only when starvation forced them to. Finally the king and Edward, with the aid of a true peacemaker, Cardinal Ottobuoni, realized that a more lenient policy was needed to restore order. Simon's death had not been in vain and in 1267 some of the reforms of Oxford were revived and Magna Carta, henceforth a symbol of English liberty, was reaffirmed. In the same year the Pope exonerated Simon and lifted the ban of excommunication.

Though Simon was headstrong and intolerant of those who disagreed with him, and though he was no saint, he was a man of honor, unshakeable in his belief and admired by the best minds of his century as well as by the common folk. Neither friend nor enemy could deny that his compelling personality raised him above the ordinary man. Like Thomas à Becket who died for the rights of the Church, Simon died for the rights of good government. He went too fast and too soon with his ideals, but they were to bear fruit later. That he had a part in the beginnings of the great English parliamentary system of government has ensured him lasting fame.

PART IV

THE LAST OF
THE MIDDLE AGES

Venice in Marco Polo's day.

The ideas of Simon de Montfort remained in the mind of the man who had slain him. When Edward I became King in 1272 he was wise enough to realize that not only the barons, high churchmen, and king should have a voice in government. By the end of his reign, summoning the "commons" to Parliament became an established practice which would have astonished the ironclad lords of earlier medieval centuries.

Other changes took place at the end of the thirteenth century. In the Holy Land the crusader domains had gradually been lost until the last Christian city, Acre, conquered so valiantly a century before by Richard the Lion Heart, fell to the Moslems in 1291. The Byzantine Empire shrank until only Constantinople and small areas in Greece remained. A huge new Tartar Empire extended from China to Hungary; Franciscan missionaries sent to Tartary brought back descriptions of an interesting Chinese invention: gunpowder. In England in the last part of the century a scholarly Franciscan friar, Roger Bacon, began experimenting with gunpowder, and by the next century, crude cannon began to shoot stone balls against castle walls. In 1271 Marco Polo, an adventurous Venetian youth, traveled in a caravan of mules and camels across the heart of Asia to the court of Kublai Khan, where he stayed for seventeen years, bringing home fantastic tales of the wealth of the Far East.

In the fourteenth century Venetian and Genoese trading posts and counting houses spread around the Black Sea and the east coast of the Mediterranean at the crossroads of great trade routes. The Italian merchants, bringing jewels, spices, camphor, ivory, drugs, and tissue-like cloth back to Europe, became a new and rising class of capitalists and bankers.

The Church was changing, too. Weakened by years of political bickering and now under pressure by France, the Papacy left Rome, its home of centuries, and moved to Avignon on the French border. There the Popes lived in palatial luxury, so much so that one of them in 1323 declared that anyone who preached St. Francis' hundred-year-old doctrine of poverty was a heretic! Traveling friars now collected money instead of rejecting it. Monks no longer worked but enjoyed the wealth from the labor of their serfs on rich monastic lands. Peasants throughout Europe and England began to mutter against the Church.

In 1347 the Black Death broke over Europe even more violently than it had in the sixth century. It raged for three years, subsided, then erupted five more times by the end of the fourteenth century. At

Coffins for victims of the Black Death.

its end, the population of the medieval world had shrunk by more than a third—and in some places by a half. Labor became scarce, and landowners sought laws to prevent surviving peasants from leaving their lands in search of high wages. But the laws were ineffective and the old system of the serf bound forever to the land of his lord was on the way out.

A final blow to the Middle Ages in Europe was the Hundred Years War between England and France. Starting in 1337 this feudal war involved the old problem of vassal and king. King Edward III of England, great-great-great-grandson of Eleanor of Aquitaine, did not wish to pay homage to the King of France for the duchy of Aquitaine. The French king had no intention of excusing this homage and losing his valuable fief.

This war was to impoverish both countries but it had its moments of glory for the English at the beginning and the French (under Joan of Arc) at the end. In 1346 at the battle of Crécy, King Edward III's green-clad yeomen, standing behind stakes with their longbows shooting steel-tipped arrows five times a minute, mowed down the mounted knights of France. In this battle a few of the new cannon were used, although they made more noise than damage.

As the Hundred Years War gathered momentum and as the Black Death thinned out rich and poor alike, an English poet, Geoffrey Chaucer, was born. He would describe vividly these last years of the Middle Ages.

GEOFFREY CHAUCER

Geoffrey Chaucer.

Geoffrey Chaucer, the great English poet of the Middle Ages, was born in London sometime between 1343 and 1345. His father, John Chaucer, was a vintner, or wine-merchant. Merchants had climbed much higher in society since the days of St. Francis' father who sold cloth in a small shop. Now only the most important businessmen—such as vintners, goldsmiths, grocers, fishmongers, and drapers—called themselves merchants, and vintners were particularly important because so many men, women, and children of the Middle Ages drank wine. John Chaucer made big profits on the barrels of wine he imported and then resold.

The Chaucers lived in the prosperous importers' district of London called Vintry Ward, close to the river Thames where foreign ships unloaded their cargoes. Here twice a year the wine fleet from King Edward III's duchy of Gascony in southwestern France arrived, heavily convoyed against pirates and the northern French enemies, and tied up at the London wharves. Young Geoffrey would go down to the docks with his father and watch as the wine barrels were pulled up from the holds by creaking winches and swung over the sides by rope cranes. John Chaucer's barrels would then be carried or rolled up the cobbled banks by porters to the big Vintry storehouse near Geoffrey's home.

A medieval picture of the Holy Family which shows a middle-class family, including the baby in his stroller.

Because the family was well-to-do, their house was far more substantial than most of the houses in London, some of which might even be only six by ten feet with two rooms, one above the other. A master vintner like John Chaucer built his house of stone and timber, with a big hall used as a parlor and dining room, a kitchen, a larder, servants' and apprentices' rooms, a counting-room or office, and a big bedroom in which the entire family slept. There were stables in the rear, a garden and fruit trees, poultry pens, and a well or a cistern to catch rainwater.

London of the fourteenth century was an exciting place to grow up in. It was by far the biggest city in England, with forty thousand people crowded into a rectangular walled area of about one and a half square miles bounded on one side by the river. Scattered within this small area were more than a hundred parish churches, and also many chapels, abbeys, guildhalls, elegant houses of the gentry—and dark slums where (as Chaucer later wrote) "the smiler with the knife under his cloak" lurked. Five hundred feet above the streets towered St. Paul's steeple with its huge golden ball topped by a fifteen-foot cross. London Bridge, with a hundred shops crowded on its narrow width, spanned the river to the south; swans swam under its arches, and fishermen caught salmon and washerwomen slapped their sheets clean on the river banks nearby. A steady stream of small rowboats (the taxis of the city) darted back and forth, while barges glided from the palace of the king upriver at Westminster to the great lords' mansions that lined the river between the king's palace and the city walls.

A butcher shop.

London was a city of contrasts. Butchers slaughtered in the streets; beggars, lepers, and pigs shared the oozing gutters. There were pillories in which wrongdoers were locked for counterfeiting or selling mouldy flour; there were executions after which the criminal's head would be carried on a pike through the crowds. There were jugglers and acrobats, and simple Biblical plays performed by guild actors on flat carts in the middle of the street. There were ceremonial processions with the mayor and his aldermen in scarlet robes, preceded by guards carrying the mayor's mace and sword. Most glorious of all the sights was the great King Edward III with his sons and his lords, riding through the streets on splendid horses.

All of these sights were loved dearly by the child Geoffrey. The noises and activities of the city were deep in his blood and for the rest of his life he never was happy to be away from London for long.

When it was time for Geoffrey to learn the alphabet and to read and write, he was probably sent to a "song-school" for very young children, for later he described a little boy sitting in such a school with his primer in his hand, chanting Latin, although he did not understand a word and feared to be beaten three times in an hour.

Later Geoffrey went to a grammar school run by one of the churches in the city. Education at these church schools was based on the same subjects taught in Pope Gregory the Great's time eight hundred years before; indeed, Pope Gregory would have recognized most of the Latin readings and mathematics. Geoffrey had an excellent memory and enjoyed reading Latin stories; he loved the sounds and rhythms of words.

At home Geoffrey heard his parents speak two languages—English and French. Although three hundred years had passed since Duke William had brought French knights to rule England, the English court and the nobility still spoke French. Anyone who had dealings with the court had to speak that language, and Chaucer's father—who supplied the court and the armies with some of their wine—had to speak it fluently.

When Geoffrey was twelve years old or so, his father secured a job for him as page in the household of the king's young daughter-in-law Elizabeth, wife of the king's second son Lionel. In this way he guaranteed an important step up in the world for his son, out of the merchant class into the world of gentlemen.

Geoffrey's first job as page was mostly that of errand boy for Countess Elizabeth and her ladies-in-waiting. He fetched their embroideries,

Chess players.

chessmen, puppies, or refreshments to their gardens or chambers. He accompanied them on walks and as they rode to the hunt. When Countess Elizabeth moved her entire household from one of her manors to another, Geoffrey was taken along. Since even in the richest castles or manors there were few rooms and little privacy, he knew everything that was going on. He heard well-born people speak cultivated French; he observed their manners, latest fashions and amusements—and he stored all of these things in his memory for future use.

Geoffrey was given food and clothes, and probably slept on straw with other pages on the big hall's stone floor. At Easter in 1357 he was given the latest spring outfit—tight breeches in red and black, a short tight coat called a paltok, and new shoes. The clothes of King Edward's court were particularly lavish: fabulous sums were spent on furs, gold-threaded embroideries, and silks; coats were either long and

A falconer.

flowing, or short with notched sleeves often slit to show shirts of another color beneath.

There was a special reason for Chaucer's Easter outfit. That spring, to the astonishment of Europe, the king's eldest son Edward the Black Prince had captured the King of France at the battle of Poitiers. All Londoners dressed up in their finest clothes, and lined the streets to welcome the returning hero and his important captive. For several years after his capture the French king lived at the English court waiting for his countrymen to pay an enormous ransom of four million gold pieces. During the truce talks and the haggling over the ransom payments, the French and English kings and many highborn French hostages took part in tournaments, feasts, hunts, and dances. Geoffrey the page had even more pomp and ritual to observe than ever before.

He was soon moved to a higher rank—squire of the king's household. No longer did all squires have to become knights; a well-educated squire like Chaucer would be more useful to the king in other ways as he grew older.

Geoffrey now lived in the king's palace and no longer slept on the floor, but shared a bed with another squire. Every day he was given meat, dark bread, and a gallon of beer; once a year he was given a robe, and shoes twice a year. King Edward III kept extravagant numbers of people about him to give an appearance of show and splendor: not only high churchmen, knights, and lawyers but a vast staff of grooms, watchmen, laundrywomen, cooks, scullions, falconers, and other servants of every description. There were many times when Chaucer and the other young people at court did not have much to do. Geoffrey used this leisurely life to great advantage. When his few duties had been done, he escaped to some corner to read. Most squires would have gone off to whack each other in the tilting yard, but Geoffrey was not going to make a career of fighting. He preferred reading to any other amusement; he must often have wakened the squire who shared his bed by his habit of reading by candlelight all through the night.

> So when I saw I might not sleep
> .   .   .   .   .   .   this other night,
> Upon my bed I sat upright
> And asked someone to hand a book—
> A romance—which I took
> To read and drive the night away;
> For I thought it better play
> Than either chess or backgammon . . .

The more he read, the more he tried to "make books, songs, and ditties in rhyme." The people at court were glad to have a squire around with a gift for clever verse. Because few of them could read or write, they liked to have stories read out loud, or better still, sung to them. Poetry was popular, for its lively rhythms held people's attention and could be accompanied by a strumming instrument such as a lute or gittern (guitar).

On cold winter days by smoking fires, with hawks sitting on their perches and hounds lying on the floor, or on summer days within

227

walled gardens, Chaucer would read his latest ballads and rhymed stories to a delighted audience. Later, Chaucer described a young squire, perhaps himself at the court of Edward III:

> Singing he was, or fluting all the day.
> He was as fresh as is the month of May.
> Short was his gown, with sleeves long and wide,
> Well could he sit on horse, and fairly ride;
> He could songs make, and well indite,
> Joust and dance, and draw and write.

The songs he wrote at first were in French, the language of culture. But French poetry had been declining since the days of Queen Eleanor of Aquitaine. The days of the famous minstrels and troubadours were over; poetry had lost its freshness and become stiff and lifeless. So Chaucer decided to give up writing French verse and to write in English—a language used mainly by the lower classes since William the Conqueror's time, but now beginning to be heard even in high places. King Edward III had finally had to allow the English parliament to conduct some of its business in English. Why then could not English be also used for poetry of the highest type? Chaucer stuck to his experiment, although he wrote in one poem,

> . . . there is such great diversity
> In English and in writing of our tongue,
> That whether you be read or sung
> I pray to God that you'll be understood!

Chaucer's English, a mixture of Anglo-Saxon and Norman-French, was very different from the English we speak today. It was far more guttural. Its *r's* were trilled, and some letters were pronounced that we no longer pronounce—like the *g* in *gnaw* and the *k* in *know*. People spelled it any old way, sometimes writing one word two or three ways even on the same page.

In spite of the difference in words and spelling, many of Chaucer's lines can be understood by the ordinary reader. For example, this is the way he describes a nun:

> She was so charitable and so pitous
> She wolde wepe if that she sawe a mous
> Caught in a trappe, if it were deed or bledde.

And an archer:

> And he was clad in cote and hood of grene.
> A sheef of pecok arwes bright and kene
> Under his belt he bar ful thriftily . . .
> And in his hand he bar a mighty bowe.

But most of Chaucer's English can be read only by scholars or readers with a special dictionary.*

In 1359 war with the French broke out again after a disagreement over the French king's ransom. King Edward III, always delighted at the prospect of battle, left his royal French prisoner in London and crossed the Channel with his sons. Geoffrey went along in the king's army.

It took King Edward eight days to unload all his baggage in France. He brought tents and pavilions, mills to grind grain, forges to make shoes for his hundreds of horses, falcons and thirty falconers to take care of them, and two hundred hunting dogs and greyhounds. He even brought over small boats sewn of boiled leather from which his soldiers could catch fish in French lakes during Lent.

In spite of these elaborate preparations, Edward's army did not succeed in conquering a French town of any consequence. Stores of food dwindled, and the English had a hard time finding food in a countryside already wrecked by war. Chaucer, riding out in a foraging party, was captured by the French and held for ransom. His importance as a king's squire is shown by the size of the ransom which the English paid for him: sixteen pounds, or over two thousand dollars in modern money.

After Geoffrey returned to the English armies, he was used as a trusted courier to go back and forth to London with papers involving

---

* When Chaucer is quoted in the rest of this chapter, modern English is used.

229

a new treaty with the French—the first of many times that he was sent on diplomatic missions for England.

In the early 1360's the young squire married Philippa de Roet, the daughter of a Flemish knight attached to the court of King Edward III. Chaucer must have been especially well thought of to make such a match, for Philippa outranked him; her own sister even became the wife of the king's son John of Gaunt.

For ten years or so the young couple continued to live at court, surrounded by luxury. The king gave Geoffrey in addition to the regular squire's salary—a yearly pension of twenty marks (about $2000 today) for life, and Philippa received a pension, too. John of Gaunt added a yearly sum and occasionally gave them magnificent presents such as three silver goblets and six silver buttons (a new popular invention).

In 1374 the King appointed Chaucer to an important position. His new title was "Comptroller of Customs and Subsidy of Wools, Skins & Hides in the Port of London." This meant that Geoffrey and Philippa had to leave the palace in Westminster and move into the city itself, a few miles downriver. Such a post added to his prestige. Wool was the main source of England's wealth. It financed Edward's wars and extravagances, for every sack of wool and sheepskins that left the port of London for export abroad was taxed.

Chaucer's office was in the Customs House close by the wharves where the wool ships tied up before they left England. Their sacks were searched, weighed, and then repacked for shipment. Chaucer was supposed to keep all the records of these transactions, in his own handwriting so that the king's officials would know he was on the job. He had to use a counting board and counters (like checker pieces), for the English still used Roman numerals which were impossible to add in columns. In one year his records show that 1,220 wool merchants weighed their wool and paid taxes amounting to over 23,000 pounds (or about three million dollars today)—a huge sum for a small medieval country.

The king granted Chaucer and his wife a rent-free house built on top of one of the old gates into the city, called Aldgate, and originally intended for garrisons of soldiers who guarded the city walls. The Chaucers lived right above huge double doors and portcullises. They had a cellar beneath the walls, and a stairway down to a garden with a little arbor and benches of fresh turf in the summertime. Their rooms, in contrast to most of the dark houses of London, were airy and light. Geoffrey and Philippa could look west and see all of London with its church towers and crooked roofs; to the east, outside the wall, they could see meadows and a long road stretching away through hedges and groves of trees. At night wagons and workers began to straggle back into the city before curfew. The warden of the gates began to call any loiterers outside the gates to hurry and drive in all their animals or else spend the night in the fields. After the last carts rumbled through, the gates clanged shut until daybreak when the gatekeeper opened them again.

Chaucer would rise at dawn and walk the half mile to the Customs House on Wool Wharf on the river next to the huge Tower of London. In the late afternoon he hurried home, anxious to get back to his books and his writing. The noises of the city, his neighbors bickering, the apprentices brawling in the taverns, his own children playing, did not break through his concentration. In a long poem, *The House of Fame,* which he wrote soon after moving to Aldgate, he described an imaginary eagle who accuses him of getting headaches from so much studying and writing at night, and who adds:

. . . . and of your very neighbors
That dwell almost at your door
You hear neither that—nor this—
For when your labor done all is
And you have made your reckonings,
Instead of rest and different things
You go back to your house anon
And then, as silent as a stone,
You sit at yet another book
Till fully dazéd is your look;
And thus you live as a hermit!

This picture of a hermit's life was an exaggeration, but Chaucer always enjoyed poking fun at himself in his poetry. He and his wife were still great favorites at the court and had friends among the important and influential men of London.

Chaucer must have spent a large proportion of his income collecting books. One fat manuscript, even with ordinary wooden slabs for covers, was costly; one decorated with delicate miniatures and borders, with its covers studded with jewels and clasped with gold, was a treasure only the very rich might afford. University libraries often had no more than fifty books on their shelves. It was rare for a person of Chaucer's class to buy a book at all.

When Chaucer wanted his own writings made into books, he had to hire a scribe and pay him for slow, laborious copying. One of his scribes, called Adam, made him so angry that he wrote a special verse to him:

> Often I must do your work over again
> And correct it, and rub and erase,
> Because of all your negligence and haste!

The years from 1374 to 1386 when Chaucer was Comptroller of the Wool Customs were the happiest of his life. He and his wife were prosperous. In addition to his salary, they both still had the generous pensions, gifts of robes, and a daily pitcher of wine from the king, and other presents from the king's son John of Gaunt. One can picture both of them at the day's end, dressed in robes from the king, drinking the king's gift of wine from one of John of Gaunt's silver goblets as the sun set over the roofs of the city,

> Both of one mind, as married people use,
> Quietly, quietly the evening through.

During these years Chaucer was often sent abroad by the king. The king's governmental departments had increased greatly from the days when a few loyal nobles, churchmen, and sheriffs were all that were necessary to help the king run his kingdom. Now the beginnings of

modern bureaucracy could be seen as lawyers, treasurers, accountants, and envoys were kept busy in Westminster. Many educated men
were needed. England had no foreign embassies and yet there were
constant dealings—from royal marriages to trade agreements—with
foreign countries. Chaucer, good at languages and a trusted official
of the king, was sent on diplomatic missions of all sorts.

Two of these diplomatic trips took him to Italy. Traveling from
the wintry north into the early Italian spring, he thought he was
looking at a new world. Italy's warmth, its bright sky and hills, its
rich and colorful cities, were a contrast to England and the other
northern European countries he had visited—but there was more to
it than that. A change was sweeping over this warm southern land.
Here, the Middle Ages were coming to an end and a new way of life
(to be known as the Renaissance) was taking the place of old feudal
ways and ideas. Italy's prosperous Mediterranean trade with the Near
East had brought wealth to her merchants, who, becoming more
powerful than feudal lords, ruled the towns; the towns in turn expanded into huge city-states with colonies around the Mediterranean
from Africa to the Black Sea. With wealth came a gayer and freer
life; philosophers, craftsmen, writers, and artists bloomed in a crea-
tive society.

Chaucer visited three Italian towns, Genoa, Milan, and Florence.
Genoa, with colonies everywhere, was at its height. The wharves in
its great curving harbor were piled high with cargoes of silks, carpets,
spices, and jewels from the East. Milan, a beautiful city bounded by
rose-colored brick walls, was crisscrossed by bustling canals; its ruling
merchant, Bernabo Visconti, was so rich that he had persuaded a
prince of England and a princess of France to marry two of his children. The paintings on the walls of his palace were by Giotto, the
Franciscan artist who used subtle colors and made people far more
alive than the flat, stiff medieval figures which Geoffrey was used to
seeing on the walls of northern halls and churches.

But it was the writers of the city-state of Florence that made the
greatest impression on the English poet. They were rediscovering the
manuscripts of ancient pagan writers that had been neglected since

the Dark Ages. These manuscripts had opened the Italian writers' eyes. Three great fourteenth-century poets of Florence—Dante, Petrarch, and Boccaccio—had broken new ground and had written startling and fresh comedies, romances, and tragedies unlike anything being written in England.

Chaucer collected manuscripts of these poets and brought them back to England. In his London gatehouse once more, after his work at the wool docks was done, he pored over the Italian writings. His own style of writing became different.

Genoa.

Life at court was changing. King Edward III died in 1377 at the end of a glorious reign of fifty years. His heir, the Black Prince, had wasted away of an incurable disease, leaving ten-year-old Richard, Edward's grandson, to inherit the throne. The people, tired of an old man, welcomed the boy-king Richard II, blond and handsome like all the Plantagenets but slimmer and less strongly built.

His reign started off well. Chaucer's life did not change for many years under the new king. Richard II let him stay on at the Customs House and granted him the same house, pension, and daily pitcher of wine.

Gradually the realm became disturbed as the king, like Henry III, became wildly extravagant and listened to the advice of unpopular favorites. Behind the scenes his powerful uncles connived for power. The kingdom was almost bankrupt, the English were losing most of their conquests in France, and peasants were muttering at harsh laws and taxes.

Chaucer let the disturbances of the realm swirl about him. Unlike Simon de Montfort, who had died a hundred years previously for an ideal, Chaucer left politics to others. He wrote a ballad in which he advised, "Flee from the crowd; don't fight to cure impossible things, or you will break yourself like a jug thrown against a wall." He kept at his work in the Customs House and wrote more poems at night.

So when the terrible Peasants' Revolt occurred in 1381, in which thousands of angry armed peasants stormed London demanding freedom from old feudal laws and money for their labor, Chaucer merely buried his nose deeper in his books, although the revolt raged below his very windows when the peasants forced Aldgate to be opened and then burned, sacked, and killed in the city at will.

The revolt died in three days. With great courage the young King Richard II rode into the center of the peasant mob and promised them all sorts of freedoms—which he had no intention of giving. The gullible peasants straggled back to their fields and families and found too late that their revolt had been in vain. The aristocrats killed the leaders and now made doubly sure that it would be hopeless to revolt again. When a group of peasants asked about their promised liberties, they were met with the king's terrible answer, "Serfs you have been, serfs you are, and serfs you shall remain."

Chaucer wrote little about serfs, for most of his life was spent among the upper classes. But he wrote a few sympathetic descriptions of those whose lot it was (so the preachers said and the lords insisted) to till the soil. He described a poor peasant widow:

> Few were the possessions she had in store.
> Three large sows had she—and no more—
> Three cows, and a sheep named Moll.
> Full sooty was her sleeping place and hall
> In which she ate many a slender meal . . .
> No dainty morsels passed through her throat,
> Her diet was as simple as her coat.
> No wine drank she, neither white nor red;
> Her table was served with milk and brown bread,
> Singed bacon, and sometimes an egg or two.
>
> A yard she had, enclosed all about
> With sticks, and a dry ditch without.

And he wrote a poem about a plowman:

> A true laborer and a good was he,
> Living in peace and perfect charity.
> God loved he best with his whole heart.

By 1385 Chaucer had completed a masterpiece, *Troilus and Criseyde,* "in which," Chaucer read to his audience at King Richard's court,

> . . . you may the double sorrows hear
> Of Troilus, in loving of Criseyde,
> And how that she forsook him ere she died.

Its setting was an ancient one, the Trojan War—but in Chaucer's descriptions of the houses, streets, walls, and crowds of ancient Troy one can recognize medieval London. Its plot was based on a story he had brought back from Italy, but greatly changed; he made its characters so complex, and he showed such understanding of human emotions and failings (most unusual in the writings of the Middle Ages) that critics have called it the first psychological novel. Many consider it Chaucer's greatest work.

The poem had more than eight thousand lines, or several hundred manuscript pages, and what with all the pauses and the slowness with which people read out loud in those days, it must have taken him many an hour at the court to get through it. A picture of Chaucer reading to the court, painted by someone who remembered him, shows him reading from a tapestried pulpit within a green bower; carefully pruned trees and a many-towered castle are behind him and his audience consists of elaborately dressed people, one of whom is certainly a prince or a king—perhaps Richard II himself.

In 1386 Chaucer and his family left the house over Aldgate to become residents of Greenwich, a suburb about four miles from London. He was promptly made a justice of the peace for the county of Kent. With other justices he had to go several times a year to the villages and coastal towns of Kent where he would listen carefully as one neighbor accused another of brawling, murdering, stealing, planting on another man's land, or fishing from another man's pond. These trials gave the observant poet a whole new set of people to use as models for stories: millers, shipmen, bailiffs, franklins, cloth-weavers, country priests, and plowmen—some honest, others rascally.

In the fall of 1386 Chaucer was also appointed Knight of the Shire and sent to the House of Commons in parliament. Since Simon de Montfort's day, the Commons had developed into a regular body of men of importance in their communities—burgesses from the towns and "knights" from the countryside. Chaucer, well-known and with influential friends, fitted well into this category. The House of Lords in this parliament seized most of the king's power, while the House of Commons merely muttered against the king's extravagance and careless rule. Chaucer was a fascinated observer of a dramatic session in which King Richard II sat glowering on his throne in Westminster Palace at the end of a long narrow hall painted with heroic scenes of the past. The great barons of the kingdom sat on his left, the high-ranking churchmen sat on his right, and Geoffrey Chaucer and the rest of the Commons faced the king at the back of the room. Chaucer watched the king's face with its thin lips, sharp nose, and narrow puffy eyes under haughty, thin eyebrows, as his triumphant royal uncle the Earl of Gloucester, head of an opposition group of powerful lords, dismissed the king's friends from office one by one.

At the end of the session Chaucer went back to Greenwich with pay for sixty-one days in his purse. He was fortunate to be out of London and safe in the countryside during dangerous months; but many of his London friends were not so lucky. Just after the king's twenty-first birthday in 1387, the big barons, with troops to back up their power, confined the king in the Tower of London, then met in a "Merciless Parliament" and sent the king's closest friends to bloody death or exile. Many were also old, close friends of Chaucer.

In his country retirement Chaucer wrote a bitter poem:

> The world has made a change
> From right to wrong, from truth to fickleness.
> Once the world was so steadfast and stable
> That a man's word was an obligation.
> Now it all is false and deceivable.
> Pity is exiled; no man has mercy.

Overlooked by the king's enemies who were trying to round up other friends of the king, he now started to write his most famous, best-loved work, *The Canterbury Tales,* an enormous project which had been in the back of his mind for many years. Its plot, refreshingly original in the days when most stories were romances of highborn ladies and lords, concerns the journey of twenty-nine imaginary pilgrims to England's most popular shrine, the tomb of the martyred St. Thomas à Becket in Canterbury. The poet Chaucer joins them at the Tabard Inn, just south of London, on an April day in 1387.

The Prologue to *The Canterbury Tales* starts with the famous line "Whan that Aprille with his shoures sote" (When April with its sweet showers). The characters on this April pilgrimage range in rank from peasant to nobleman. A religious pilgrimage was one of the few occasions in the Middle Ages when all classes of people got together, so Chaucer could include on the same trip a plowman, bailiff, yeoman, members of craft guilds, a merchant, scholarly clerk, monk, nun, and a knight with his squire son—the medieval social scale from peasant to lord.

Richard II.

Chaucer first described a Knight who had just come back from the wars; in fact, his tunic still showed stains from his armor.

> . . . . he loved chivalry,
> Truth and honor, freedom and courtesy.
> He never yet had said a rude word
> In all his life to any sort of person.
> He was a true and perfect, courteous knight.

The aristocratic Prioress came next, as befitted her rank. Chaucer drew a fond picture of her, although he admitted that she cared too much how her headdress was arranged so as to show off her beautiful forehead and eyes as gray as glass. He was not so kind to four of the other churchmen, and his satire became stronger with each one. The Monk, riding to Canterbury on the finest palfrey, and with his sleeves lined in fur, was a far cry from the early days of monastic life. Chaucer's monk thought St. Benedict's rule "not worth an oyster," and instead of working in the fields he went hunting, and fed many beautiful horses and greyhounds when he should have fed the poor.

Chaucer's description of the Friar shows how far, by the end of the Middle Ages, the Franciscans and other orders had departed from the ideals of St. Francis. Hubert the Friar saw no point in knowing lepers or people without money; he only bothered with people who would give him something. He was such a skillful talker, with an affected lisp and a good singing voice, that

> Though a poor widow did not own a shoe
> Yet he would have a farthing ere he left.

The Friar did not follow St. Francis' command that brothers should wear mean garments patched with rags and sacks, but was dressed like a pope, with a soft woolen cape rounded like a bell.

Then there were the Summoner with a bad complexion and garlic breath, and the Pardoner with glaring rabbits' eyes. One summoned gullible people to church courts for imaginary offenses, unless they bribed him; the other sold pardons for sins, and false relics:

> In his bag he had a pillow case
> Which he claimed was Our Lady's veil;
> He said he had a portion of the sail
> That St. Peter had, when he went
> Upon the sea . . . and in a glass he had pigs' bones.
> But with these relics, when he found
> A poor person dwelling in the land
> In one day he got more money
> Than that person earned in two months!

Chaucer did include a churchman who led a completely blameless life—a poor country priest who gave away all he had and trudged in the rain to take care of his people.

> To draw folk to heaven by fairness
> And good example, was his business.

One of the favorite characters in all literature is Chaucer's Wife of Bath, the bold, red-faced jolly woman who had had five husbands and hoped to find a sixth on this pilgrimage. There is also the thread-

240

bare Oxford student who spent all his money on "twenty books bound in black and red," and "gladly would he learn, and gladly teach."

After describing the rest of the pilgrims, Chaucer started them off on the way to Canterbury, joined by the Innkeeper. He originally planned to have each pilgrim tell two tales going and two more returning, to amuse the other riders on the trip. As this would have been 120 stories, and as Chaucer was getting on in years, he never finished his master plan; in fact, he never quite got his pilgrims to Canterbury. But he wrote twenty-four famous tales, ranging from comedy and satire to tragedy and moral sermons.

Before Chaucer had written half of these tales, he was given a new position as Clerk of the King's Works, in charge of the upkeep of all the royal buildings from falcon cages to palaces. In addition King Richard renewed his pension and sent him a yearly barrel of wine. Another powerful lord, the king's cousin Henry—who was later to become King Henry IV—rewarded him for a special job with a very expensive scarlet robe trimmed with fur.

Chaucer welcomed the salary, the travel money, the rent-free house and the gifts. But there was little time left in which to work on *The Canterbury Tales.* He had to supervise many people: the purveyors who chose the bricks and stone, the master masons (architects), sergeant plumbers (leadworkers), and accountants. He was responsible for all sorts of equipment belonging to the king, from a hundred stone cannonballs stored in the Tower of London to the stands for the king's tournaments.

In 1390 he had to assemble the stands for a magnificent tournament held by King Richard II in Smithfield, outside the walls of London. The scaffolding, tents, pavilions, and fences that Chaucer set up enclosed an area of smooth green grass about the size of a modern football field. All the king's officials (including Chaucer) were dressed in the King's livery, with embroidery of a white deer and golden chains.

Tournaments were no longer as vicious as in the days of Richard the Lion Heart, but though lances were blunted, and armor was especially made for jousting, they were rough enough. There were many broken bones as horses approached each other at a full gallop while each rider aimed for the other's helmet with his lance.

Probably some parts of the tale the Knight told in *The Canterbury Tales* are about this very tournament at Smithfield in 1390:

> The herald in the stands made a "Ho!"
> Till all the people's noise was done.
> Then were the gates shut, and the cry was loud:
> "Do your duty, young knights proud!"
> Now rang the trumpets loud, and clarion.
>
> The spears sit firmly in their holsters,
> The sharp spur goes in the horse's side,
> These are the men who know how to joust and ride!
> There shiver shafts upon shields thick,
> One knight's breast-bone feels the spear's prick.
> Up spring spears twenty foot long
> Out go the swords as bright as silver.
> The helmets are hewed to shreds and pieces
> Out bursts the blood with gruesome red streams . . .

Chaucer may even have been describing King Richard II riding when he wrote:

> Upon a bay steed in steel armor
> Covered in patterned cloth of gold.
> His armor was decorated with great pearls,
> His saddle of newly wrought gold,
> A mantle on his shoulder hanging
> Brimful of rubies red as fire sparkling.
>
> His hair was yellow, and glittered as the sun
> His nose was high, his eyes lemon-colored
> And as a lion he looked about him . . .
> Of five and twenty years of age, I guess.

Chaucer loved to write about knights, fair ladies, tournaments, and battles. Many of his long poems and stories, less well known to us today but very popular in his time, were about these things. He did not recognize, any more than the knights did, that the days of chivalry were ending.

Late medieval tournament.

The tournament took a week, with awards and dancing and feasting at the end. When everybody went home, Chaucer had to see that everything was dismantled and brought back to the Tower for storage.

He continued to ride from one of the king's buildings to another —a lot of travel for a middle-aged, not very athletic poet who was growing heavy and preferred writing to all this routine—which could also involve him in danger. One day as he rode on the king's business through the woods near Foul Oak in Kent, robbers fell on him. On the same day he was again robbed of a large payroll, his horse, and gear. This was the last straw and he quit his job.

Another job was immediately found for him, and he became Master Forester of an estate in Somerset. It did not matter whether he knew anything about forests, for he had two yeomen under him who did the actual patrolling of the vast forest and its game. Probably the king insisted that his finest poet should have an easy job, house, and salary so that he would be able to finish *The Canterbury Tales*. The first part of the *Tales* had been circulating and was making a great hit. With money to live on and some leisure time, Chaucer might finish this great work.

So the aging poet was well taken care of. But he was not fond of country life; he had been in the midst of the hurly-burly of Westminster or London for forty-five years and disliked being away from the center of things. He complained that he was "dull as dead, forgot in solitary wilderness." He remembered reading his poetry to crowds in the midst of high life at court, but now he wrote that he was fat and gray-haired, with his poetry rusting away like an unused sword in a sheath.

As usual, he exaggerated. He was far from forgotten. His works had a big circulation; in fact, so many copies of his manuscripts survive today that there must have been hundreds more that were worn out or lost. The English court waited eagerly for his latest *Tale*. He was even famous abroad, where an important French poet wrote a ballad in his honor, comparing him to great writers of ancient times. One young English poet so admired his "dear master" that he had a small portrait of him painted on the margin of a manuscript so that other men would know what Chaucer looked like—a short, round figure with gray hair cut short, a moustache and small forked beard, a rather large curved nose, and heavily lidded eyes; dressed in a dark robe and conservative hat.

The year 1397 was a violent one—the last of King Richard II's reign. The rage that had been simmering underneath the king's outward calm finally boiled over against the lords who had once dared to cut his power and murder his friends; he killed some of these lords, banished others, and confiscated their property. Then he began to live more magnificently than ever, sending officials to tax and fine and seize more property. Finally powerful barons took arms against him, Parliament deposed him, and he died mysteriously in prison. His cousin Henry Bolingbroke succeeded him as Henry IV.

Chaucer might have been reduced to beggary by the downfall of his patron King Richard II. He depended on a job or a pension to keep him alive; his poetry brought him popularity but no money—and he was getting old. So he sent a short poem to the new king, complaining that his purse was light:

To you, my purse, and to no other person
I complain . . .
I am so sorry now that you are light;
Be heavy again, or else I must die!

King Henry IV was glad to aid the famous poet in his last days. He even doubled King Richard's pension and continued to send the yearly barrel of wine.

Chaucer had no more worries. He left the countryside, hastened back to his beloved London, and leased a small house in a garden near the Abbey of Westminster. He was again in the midst of the noise and activity which he loved. The monks of the Abbey were there to take care of him when his health began to fail.

Perhaps the tolling of the Abbey bells made him worry about his soul, but more probably like everyone in the Middle Ages he feared Hell and hoped for Heaven now that he approached death. In any case, he wrote a typically medieval ending to his wonderful *Canterbury Tales,* apologizing to God for writing such sinful stories, pointing out that he had also translated saints' legends and moral tales, and praying that at the Day of Judgment his soul might be saved. He died within a year, on October 25, 1400, and was buried in the huge Abbey, where his tomb may be seen in the Poets' Corner today.

Fortunately no one agreed with the old poet that his works were harmful. Gradually he was recognized as a genius, one of the great poets of all time. Though he spent much of his life at the most medieval and elegant of courts, he wrote of the commonest people as well as the most chivalrous, the wicked as well as the good. He wrote about real individuals, not shadowy storybook knights, ladies, and saints. He understood why people behave as they do and was tolerant of their weaknesses; although he poked fun at them, he loved them.

During his lifetime, Europe's old patterns were breaking up. Feudalism was dying as the strong bonds between vassal and lord were weakening. The knight on horseback was losing ground to the infantryman with his longbow, and castle walls were tumbling before the artilleryman with his cannon. Merchants were becoming as powerful as princes; monasteries were losing their importance as bulwarks of medieval life. In the next century sailors would discover new continents, and the invention of printing would bring reading within everyone's grasp; the great Renaissance, when people looked outward instead of inward, was on its way.

But Chaucer was not influenced by the winds of change, and perhaps did not even notice them. He was a medieval man, with medieval thoughts; the world was a pageant to him, and he recorded it in brilliant detail. He makes the glory of the Middle Ages come alive to us.

An attack with cannons in late medieval times.

BIBLIOGRAPHY

(Books especially recommended for younger readers are starred)

ADAM, HENRY H. *Mont-St. Michel and Chartres.* Garden City, N.Y.: Doubleday Anchor, 1950.

ARCHER, T. A. *Crusade of Richard I* (fragments of chronicles). New York: G. P. Putnam's, 1889.

ASHDOWN, C. *Arms and Weapons in the Middle Ages.* London: Harrap Co., 1925.

BARK, W. C. *The Origins of the Medieval World.* Garden City, N.Y.: Doubleday Anchor, 1960.

BARLOW, FRANK. *William I and the Norman Conquest.* London: English Universities Press, 1965.

BATESON, MARY. *Records of the Borough of Leicester.* Cambridge University Press, 1899.

BEDE. *Ecclesiastical History of the English Nation.* Translated by J. E. King. Cambridge: Harvard University Press, 1954.

BÉMONT, CHARLES. *Simon de Montfort, Earl of Leicester.* Translated by E. F. Jacob. Oxford: Clarendon Press, 1930.

BENNETT, H. S. *Life on the English Manor. A Study of Peasant Conditions.* New York: Cambridge University Press, 1962.

BLOCH, MARC. *Feudal Society.* Chicago: University of Chicago Press, 1961.

BOWDEN, MURIEL. *A Commentary on the General Prologue to the Canterbury Tales.* New York: Macmillan, 1964.

BROOKE, CHRISTOPHER. *Europe in the Central Middle Ages 962-1154.* London: Longmans, 1964.

*———. *Saxon and Norman Kings.* New York: Macmillan, 1963.

*BRYANT, ARTHUR. *Story of England.* London: Collins, 1961.

*———. *Age of Chivalry.* New York: Doubleday, 1964.

*BUEHR, W. *Warriors' Weapons.* New York: Thomas Y. Crowell, 1963.

BUSCH, H., AND LOHSE, S. *Romanesque Europe.* New York: Macmillan, 1960.

CANTOR, N. E. *Medieval History: The Life and Death of a Civilization.* New York: Macmillan, 1963.

CHAMBERS, FRANK. *Some Legends Concerning Eleanor of Aquitaine.* Cambridge: Medieval Academy of America. *Speculum XIV,* 1941.

CHAUCER, GEOFFREY. *Complete Works,* ed. F. M. Robinson. Boston: Houghton Mifflin, 1933.

———. *Selections,* ed. W. A. Neilson & H. R. Patch. New York: Harcourt Brace, 1921.

———. *Major Poetry,* ed. A. C. Baugh. New York: Appleton-Century-Crofts, 1963.

*———. *Canterbury Tales,* ed. A. K. and Constance Hieatt. New York: Bantam Dual Language Book, 1964.

*CHUTE, MARCHETTE. *Geoffrey Chaucer of England.* New York: Dutton, 1946.

*COSTAIN, THOMAS. *The Conquerors.* New York: Doubleday, 1949.

*———. *The Last Plantagenets.* New York: Doubleday, 1958.

*———. *The Magnificent Century.* New York: Doubleday, 1961.

*———. *The Three Edwards.* New York: Doubleday, 1958.

COULTON, G. G. *Medieval Panorama, Society and Institutions.* London: Fontana Library, 1961.

———. *Medieval Panorama, The Horizons of Thought.* London: Fontana Library, 1961.

———. *Chaucer and His England.* London: University Paperbacks, 1963.

CREIGHTON, M. *Simon de Montfort.* London: Rivingtons, 1876.

CROSBY, S. M. *The Abbey Church of St. Denis.* New Haven: Yale University Press, 1942.

———. *L'Abbaye Royale de St. Denis.* Paris: Paul Hartman, 1953.

DAVIS, H. W. C. *Charlemagne. The Hero of Two Nations.* New York: G. P. Putnam's, 1900.

DAVIS, R. H. C. *A History of Medieval Europe from Constantine to St. Louis.* New York: David McKay, 1962.

DAWSON, C. *The Making of Europe.* New York: Meridian Books, 1960.

DENHOLM-YOUNG, N. *Studies in Medieval History.* Oxford: Clarendon Press, 1948.

DEVIZES, RICHARD OF, AND VINSAUF, GEOFFREY OF. *Chronicle of the Crusades.* London: H. C. Bohn, 1848.

DOUGLAS, D. C. *William the Conqueror.* Berkeley: University of California Press, 1964.

DOWNS, NORTON. *Basic Documents in Medieval History.* Princeton: D. Van Nostrand, 1959.

DUCKETT, E. S. *Carolingian Portraits.* Ann Arbor: University of Michigan, 1962.

———. *Gateway to the Middle Ages* (3 vols.). Ann Arbor: University of Michigan, 1938.

DUDDEN, F. H. *Gregory the Great: His Place in History and Thought.* London: Longmans Green, 1905.

*DUGGAN, A. *Growing Up in Thirteenth Century England.* New York: Pantheon, 1962.

*———. *The Story of the Crusades.* New York: Pantheon, 1964.

DURANT, WILL. *Age of Faith.* New York: Simon and Schuster, 1950.

EASTON, S. C., AND WIERUSZOWSKI, H. *The Era of Charlemagne.* Princeton: Anvil Books, 1961.

EGINHARD AND MONK OF ST. GALL. *Early Lives of Charlemagne.* Translated by A. J. Grant. London: Chatto and Windus, 1926.

*EINHARD. *The Life of Charlemagne.* Translated by S. E. Turner. Ann Arbor: University of Michigan Press, 1960.

EVERYMAN'S LIBRARY. *The Little Flowers of St. Francis, The Mirror of Perfection, and The Life of St. Francis.* London: Dent, 1963.

FARNELL, IDA. *The Lives of the Troubadours.* London: D. Nutt, 1896.

FREEMAN, E. A. *The History of the Norman Conquest of England* (5 vols.). Oxford: Clarendon Press, 1873.

*FREEMANTLE, ANNE. *Age of Faith.* New York: Time-Life, Inc., 1965.

FROISSART, SIR JOHN. *The Chronicles of England, France and Spain.* New York: Dutton, 1961.

GILMAN, M. *Eleanor, By the Wrath of God.* Ms. Cambridge: Widener Library, Harvard University.

GREGORY I (POPE). *Dialogues.* Translated by O. J. Zimmerman. (Fathers of the Church Series.) New York: Fathers of the Church, Inc., 1959.

———. *The Book of Pastoral Rule and Selected Epistles of Gregory the Great.* Translated by J. Barmby. New York: Select Library of Christian Literature, 1895-98.

248

HALPHEN, L.   *Paris sous les Premiers Capetiens.* Paris: Albin Michel, 1909.

————. *Charlemagne et L'Empire Carolingien.* Paris: Albin Michel, 1949.

*HARTMAN, GERTRUDE.   *Medieval Days and Ways.* New York: Macmillan, 1958.

HASKINS, C. H.   *Renaissance of the Twelfth Century.* Cambridge: Harvard University Press, 1957.

————. *The Rise of the Universities.* Ithaca: Cornell University Press, 1957.

HAY, DENIS.   *The Medieval Centuries.* London: University Paperbacks, 1964.

HEER, F.   *The Medieval World.* Cleveland: World Publishing, 1961.

HENDERSON, P.   *Richard Coeur de Lion.* New York: W. W. Norton, 1959.

HODGIN, THOMAS.   *Charles the Great.* New York: Macmillan, 1897.

*HOLMES, U. T.   *Daily Living in the Twelfth Century.* Madison: University of Wisconsin Press, 1962.

HUTCHISON, H. F.   *The Hollow Crown, A Life of Richard II.* New York: John Day Co., 1961.

HUTTON, W. H.   *Simon de Montfort and His Cause.* London: Putnam's, 1841.

JACOB, E. F.   *Studies in the Period of Baronial Reform and Rebellion.* Oxford: Clarendon Press, 1925.

KAZANTZAKIS, N.   *Saint Francis.* Translated by P. A. Bien. New York: Simon and Schuster, 1962.

KELLY, AMY.   *Eleanor of Aquitaine and the Four Kings.* Cambridge: Harvard University Press, 1952.

————. *Eleanor and Her Courts of Love.* Cambridge: Medieval Academy of America. *Speculum* XII, 1937.

KINGSFORD, C. L. ed.   *The Song of Lewes.* Oxford: Oxford University Press, 1890.

KLEINCLAUSZ, A.   *Charlemagne.* Paris: Libraire Hachette, 1934.

LaBARGE, M. W.   *A Baronial Household in the Thirteenth Century.* New York: Barnes and Noble, 1965.

————. *Simon de Montfort.* Toronto: Macmillan, 1963.

*LAMB, CHARLES.   *Charlemagne.* New York: Doubleday, 1954.

LEMMON, C. H.   *The Field of Hastings.* St. Leonard's on Sea: Budd and Gillatt, 1957.

LE MONNIER, ABBÉ LÉON.   *Histoire de St. François d'Assise.* Paris: V. Licoffre, 1889.

LEWIS, A.   *Naval Power and Trade in the Mediterranean 500-1100.* Princeton: Princeton University Press, 1951.

LEWIS, C. S.   *The Discarded Image.* New York: Cambridge University Press, 1964.

————. *Medieval Bestiary.* New York: G. P. Putnam's, 1960.

LLOYD, ALAN.   *The Making of the King, 1066.* New York: Holt, Rinehart and Winston, 1966.

LOT, FERDINAND.   *End of the Ancient World and Beginnings of the Middle Ages.* New York: Harper Torchbook, 1961.

LUNT, W. E.   *History of England.* New York: Harper's, 1951.

MacDONALD, W.   *Early Christian and Byzantine Architecture.* New York: Braziller, 1965.

McKISACK, MAY.   *The Fourteenth Century, 1307-1399.* Oxford: Clarendon Press, 1959.

McNEILL, W. H.   *The Rise of the West.* Chicago: University of Chicago Press, 1964.

MAYNARD, T.   *Richest of the Poor.* New York: Doubleday, 1948.

*MILLS, DOROTHY.   *The Middle Ages.* New York: G. P. Putnam's, 1935.

*MORRISON, SEAN.   *Armor.* New York: Thomas Y. Crowell, 1963.

MOSS, H.   *The Birth of the Middle Ages, 395-814.* Oxford: Clarendon Press, 1935.

NICHOLSON, H.   *Kings, Courts and Monarchy.* New York: Simon and Schuster, 1962.

NORGATE, KATE. *England Under the Angevin Kings* (2 vols.). London and New York: Macmillan, 1887.

———. *Richard the Lion Heart*. London: Macmillan, 1924.

OAKESCHOTT, R. E. *Archeology of Medieval Weapons*. New York: Praeger, 1963.

OMAN, C. W. C. *The Art of War in the Middle Ages*. Ithaca: Cornell University Press, 1953.

ORDERICUS VITALIS. *The Ecclesiastical History of England and Normandy*. Translated by T. Forester. London: H. G. Bohn, 1853-56.

PAINTER, S. *French Chivalry*. Ithaca: Cornell University Press, 1957.

PANOFSKY, ERWIN. *Abbot Suger on the Abbey Church of St. Denis and Its Art Treasure*. Princeton: Princeton University Press, 1946.

PARIS, M. *Historia Anglorum*. Translated by J. A. Giles. London: H. G. Bohn, 1853.

PAUL THE DEACON. *History of the Longobards*. Translated by W. D. Foulke. Philadelphia: University of Pennsylvania Press, 1907.

PERROY, E. *The Hundred Years War*. Indianapolis: Indiana University Press, 1959.

PEVSNER, NIKOLAUS. *An Outline of European Architecture*. Baltimore: Penguin Books, 1960.

PIRENNE, H. *Economic and Social History of Medieval Europe*. New York: Harcourt Brace, 1937.

———. *A History of Europe*. New York: Doubleday Anchor, 1956.

———. *Medieval Cities*. Princeton: Princeton University Press, 1925.

———. *Mohammed and Charlemagne*. New York: Meridian Books, 1957.

POËTE, N. *L'Enfance de Paris*. Paris: A. Colin, 1908.

POOLE, A. *Domesday Book to Magna Carta*. Oxford: Clarendon Press, 1955.

*POWER, E. *Medieval People*. Garden City: Doubleday Anchor Books, 1954.

POWICKE, F. M. *The Thirteenth Century, 1216-1307*. Oxford: Clarendon Press, 1953.

———. *King Henry III and the Lord Edward*. Oxford: Clarendon Press, 1947.

PRÉVITE-ORTON, C. W. *The Shorter Cambridge Medieval History*. New York: Cambridge University Press, 1960.

PROTHERO, G. S. *The Life of Simon de Montfort, Earl of Leicester*. London: Longmans Green, 1877.

RICHARD, A. *Histoire des ducs et des comtes de Poitou, 778-1202*, 2 vols. Paris: A. Picard et fils, 1903.

RICKERT, E. *Chaucer's World*. New York: Columbia University Press, 1948.

ROSENBERG, M. *Eleanor of Aquitaine*. New York: Houghton Mifflin, 1937.

ROSS, J. B., AND McLAUGHLIN, M. M. *Medieval Reader*. New York: Viking, 1949.

RUNCIMAN, S. *A History of the Crusades*, 3 vols. New York: Cambridge University Press, 1954.

RUSSELL, C. B. *Charlemagne, First of the Moderns*. New York: Simon and Schuster, 1930.

SAALMAN, HOWARD. *Medieval Architecture*. New York: Braziller, 1962.

SAYERS, D. L. *The Song of Roland*. Baltimore: Penguin Books, 1953.

ST. FRANCIS. *The Writings of St. Francis of Assisi*. Translated by Father Paschal Robinson. Philadelphia: Dolphin Press, 1906.

SLOCUMBE, G. *William the Conqueror*. New York: G. P. Putnam's, 1958.

SMAIL, R. C. *Crusading Warfare*. New York: Cambridge University Press, 1956.

SMYTHE, B. *Trobador Poets*. New York: Duffield Co., 1911.

SOUTHERN, R. W. *The Making of the Middle Ages*. New Haven: Yale University Press, 1963.

STENTON, F. M. *William the Conqueror and the Rule of the Normans.* New York: G. P. Putnam's, 1908.

———— (ed.) *The Bayeux Tapestry.* London: Phaidon Press, 1957.

STEPHENSON, C. *Medieval Feudalism.* Ithaca: Cornell University Press, 1961.

STONE, E. N. *Three Old French Chronicles of the Crusades.* Seattle: University of Washington, 1939.

STRAYER, J. R., AND MUNROE, D. C. *The Middle Ages.* New York: Appleton-Century-Crofts, 1959.

*TAYLOR, DUNCAN. *Chaucer's England.* London: Dobson, 1959.

THOMAS OF CELANO. *The Lives of St. Francis of Assisi.* Translated by A. G. F. Howell. London: Methuen, 1908.

*TOY, S. *The Castles of Great Britain.* London: Wm. Heinemann, 1959.

TREHARNE, R. F. *The Baronial Plan of Reform.* Manchester: Manchester University Press, 1932.

————. *The Personal Role of Simon de Montfort in the Period of Baronial Reform and Rebellion.* London: From the Proceedings of the British Academy, Vol. XI. Cumberlye, 1954.

*TUNIS, E. *Weapons, a Pictorial History.* New York: World Publishing, 1954.

*TREVELYAN, G. M. *History of England.* New York: Doubleday Anchor Books, 1953.

*TREVOR-ROPER, H. *The Rise of Christian Europe.* London: Jarrod, 1965.

TURNER, S. E. *A Sketch of the Germanic Constitution.* New York: G. P. Putnam's, 1888.

VILLEPREUX, L. DE. *Eleanore de Guienne.* Paris: Hachette, 1862.

VIOLLET-LE DUC. *An Essay on Military Architecture of the Middle Ages.* Translated by M. Macdermott. Oxford and London: J. H. & J. Parker, 1860.

VON SIMPSON, O. *The Gothic Cathedral.* New York: Bollingen, 1962.

WADDELL, H. *Medieval Latin Lyrics.* London: R. R. Smith, Inc., 1929.

WALLACE-HADRILL, J. M. *The Early Middle Ages.* New York: Harper's, 1962.

WHITE, LYNN. *Medieval Technology and Social Change.* Oxford: Oxford University Press, 1962.

WILLIAM OF JUMIÈGES: *Gesta Normannorum Ducum.* Translation, "Histoire des Normands, Collection des Memoires relatifs a l'histoire de France." Paris: F. P. G. Guizot, ed., 1829.

WILLIAM OF MALMESBURY. *Gesta Regum.* Translated by Rev. J. Sharpe. London: Seelays, 1854.

WILLIAM OF POITIERS. *Gesta Willelmi Ducis Normannorum.* Translated and edited by F. P. G. Guizot, "Vie de Guillaume le Conquerant." Paris: 1826.

WILLIAMS, JAY. *Knights of the Crusades.* New York: American Heritage, 1962.

WINSTON, RICHARD. *Charlemagne, from the Hammer to the Cross.* New York: Vintage Books, 1960.

WRIGHT, T. *Political Songs of England.* London: Camden Society, 1839.

INDEX

Aachen, 63, 71, 75
abbots, 28, 32
Abelard, Peter, 111
Abul-Abbas, 67, 70
Acre, 140-153, 179, 218
Adrianople, battle of, 16
Agilulf, King, 39
Albigensian Crusade, 189
Alboin, King, 26
Alcuin, 59, 60, 61, 65, 70
Alexander II, Pope, 87
Alfred the Great, King, 77
Angles, Anglo-Saxons, Angleland, 16, 19, 30, 38, 76, 77, 86
Anjou, 104, 105, 119, 120, 122, 130, 185
Aquitaine, 50, 105-120, 126, 130, 185, 200
Aquitanians, 49, 108, 124
Arabs, 102, 104
architecture, 62, 63, 66, 79, 81, 82, 95, 96, 97, 110, 113-114, 155-157, 196-197
armor, arms, 14, 16, 42-43, 52, 91, 136, 137, 142-144, 145, 147, 149, 150, 191, 218, 219, 245
Arsuf, battle of, 146
Assisi, 161-183
Augustine, St. (A.D. 354-430), 24
Augustine of Canterbury, St., 38
Avars, 62

Bacon, Roger, 218
barbarians, 13-17, 19, 20, 40
Barbarossa, Frederick, Emperor, 135, 138
Barons' War, 205
Bavaria, 47, 62
Becket, Thomas à, 125, 216, 238
bell, book and candle, 212
Benedict I, Pope, 30
Benedict, St., 20, 28
Benedictine monks, 20, 21, 28-29, 38
Benedictine Rule, 20, 28, 240
Berengaria, Princess, 138, 139
Bernard, St. (Abbot), 115, 116, 120, 137
Bernart de Ventadour, 120
Black Death, 26, 32, 218, 220
Black Prince, 226
Blanche of Castile, 159
Boniface, St., 44, 51
Bordeaux, 108, 109, 159

Britain, 30
Brittany, 84
bull, (papal), 206, 212
Burgundians, 16
Burgundy, 116
Byzantine Emperor, 21, 22, 26, 31, 39, 67, 102, 103; Empire, 21, 42, 102, 218; troops, 23, 30, 31
Byzantines, 67
Byzantium, 15

cannon, 218, 220, 245
Canterbury Tales, The, 238-245
"Canticle of the Sun, The," 182, 183
Carloman, 49-51
castles, 79, 96, 155-157, 196-198, 225, 237
Charles the Great (Charlemagne), 45, 47-72, 73, 74
Charles the Hammer, 42, 43
charters, 155, 159, 192
Château Gaillard, 155-157, 159
Chaucer, Geoffrey, 220-246
China, 218
Chinon, 132, **157**
chivalry, 121, 127, 128, 151, 158, 239, 242
Christians, Christianity, 15, 17, 38, 51, 55, 56, 58, 59, 62, 64, 65, 66, 72, 74, 76, 77, 111, 112, 117, 121, 131, 145, 146, 147, 150, 151, 155, 165, 174, 176, 179, 218
Church, the, 33, 34, 37, 38, 40, 43, 45, 50, 60, 98, 103, 104, 125, 133, 136, 155, 173, 174, 177, 178, 189, 193, 194, 218
Conrad, Lord of Tyre, 147, 151, 153
Constantine, Emperor, 15, 31
Constantinople, 15, 16, 31, 42, 116, 117, 218
Crusades, I, 102, 104; II, 115-118; III, 131, 133-151, 195; IV, 174; V, 179-180
court of love, 127
crossbow, 136, 149, 157

Dante, 184, 234
Dark Ages, 19, 21, 40, 45, 72, 77, 234
Day of Judgment, 26, 99, 245
Denis, St. (abbey church), 113, 114
Desiderius, King, 53, 55
Domesday Book, 98, 99
dress, 13, 14, 25, 31, 33, 48, 66, 83, 123,

133, 163, 172, 225, 226

education, 17, 25, 26, 28, 36, 37, 48, 60, 77, 82, 104, 108, 111, 162, 224
Edward the Confessor, King, 77, 79, 83, 85, 86
Edward, Prince (later Edward I), 204, 206, 208, 209, 210, 211, 213, 214, 215, 216, 217
Edward III, King, 219, 221, 224, 225, 227, 228, 229, 235
Eleanor of Aquitaine, 105, 107-134, 152, 153, 154, 194, 219, 228
Eleanor, wife of Simon de Montfort, 194-213
Elizabeth, Countess of Ulster, 225
Ethelbert, King, 38
Evesham, battle of, 214, 215
excommunication, 112, 185, 212, 216

feudal and feudalism, 43, 74, 76, 79, 85, 96, 103, 104, 107, 122, 127, 162, 186, 191, 219, 245
fiefs, 43, 105, 118, 119, 120, 186, 219
Francis, St., 161-184
Franciscan missionaries, 193, 218; Rule, 172, 174, 240; schools, 181, 193
Frankland and Franks, 16, 17, 20, 37, 42-45, 47-72, 73, 74
Frederick Barbarossa, Emperor, 135, 138
friars, 174, 175, 177, 178, 181, 193, 207, 211, 240

Gascony, 198, 200, 202, 221
Gaul, 20
German, Kings and Emperors, 74, 104, 135, 153, 165, 203, *see* Holy Roman Emperor
Giotto, 183, 233
Gothic, 113-114
Great Parliament, the, 212
Greek fire, 142, 144
Gregorian chants, 37
Gregory I, Pope, 22-40, 167, 224
Grosseteste, Bishop, 193, 199, 200

Hadrian I, Pope, 52
Harold, Earl (later King of England), 83-95
Harold Hardraada, King of Norway, 86
Hastings, battle of, 90-94
Henry I, King of England, 100
Henry II, King of England, 118-132
Henry III, King of England, 187, 188, 191-197, 199-216

Henry IV, King of England, 241, 245
Henry VI, Holy Roman Emperor, 153
Holy Land, 101-103, 117, 131, 137, 139, 150, 151, 218
Holy Roman Emperor, 104, 135, 153, 193
Holy Roman Empire, 48, 72, 87, 104, 202
Honorius III, Pope, 177
House of Commons, 212, 217, 237
House of Lords, 237
Hundred Years War, 219-220, 226, 229
Hungarians, 74
Huns, 15, 16

Ibn-al-Rabi, 56
Innocent III, Pope, 165, 185
Innocent IV, Pope, 202
Irminsul, 51

Jaffa, 145, 146, 149, 150
Jerome, St., 24
Jerusalem, 42, 67, 79, 102, 103, 117, 118, 131, 139, 146, 147, 150, 179, 196
Joan of Arc, 219
John, King, 124, 130, 131, 132, 134, 152-155, 158, 159, 185-187
John of Gaunt, 230, 232
justice, 17, 67, 95, 98, 123, 124, 133, 204, 205
Justinian, Emperor, 21-22
Jutes, 38

Kenilworth castle, 196-199, 214, 216
knighthood, knights, 43, 52, 55, 69, 74, 87, 90-94, 96, 102, 103, 119, 127, 128, 135-139, 144-147, 150, 158, 164, 165, 166, 190, 191, 206, 210, 215, 239, 242, 245
Kublai Khan, 218

Lanfranc, Archbishop, 99
law, 14, 17, 40, 66, 67, 68, 98, 159, 186, 187, 199, 204
Leicester, Earldom of, 191, 192
Leo III, Pope, 64-66
Leopold, Duke, 144, 152-153
Llywellyn, Prince of Wales, 214
Lombardy, 55, 138
Lombards, 26, 27, 30, 32, 38-40, 45, 47, 50, 51-55
London, 95, 123, 133, 206, 208, 222-224, 231, 236
longbow, 219, 245
Louis VI, (Louis the Fat), King of France, 104, 105, 107, 108
Louis, Prince, (later Louis VII, King of France), 108, 109, 110, 112-120, 122,

125, 128, 131
Louis IX, King of France, 159, 202, 208, 209

Magna Carta, 186, 187, 204, 216
Malik al-Kamil, al-, 179, 180
manuscripts, 25, 28, 61, 75, 232-234, 244
manors, 99, 191, 192
Marie, Countess of Champagne, 127, 129
Marsh, Adam, 199, 200
Matilda, Queen, 81, 87, 96, 99
medieval, 25, 40, 43 59, 98, 99, 100, 124, 194, 219, 230, 245, 246
Middle Ages, 18, 19, 26, 28, 36, 40, 48, 57, 64, 72, 82, 85, 100, 104, 112, 158, 181, 184, 197, 198, 220, 221, 233, 236, 238, 240, 246
miracles, 36, 52, 72, 182, 215
missi, 67
Mohammed, 41
Mohammedans, 178
monasteries and monks, 18, 28-29, 32, 33, 34, 38, 55, 81, 239-240, 245
Montfort, Simon de, Earl of Leicester, see Simon de Montfort
Montfort, Simon de (father of the Earl), 189, 190, 191
Montfort, Simon de (son of the Earl), 213, 214, 215
Moslems, 41-43, 56, 74, 101, 102, 104, 131, 139, 145, 150, 151, 218
motte and bailey, 97

Norman, Normans, Northmen, 75, 76, 77, 78-84, 91, 100
Normandy, 76-100, 110, 120, 128, 130, 155, 185, 191

Odovacar, 16, 19
ordeal of the cross, 68
Otto the Great, 74
Ottobuoni, Cardinal, 216
Ostrogoths, 16, 21-23
Oxford, 181, 193, 204, 205; Provisions of, 204-206, 209; University, 193

page, life of, 190, 224-225
Papacy, Popes, 25, 33-34, 37, 44, 45, 54, 55, 64-65, 87, 98, 103-104, 112, 115, 118, 154, 178, 185, 194, 199, 202-203, 218
Paris, 110-112, 123
Parliament and parliamentary systems, 187, 201, 203, 204, 206, 212, 216, 217, 228, 237, 238
Paul's Cathedral, St., 208, 223

Pavia, 53-54
Pax Romana, 15
peasants, see serfs
Peasants' Revolt, 235
Pelagius II, Pope, 30, 32
Pepin the Short, 44-45
Peter's pence, St., 98
Peter, St., 25, 30, 36, 37, 154, 240
Peter's basilica, St., 25, 33, 37, 40, 54, 64, 65, 66, 74, 167
Petrarch, F., 234
Philip Augustus, 125, 131, 132, 135-159
Philippa de Roet, 230
Plantagenet, 120, 128, 130, 134, 159, 187, 195
Poitiers, battle of, 226
Polo, Marco, 218
Popes, see Papacy
Prefect of Rome, 27, 28

quintain, 190

relics, 36, 63, 85, 91, 183, 240
Renaissance, 18, 61, 198, 233, 246
Richard II, King, 235-237, 241, 242, 244
Richard, King of the Germans, 203, 210
Richard the Lion Heart, King, 124, 126, 128, 130-134, 135-158, 218
Robert the Magnificent, 78, 79
Roland, Count, 57-58; Song of, 57-58, 102
Rollo, Duke, 76
Roman Catholic, 20, 37, 50, 178
Roman Empire, 13, 14, 15, 16, 17, 19, 21, 37, 38, 42, 48, 66; government, 14; law, 188; Senate, 20, 22
Romanesque, 109, 114
Romans, 13, 17, 19, 24, 25, 40, 45, 60, 66
Rome, 15, 19-40, 45, 55, 64-66, 186, 194, 218
Roncesvalles, 57
Rouen, 76, 79, 155
Runnymede, 186

Saladin, 131, 139-151
Sancta Sophia (basilica), 31
Saracens, 139, 140-146, 149-150
Saxons, Saxony, 16, 51, 52, 55, 58, 59
Senlac Hill, 90
serfs (peasants), 34, 68-69, 74, 81, 96, 99, 163, 192, 193, 218-219, 235, 236
ships, 69, 75, 87-88, 89, 90, 137-138
Sicily, 202, 203
siege weapons, 136, 142-144
Simon de Montfort, Earl of Leicester, 188-216, 217, 237

slaves, 20, 34, 63, 69, 74, 99, 116
Song of Lewes, 211
Song of Roland, 57-58, 102
Spain, 56, 74, 102
squire, life of, 190, 226-227, 229
Stephen, Pope, 45
stigmata, 181
stirrups, 43
Suger, Abbot, 112, 113, 114, 118

Tartar Empire, 218
Theodelinda, Queen, 39-40
Theodoric the Ostrogoth, 20
Thomas à Becket, 125, 216, 238
Tiberius, Emperor, 31
tournaments, 109, 155, 241-243
Tower of London, 95, 241
trade, 42, 48, 63, 75-76, 104, 230, 233
troubadours, 108, 112, 116, 120, 162, 228
Troilus and Criseyde, 236-237
Truce of God, 131
Turks, Seljuk, 102, 146

Ugolino, Cardinal, 177, 178
Urban II, Pope, 102, 104

Vandals, 16, 20
vassals, 43, 49, 52, 79, 96, 104-105, 120, 154, 159, 202, 219, 245
Venice, Venetian, 67, 151, 162, 218
Vikings, 70, 72, 74-77
Virgin Mary, 63, 121
Visigoths, 15, 16, 20

Wales (Welsh), 203-204, 211
weapons, *see* armor, arms
wergeld, 68
Westminster Abbey, 86, 95, 133, 245; Palace, 123, 223, 232, 237
Widukind, 55, 58
William I, King (The Conqueror), 77-100, 105, 224
William II, King (Rufus), 100
Witan, 86